Wake Me When It's Funny

Wake Me When It's Funny

How to Break into Show Business and Stay There

•

Garry Marshall

with Lori Marshall

A

ADAMS PUBLISHING • HOLBROOK, MASSACHUSETTS

*Published by Adams Media Corporation
260 Center Street, Holbrook, MA 02343*

ISBN: 1-55850-526-1

Printed in the United States of America

FIRST EDITION
J I H G F E D C B A

*Library of Congress Cataloging-in-Publication Data
Marshall, Garry.
Wake me when it's funny: how to break into show business and stay
there/by Garry Marshall with Lori Marshall
p.   cm.
Includes index.
ISBN 1-55850-526-1
1. Marshall, Garry. 2. Television producers and directors—United States—
Biography. 3. Performing arts—Vocational guidance—United States. I.
Marshall, Lori. II. Title
PN1992.4.M37A3   1995
791.45'0232'092—dc20   95-6630
[B]   [CIP]*

*Produced by K&N Bookworks
Designed by Liney Li*

For Barbara Sue Wells

Laverne Writes
About Her Brother

Foreword by Penny Marshall

I've known my older brother Garry my whole life. With a lot of people, he's known for his television shows and movies. But in our family he was known most for his sneezing.

Garry was a sick baby. A sick little boy. And a sick teenager. Along with the Egyptian pyramids and the fact that I can't stop smoking no matter how many patches I stick under my damn arms, one of the great mysteries of the modern world is how my brother ever made it out of the Bronx alive. I mean, yeah, he's a success in show business now, but he was so ill growing up that most of the time he couldn't even get up out of bed. For him just to yell down the hall from his bed, "Penny, you wanna play Monopoly?" was a big deal.

I gotta be honest, my brother was very skinny and looked so green all the time that he could have been a body double for Gumby. If he wasn't scratching an itchy rash or throwing up into

a garbage can from some strange food allergy, he was getting hit
by a moving object. My mother said that by the time he was ten,
Garry had gotten smacked with a golf ball in the eye (two
stitches), cut in the right thigh after wrestling with a rotten little
boy who had a sharp compass in his back pocket (four stitches),
belted by a baseball bat in the head (five stitches), knocked off the
top of a jungle gym at the playground (eight stitches), and
rammed his head into a moving blue Oldsmobile (fifteen stitches).

I was born Carole "Penny" Marshall nine years after my
brother and it was pretty common around our apartment to hear
Garry referred to as "the sick one." Then there was my amiable
sister, Ronelle Lynne, three years younger than Garry, who was
dubbed "the nice one" and—ta da!—I myself earned the title "the
bad one" or "the bad seed." Why, you ask? Was it because I was
always getting into trouble? Yes! Well, not bad trouble by today's
standards, but I could count among my various offenses such
things as precariously walking along the edge of the roof of our
six-story apartment building to try to give my mom a heart attack
and getting caught sneaking into the movies through the backdoor
and having the Hitler-faced usher try to pull my hair out. Add
these to my dating a known hoodlum named Lefty, who could spit
farther than any boy I ever saw, and you get the picture of my
charming childhood.

The three of us grew up in an apartment building along the
Grand Concourse in the Bronx. Our cohabitants included our parents, Marjorie and Tony, and our grandparents (mother's side),
Willie and Margie Ward, all in this little apartment. Dad worked
both in industrial films and the advertising business and Mom
taught dance (tap, ballet, and jazz) to neighborhood kids in the
basement of our building, which we called the "cellar." Mom
always put on shows for the neighborhood. In one memorable
recital, I spelled out the word "moth" with my whole skinny body
while Garry played the drums loudly. For the Bronx in the 1950s,
that was show business.

I remember that my brother spent a lot of time staring into
space when he was sick and sometimes when he wasn't sick.
Nobody knew what he was thinking about, but I'd like to believe

that Garry was dreaming up all of the comedy material that he would later use in his career, but God knows around our apartment there was plenty of material to begin with. All three of us agreed that our mom was funny, and most of our friends thought she was funny, too. She was one of the only working moms in the neighborhood and the only mom who wore slacks every day and hated to cook. She was sort of the Gloria Steinem of the Grand Concourse, not in what she said but in what she did. And she wasn't a shy, coy woman, either. Although she was never much of a traveler, I don't think she ever would have made it in one of those third world countries where women are made to walk a few steps behind the men. Instead of obeying an order to walk behind a guy, she would have run up alongside him, tapped him on the shoulder, and said, "Hey, buddy, where are you going? If it's going to be boring, then I'm not following you."

My mother's jokes were usually derogatory cracks about our family members. For his birthday one year she congratulated Garry on celebrating eleven years of being round shouldered. Ronny had such a round, chubby face as a little girl that Mom would sometimes say, "Ronny, are you storing food for the winter in those cheeks?" And I had buck teeth and my mother used to say that my overbite "could open a Coke bottle."

My dad, on the other hand, was known for his white lies. For as long as we could remember, he had told us that our relatives had come over to America from England on the *Mayflower*. I remember every Thanksgiving in elementary school my teacher would pass around a book with lots of pictures of the Pilgrims in their little white-and-black outfits and funny pointy hats and I would think, "Those there folks are my relatives." However, I soon found out that I had been duped.

My father's parents, Joseph and Ann, lived in the east Bronx and several times a year we would go to their house for Sunday dinner. It was during these visits that Garry, being the oldest child, slowly but surely started to put together some of the pieces of our mixed-up family history. The first clue was that we always ate spaghetti at their house. The second clue was that they listened to opera and had red tomatoes growing along stringy vines on their back porch. And here's the kicker: They spoke Italian, not English. For a long time we ignored the clues and smiled like idiots and said, "Our relatives came over on the *Mayflower*."

But then one day I remember we were over at Grandpa Joseph and Grandma Ann's house eating a big bowl of linguini with fresh tomato sauce when I learned the truth. Garry leaned over to Ronny and me and, just before he sneezed, whispered, "We're Italian. Dad's name used to be Masciarelli. I saw it in a scrapbook. We didn't come over on the *Mayflower*. We came through Ellis Island." And sure enough it was true. When my father turned eighteen he changed his name to Marshall because he thought it would help him get a more prestigious job than the low-paying labor positions usually filled by Italian immigrants. And he was right. But Dad should have told us. I've never been able to look at a picture of a pointy-hatted Pilgrim again without somehow feeling cheated.

God, praying, and religion were another gray area in our family. We lived in the last apartment building on the Concourse between Villa Avenue, which represented the Italian-Catholic neighborhood, and the Parkway, where most of the Jewish families lived. Half our neighbors thought we were Catholic and the other half thought we were Jewish, but nobody believed for a New York second the rumor that we had come over on the uppity *Mayflower*. The truth was that my parents were atheists but they never told anybody, including us. Even though we were all three christened Episcopalian, we ended up going to a Presbyterian church in our neighborhood until we turned thirteen. After that, we were on our own. The reason we went to the Presbyterian church was because it had a spacious stage in the basement and the minister agreed to let Mom hold several dance recitals there.

During his final year of church, Garry used to slip Ronny a quarter to tell our parents that he went to church with her while instead he would put on his helmet and uniform and go to his Sunday football game with his team, the Bronx Falcons. Even though he spent most games hurt and sidelined by injuries, Garry loved to play all kinds of sports, from baseball to stickball, basketball to punchball, and roller hockey to association. (Association, for those of you not from the Bronx, is a game of touch football played in the street often with a rolled-up wool hat as the ball. We weren't a rich bunch of kids.) When it came to football, Garry was easy to spot on the field: He was the one playing left end with a Kleenex in his hand.

His little church/football scam was working well until Mom grew suspicious about his hair. She didn't understand why his hair was so sweaty and matted down when he came home from church. One day she confronted him with it.

"What's wrong with your hair?" Mom asked. "What are they doing to you at church?"

Quick on his feet and not wanting to confess that he had been wearing a helmet to play football, Garry said: "It's the minister. He presses down very hard on my head during communion."

The next day Mom, dressed in her best pair of slacks, marched down to the church and told the minister not to press so hard on her kid's head.

And so, we were an Italian, Protestant family living in a predominantly Jewish building with a mother who liked to order Chinese food because it was fast and a father who insisted we were distant cousins of the British royal family.

Everybody always asks me why my brother, sister, and I get along so well. Ronny, by the way, was one of the producers on *Happy Days* and since has been a producer for Miller/Boyett at Warner Bros. television. We all work in show business, each has bad gums, and often swap painful dentist stories. Many people also say that Garry and I talk alike, but I don't think so. He has a terrible accent. Ronny speaks beautifully. However, the main reason we bonded was our parents. Their marriage was not cut from the Ward and June Cleaver mold. If they had been married about forty years later, they probably would have gotten a quickie divorce in Reno and moved on to find somebody else to love. But instead they stayed together and made our daily lives very similar to sitting in the front row of an action-adventure movie: It's nice

to be able to see the chase scenes without anybody's head block-
ing your view, but you quite often wish you were a little farther
back. I mean they both loved us but other than that, there was
very little they could agree on. At some point we all decided that
if both our parents were going to be eccentric, we better stick
together if we had a prayer of surviving.

My brother went away to college in Chicago when I was only
nine years old, so I didn't really get to know him again until I
moved out to Los Angeles in 1967. At the time, Garry was a hot-
shot television comedy writer, along with his partner Jerry Belson,
and the two were trying to break into features by writing screenplays. When I came to town, Garry asked me what I wanted to do
with my life.

"I don't know," I said.

I had gone to the University of New Mexico as a math and psy-
chology major, but instead of getting a degree, I ended up with a
husband and a baby girl. Of the three of us, only the baby decided
that we were meant for each other. However, I had to leave her in
New Mexico with my ex-husband's family while I went to
California to try to look for a job. My previous work experience
had been achieving the goal that I had set for myself in my high
school yearbook: secretary.

"Think," said Garry when I arrived on his doorstep in Los
Angeles, "when was the last time you were happy doing something?"

"When I was sitting on the Parkway fence watching the boys
play stickball," I said.

"We're looking for a career here, Penny. Think more. When
were you happy doing something? Anything?" he asked.

I thought for a minute and then came up with this: "In New
Mexico I was in a production of *Oklahoma!* where I played Ado
Annie. I made the audience laugh and that made me happy. Does
that count?"

"Yeah. That's acting. That's good," he said.

But I thought that to be an actress you had to look like
Elizabeth Taylor and I told Garry that I wasn't pretty enough. But
he said all I needed was some training, so he helped me enroll in
Harvey Lembeck's acting class. Those damn classes were hard,

but I stuck with it and finally got the call for my first job: a Head & Shoulders shampoo commercial. I went down to the set and was told I was to play a character with limp, stringy, dandruff-specked hair and that my costar, an up and coming actress named Farrah Fawcett, would play a character with thick, bouncy hair without a speck of dandruff.

While Farrah and I were having our makeup done, the director put two stand-ins on the set so the crew could light the shot. Farrah's stand-in had a sign around her neck that read BEAUTIFUL GIRL and my stand-in had another that read HOMELY GIRL. When Farrah saw this, she quickly ran over with a pen and crossed out "homely" and replaced it with the word "plain." It was a nice try but my self-esteem had already sunk as low as buried treasure. When I got home, I called up Garry.

"Well, how did the commercial go?" he asked.

"Today I went from homely to plain," I said.

"You're on your way," he said.

"But all they want is perky and pretty and I'm neither."

"Don't worry. You are pretty and you don't have to be perky if you don't want to be," he said. In between scratching, sneezing, and bleeding, he was a pretty nice brother.

I used to come home crying all the time, thinking that I would never make it as an actress and should probably turn right around and get on the next Greyhound for New Mexico. Working as a secretary looked pretty good compared with the rejection that went along with being an actress. But my brother kept encouraging me and gave me a small part in his movie *How Sweet It Is.*

I was cast in a scene set in Paris's Louvre where a tour group of girls took turns smiling in front of the Mona Lisa. I really got the part because I was the only actress Garry could convince to put *real* wire braces on her teeth and smile in front of the painting. But slowly I started getting other small parts on television, some which did not require orthodontia, until Garry gave me my big break when he cast me in his TV show *The Odd Couple.* I was Oscar Madison's constantly whiny secretary, Myrna Turner.

At first I thought Garry hired me just to be nice.

"No one's that nice," he said. "You're good. You aren't perky, but you're good."

And a few years later Garry, along with writers Lowell Ganz and Mark Rothman, created *Laverne & Shirley* for me and Cindy Williams and I had a steady job for almost eight years. During *Laverne & Shirley*, I spent a lot of time learning what was going on behind the camera and now I work behind it full time as a director, a job I like even more than playing Ado Annie. I'm just thankful that Garry encouraged me to go forward and make a life for myself in show business, but I must confess there were days on *Laverne & Shirley* when being a secretary looked mighty calm and peaceful.

Over the years Garry has sort of been my muse because when I was starting out in this business I didn't have many women directors to look to for inspiration. Now that I think about it, my muses were all men. I guess the Seven Dwarfs got to Hollywood before the nine Muses and there's been a testosterone imbalance ever since. But I think I've managed to win over most of the dwarfs by now, too.

My brother showed me how to gather up the confidence and self-esteem to build a career in show business and how to swim the tricky waters of industry politics. That in a nutshell is the point of this book. If he can do it for me, maybe he can do it for you, too. He's certainly done it for others. Like me, my sister, Ronny, came out to California, divorced with three little girls, and my brother helped her become a producer. After watching him also help launch the careers of people like Henry Winkler, Robin Williams, Julia Roberts, and Mayim Bialik, to name a few, many think, "Maybe he'll turn me into the next Fonz or Pretty Woman."

Radio shock jock Howard Stern once said, "Garry Marshall is a man who made a lot of unfunny people funny." I don't know if that's true but he has certainly helped a lot of actors be amusing. On the first day of *Happy Days*, Ron Howard pulled my brother aside and said, "I'm really glad to be doing this show, but I'm not very funny." But a few months later he was singing that Blueberry Hill song and making audiences laugh. Before *The Flamingo Kid*, Matt Dillon was apprehensive about comedy, and before *Frankie and Johnny*, Al Pacino wasn't exactly the godfather of humor, either. But Garry gave each of these actors the confidence to give it a shot at making audiences laugh.

There are some things about my brother that aren't in this book because he doesn't like to brag. But I'm his sister, so it's okay if I do it:

- During the week of January 28, 1979, four of the top five rated Nielsen shows were produced by my brother. *Laverne & Shirley*, *Happy Days*, and *Mork & Mindy* were rated one, two, and three, and *Angie* was rated number five. When you're a television creator and producer, it doesn't get much better than that.

- He's produced more than a thousand television shows, written more than one hundred television scripts, directed eight movies, and written three plays. His television series and their performers have been nominated for and won several Emmys, Golden Globes, and Writers Guild awards. He was most proud in 1995 when presented with one of the Writers Guild's most prestigious honors: the Valentine Davies Award, given to a member whose "contributions to the entertainment industry and the community at large have brought dignity and honor to writers everywhere."

- My brother has a star on the Hollywood Walk of Fame, near those of Ron Howard and Burt Reynolds, right in front of the El Capitán theater. While some celebrities have fan clubs that clean their stars, Garry doesn't. So when you walk by his star, watch out or you might step in some old bubble gum.

- Garry likes to build buildings. I don't know if it was all those years we spent playing Monopoly or what but when it comes to saying "thank you," Garry likes to do it with a concrete structure. His favorite one is Northwestern University's Marjorie Ward Marshall Dance Center, which he built for our mother, who died of Alzheimer's disease in 1983. There's also the Barbara and Garry Marshall studio wing for film and television production at Northwestern and the Marshall Center for Arts and Athletics at the Harvard–Westlake School in Los Angeles.

- In a town where men change their wives as fast and as often as they change their favorite restaurants, Garry has been married to the same woman for thirty-two years. The reason is not some big mystery: She's a nurse and can take care of him. They've also managed to raise three children in Hollywood without having them grow up to be drug addicts, nude center-folds, or agents.

- He's been honored as Man of the Year by several different groups, inducted into the Broadcasting and Cable Hall of Fame, and lectured at major universities from UCLA to NYU to Yale and Northwestern. And even though he has received several Lifetime Achievement awards he's still going strong, preparing two movies, a new TV series, and writing another play with Lowell Ganz.

And so now that I've given you a little background about Garry, it's time to let him take over because after all, it's *his* book. The truth is that Garry managed to overcome the obstacles and not only make a career for himself in show business, but in thirty-five years—and this amazes me—he was only out of work for eight weeks. All this and he also got jobs for the rest of us, too. The fact that he pops Actifed while others are popping Prozac is just one of the things that sets him apart from the pack in Hollywood. He's a writer, producer, director, actor, and teacher, but to me he'll always be my older brother—the sick one.

ACKNOWLEDGMENTS

This book would not have been possible without the guidance and encouragement of Willie Ward, Dan Weaver, Esther Newberg, Tom Dyja, Joan Nagy, Bill Fricker, and the mysterious lady in the dark apartment.

Thanks also must go to Diane Frazen, Karen Stirgwolt, Sam Cohn, Jim Wiatt, Diane Cairns, Nancy Seltzer, Peter Mayer, Suzanne Gluck, Barbara Nabozny, Robert Malina, Nanny and the Marshalls—my children Kathleen and Scott, and my sisters Penny and Ronny—for reading the manuscript or helping with it at various stages and generously offering their advice.

Over the years so many people have contributed to my career, but I wouldn't have a career to write about if it had not been for my early mentors Phil Foster, Joey Bishop, Sheldon Leonard, Milt Josefsberg, and Carl Reiner, and my ambitious writing and producing partners Fred Freeman, Jerry Belson, Tom Miller, Eddie Milkis, Lowell Ganz, Alexandra Rose, and Bob Brunner. And three men who helped me when I needed it most, Joel Cohen, Marshall Gelfand, and especially Martin Garbus.

I'm forever grateful to my mother, who taught me all about humor, my father, who taught me how to be a boss, and the Bronx Falcons, who taught me the things my mother and father wouldn't discuss.

And finally no amount of thanks is enough for my oldest child and partner, Lori, for writing this book with me even though her discipline and persistence to meet deadlines cut heavily into my basketball, tennis, softball, and nap time.

CONTENTS

Wake Me When It's Funny

Chapter One

Starting out with a Flaming Rejection

Allow Thirty Minutes of Self-pity a Day

Early in my career when I finally made some money, I thought I would do something nice for my parents.

I went to my father and said, "Dad, I'm doing pretty well now and I want to get you something. Tell me one of your dreams."

"I always dreamed of owning a white Cadillac," he said.

"Okay, you've got it."

Then I went to my mother and said, "Mom, I'm doing well and I want to give you one of your dreams. Pop said his dream is to own a white Cadillac. What's yours?"

Without a moment's hesitation, she said, "My dream is that your father doesn't get the white Cadillac."

I ended up buying my father a white Cadillac anyway, and sending my mother to Hawaii on a vacation so she could get away from my father. The experience was an epiphany for me: I realized that I couldn't spend my whole life trying to please people. But even though I knew I couldn't please everyone, especially my parents, I decided that it shouldn't stop me from trying to please myself and as many other people as I could too.

When Paramount executive Mel Harris told me in 1983 that one of my television series was playing in syndication somewhere in the world every minute of every day, I happily pictured Fonzie in Frankfurt, Laverne and Shirley in London, and Mork in Moscow. What I didn't picture was that almost every hour of every day one of the millions of people who'd been watching my shows and going to my movies would come up to me and ask me how he could break into show business.

Most of the time they catch me off guard. One afternoon I was fishing off the Malibu pier with my then six-year-old son when the weather turned cold and I went to our car to get him a jacket. When I came back my son was holding a script for a TV pilot. "What's that?" I asked him. "A man said to give it to you, Daddy."

Another time I was standing in one of the endless lines at the California Department of Motor Vehicles in Glendale. My line had not moved in twenty minutes and I was about to faint from heat when a clerk at another counter suddenly waved me over. When I got to her counter, she said, "I know who you are. I'll be right back." I wondered where she was going and thought maybe I was in trouble for some old parking tickets. Several minutes later, she came back and handed me her acting résumé and head shot. She then quickly renewed my driver's license, which drew jealous stares from the other drivers. I later returned the favor by casting her as a night-shift waitress in my film *Frankie and Johnny*.

A few years later, *Wrong Turn at Lungfish*, the play I cowrote with Lowell Ganz, was running Off-Broadway in New York City. One afternoon I was playing softball in a Broadway show league game in Central Park and I had just hit a double. I took a lead off second base and watched out of the corner of my eye as the shortstop began to inch toward me. I thought he might try a pick-off play when suddenly he leaned forward and said, "Can I audition for you, Mr. Marshall?" I was more interested in scoring a run than in discovering a new star, so I told him to give me his photo and résumé after the game.

People have approached me in restaurants, slipped me notes on airplanes, and one even placed a whole script underneath the windshield wiper of my car at the supermarket. My wife has fielded her share too, most recently from our plumber and the postman's son-in-law. The bold and pushy even scribble me notes in the middle of their Christmas cards: "May the Lord bless you and your family on this joyous holiday and let me audition for you in the New Year." While the methods vary, the questions remain the same: "How do I get into show business, Mr. Marshall?" or "How do I get my kid in?"

Even as I enter my fourth decade in the business, I still can't give any of these people the magical change-your-life kind of answer they want. But over the years, through luck, some design, and the help of many tremendous teachers, I have uncovered some trade secrets and insights that might benefit others who are struggling to break into show business or trying to figure out a way to stay there. Working in the entertainment business is like traveling in a foreign country where you don't speak the language. At first, you muddle through with hand signals, but if you stay there long enough you can learn to speak the language, or at least learn how to ask where the restroom is. This book is about how I deciphered some of the language of Hollywood.

Starting out in any field is never easy but it's especially hard if you don't know where you want to go. Many people say to me, "I'd really like to work in show business but I don't know which job is best for me." In response I've developed a baseball analogy to give people a sense of what they might be best suited for: It's the bottom of the ninth, the score is tied, and the other team has the bases loaded with two outs and you're playing shortstop. What you're thinking at this moment is an indicator of which job you have an aptitude for.

If you're thinking: "Hit the ball to me. I'll get the out. Hit the ball to me. I'll handle it."

. . . then you should be a director.

If you're thinking: "The crowd's on their feet. They're looking at me. Is my uniform clean? Is my shirt tucked in? I'll push my hat back."

. . . then you should be an actor.

If you're thinking: "A hard ground ball will take a bad bounce and hit me in the mouth, but it'll drop right in front of me and I'll crawl forward and grab the ball and as I spit blood I'll tag the runner out going to third."

. . . then you should be a writer.

If you're thinking: "What a tight battle. It's a great game but the stadium is only half filled. They didn't advertise the game worth a damn. We should have a larger crowd here."

. . . then you should be a producer.

If you're thinking: "There will be a ground ball hit in the hole, I'll do a somersault, and bare hand the ball as I'm flipping over. Then I'll land on one foot, pivot, and make a perfect throw to first base."

. . . then you should be a stunt man.

If you're thinking: "If the ball is hit to me, I have choices. I can throw to first or I can force the guy out at second or I also have a force at third, although the slowest runner is at third, so I could throw home. I'll just have to see what happens and decide."

. . . then you should be a film editor.

If you're thinking: "God it's a tight game. I better fake an appendicitis attack and have them put a substitute in for me right now so if we lose the game it won't be my fault."

. . . then you should be a television network boss or run a movie studio.

If you're thinking: "I hope they hit it to left field because that clown out there will miss it and they'll bench him and I can get my cousin the job as the left fielder."

. . . then you should be an agent.

And finally, if you're thinking: "What a tight game. For this kind of stress I have to ask for more money."

. . . then you should become a professional baseball player.

If you're not a sports person, the best thing to do is reflect on your youth. I wasn't one of those young filmmakers who grew up running around the house with a little movie camera, shooting my mother taking out the garbage. I didn't dream of creating television shows while eating from my baby jar. And I didn't make my toy soldiers act out dramatic character-driven plays I had written in my playpen. That wasn't the way I started out. When I was little I didn't know what I wanted to be when I grew up. The truth was that I wasn't even sure I would *make* it to adolescence.

So how did I start? I was born Garry Kent Marshall in New York on November 13, 1934, and grew up in the Bronx. When my mother, Marjorie, was growing up she had dreams of becoming a dancer, but in those days most women in show business were considered harlots. Mom studied to be a gym teacher instead at the Savage School of Physical Education in New York, and she later became a dance teacher. She was a down-to-earth woman with a natural ear for music, a sharp sense of humor, and one of the greatest laughs of all time.

My father, Anthony, on the other hand, was a dignified advertising account executive who invented his middle name—"Wallace"—because he thought it made him sound more upscale. Dad had a business degree from New York University and found laughter pretty much a waste of breath. Mom married Dad because she thought he was a good dancer, and Dad married Mom because he thought her parents had money. As it turned out, they were both disappointed. They had nothing in common but their kids.

As a little boy, I was sick all the time. I mean coughing, wheezing, burning with a fever sick because of allergies—not small allergic reactions to rare things but major reactions to an awesome number of common things that most people take for granted. One doctor diagnosed my allergic reaction to a list of 128 foods and pollens, including orange lollipops, asparagus, bran, cabbage, navy beans, strawberries, walnuts, radishes, canary feathers, and all condiments except ketchup.

My mother was always trying to get me to sing and dance, but I couldn't carry a melody. When I was four years old, she gave up and bought me a set of drums for Christmas. The drums suited me because they were an instrument I could play even when I was stuck in bed, and I've played them ever since. When I was five, my mother thought I had the potential to become a child model after I won a beauty contest and had my picture in the local newspaper. My modeling career was to be short-lived: My first job was a milk commercial and each time I drank the product under the hot lights I got nauseous.

Once I knew I was allergic to nearly everything around me, my life became quite simple. If I woke up in the morning and didn't throw up or itch, then I knew it was going to be a good day. This is a valuable lesson for show business. If your expectations are low, you can't possibly be disappointed. When *Pretty Woman* was released in 1990, I thought it would sell a few tickets or, at the very least, start a new fashion trend in black thigh-high boots. But I never dreamed that one Saturday morning at seven as I was dressing for my softball game that I would get a phone call from Dick Cook at Disney's marketing department to say that *Pretty Woman* had surpassed the $100 million mark. The film would go on to make more than $450 million worldwide and earn a Best Actress Academy Award nomination for Julia Roberts.

Following the success of *Pretty Woman*, I celebrated with my family and then flew to Chicago to direct a play. Why did I leave Hollywood when my film was the toast of the town? I'm a firm believer in taking time out to bask in my success because everybody needs a little basking time once in a while. But soon it's time to get back to work. Maintaining a professional balance has always been crucial for me. I never wanted to be Louis B. Mayer and run a studio. I just wanted to have a steady job and get through the day without suffering a violent death.

Once when I got hit by a car and lay bleeding on the sidewalk, my grandmother leaned over me and said, "Garry, I'll give you a dollar if you'll stop bleeding." In my family, everybody had his own way of dealing with a crisis.

To pass the time when I was sick in bed, I used to clip out cartoons from my comic books and newspapers. I would paste my favorites in a book and rate them according to my own humor barometer: "G" was for *good*, "F" was for *very funny*, and "E" for *excellent*. Days and sometimes weeks later, I would review the jokes and those that made me laugh a second or even third time were ranked the highest of all. Somehow, even though I was just a little kid, I understood the concept that jokes that could stand up over time were better than jokes which just made you laugh the first time. I also learned that possessing a sense of humor could help me survive in the world. But I never thought this would lead to a career. It was simply something to make me smile when I was feeling blue.

As I grew older, my neighborhood in the Bronx became a place that applauded boys who could hit home runs during the day and then beat up people at night. I couldn't do either, but my parents had other plans for me. At home my mother taught me about comedy and musical theater, and my father often counseled me on how important it was to become a boss. However, he *didn't* say a boss of what. The only thing I liked doing was making people laugh and I didn't see how I could become a boss doing that.

I remember the first time I made my sisters, Ronny and Penny, laugh. I was fourteen years old. The whole family was at a restaurant called Mort's Port in New York City eating lobsters and wearing bibs. In the middle of the meal, I let out a big burp. My father looked at me in horror. Staring back at him, I said, "What'd you expect, chimes?"

Both my little sisters burst out laughing. I was quite pleased with my delivery of this line, from the play *The Man Who Came to Dinner*, which I had read in a joke book. My mother also roared with laughter, although she tried to muffle it with her lobster bib. My father didn't laugh at all. He found it foolish and undignified. Yet from that moment on, listening to my sisters giggle, I knew I had an audience of at least two.

Unfortunately, my teachers at De Witt Clinton High School in the Bronx were not as amused as my sisters were. My report cards most often contained the phrase "could do better," but I did manage to find a few teachers who thought I had potential. Raphael Philipson, the adviser for the school newspaper, was a stiff, strait-laced intellectual who wore a bow tie and showed absolutely no sense of humor. I was sure that people who wore suits and ties, like my father, were people who didn't laugh and Mr. Philipson seemed to support my theory. I used to stand over his shoulder and watch as he edited my sports and humor column with the grim expression of someone proofreading obituaries.

At first, I worried that Mr. Philipson was going to ruin my life with one quick stroke of his familiar blue editing pencil. But I was wrong. Instead of putting me down for my humor he tried to make it better by fixing the grammar or proposing a better phrase or word. I once wrote "Eye droppers are careless folks" and Mr. Philipson suggested changing the word "folks" to "people" to make it less provincial. His patience and attention to detail made me realize that I shouldn't be afraid of intellectuals or stuffy men in suits and ties. They were not always the enemy, as I had suspected, and years later the Mr. Philipsons of the world would prove important to my career.

Strangely enough, many of the people who grew up in the Bronx with me chose the careers of comedian or clothing designer. Calvin Klein and Ralph Lauren lived in the neighborhood, but back then Ralph's last name was Lifshitz. It was probably a wise move that he changed his name because Polo by Lifshitz doesn't have quite the same ring. The comedians and entertainment types included Rob Reiner, Carl Reiner, Robert Klein, Neil Simon, and Jeff Wald. I think the Bronx was a place where it was an asset to have a sense of humor to survive: When a guy is laughing, he's less likely to punch you in the face. I have no explanation for the run on clothing designers, except to say that we all probably dressed badly.

If not for two other teachers, Lou Katz and Doc Guernsey, I might have ended up working as a drummer on the strip-joint circuit. Katz was a witty and rebellious man who was the favorite of the senior class. Doc, the ultimate educator, was a heavyset teacher with white hair who had been crippled from polio and walked with two canes. Katz and Doc seemed to believe that I was brighter than I thought myself. They were always pushing me to go beyond my limits. I earned fair grades, but Katz and Doc expected more. When it came time to apply to college, I took the conservative road and considered City College of New York, New York University, and Queens College. But Katz and Doc encouraged me to shoot for the Ivy League and the Big Ten.

Even as I started sending away for college applications, though, I still had no idea exactly what it was I wanted to be. I played the drums, but not well enough to make it a full-time career (I used to do a bad drummer joke, "I'm not Buddy Rich. I'm Buddy Poor"). I played basketball and baseball, but wasn't strong enough to play at the college level. I wrote a column for my school newspaper where I tested out my new jokes. But when I wasn't sharing my jokes with other people, I was simply amusing myself. I spent most of my time daydreaming. Sometimes I would think of jokes and situations while sitting in class and begin to flinch, twist, and talk to myself as I acted them out in my mind, which caused more than one of my teachers to suspect that I might have epilepsy. But daydreaming didn't seem to be a viable career path either. The want ads didn't have a subheading for daydreamers, so I decided to go to my father and ask his advice.

"Dad, what should I be?"

"Choose a profession that you could do if you had a toothache," he said matter-of-factly and poured himself a drink.

"What are you talking about, Dad?"

"Garry, you're probably going to be sick for the rest of your life. You'd better pick a job you could do with a toothache, stomachache, headache, or whateverache."

That I understood. I decided that writing might be a job I could do if I was in bed with a fever or holding an ice bag to my mouth. And my penchant for daydreaming could be an asset. So I applied to colleges with journalism programs. The first time I saw my byline in print was in the school newspaper on a story about a pet shop that I had written when I was seven years old. Even though the teacher managed to misspell my name by leaving one *r* out of "Garry," I still found seeing my name in print a thrill. I decided that it wouldn't be such a bad way to make a living either, even if I would have to spend the rest of my life reminding people that it was "Garry" with two *r*s.

When I was applying to college my father urged me to get out of New York and see the rest of the world while my mother, although worldly when it came to the arts such as music, dance, and theater, wanted me to stay close to home because she was afraid of the rest of the world. I compromised and went as far as Chicago. In the fall of 1952, I boarded my first airplane and headed off to Northwestern University in Evanston, Illinois, to study journalism.

During my freshman year, I learned a valuable lesson: There was no way I was going to be a journalist. In my writing classes, I was constantly getting into trouble because I couldn't get the facts straight, even on my first story. Each member of the class was assigned to write a different living person's obituary. I got Danny Kaye. Our professor gave us a few hours to search the university library, collect material, and write the obit. I got side-tracked by a girl and ended up not doing the assignment, but I knew I had to hand in something so I typed out the words, "Danny Kaye, who was reported dead earlier today, didn't die at all. It was a false alarm. He was sick, but he recovered."

My teacher said, "What is this?"

"You made up that he was dead, so I made up that he was alive."

The teacher gave me a D. I should have taken this as an early sign that journalism wasn't for me. But I was an idealistic fresh-man, so I didn't give up right away.

While many of my classmates found my journalism antics amusing, my teachers usually responded with the phrase "You fool around too much, Marshall." I was always looking for ways to put my own spin on a straight news story. Instead of writing a dry, fac-tual lead, I wrote openings like "Rumors flew around the White House like golf balls yesterday as President Eisenhower prepared to hold his press conference." Another time I wrote a piece on baseball about an obscure catcher named Matt Batts. I revealed to my readers that his real name was Matthew Batthew. This kind of writing will not get you a job at The *New York Times*.

My less than impressive performance as a journalist in college didn't come as a surprise to me because I had had some trouble before I even arrived. Based on the success of my high school sports column I had been hired as a sports stringer for the *New York Journal-American*. I was the paper's De Witt Clinton corre-spondent and one day after a big game the paper was on deadline, so I called in my story from a corner pay phone.

"Hello, this is Marshall here at the Clinton–Evander game and I have a story to file," I said.

"Wait a second, Marshall," said the sports editor. "I've got another call ahead of you. Give me your number and I'll call you right back."

I rattled off a number and as I was hanging up the phone I realized that instead of giving him the number of the pay phone, I had recited the number to my *parents'* apartment. I started to call him back but discovered that I had just used my last dime. Panicked, I managed to track down a policeman, who gave me a dime. My hands shook nervously as I redialed the newsroom number.

"It's me again," I said.

"Hi, Marshall," the sports editor said archly. "I just had a nice chat with your mother, but she didn't know the goddamned score of the game!"

Even though I was busy butchering the traditional rules of journalism, Northwestern did manage to teach me something else—not to be afraid of failure. College encouraged me to try different things outside my major without the fear of being yelled at if I flopped. When I was growing up, my mother taught me that the biggest sin was to be boring. Northwestern seemed to agree with Mom. There were fraternities, intramural sports teams, and musical theater and I tried them all. Classmate Joel Sterns and I wrote a comedy skit about exchange students going to Mexico for Northwestern's annual Waa-Mu show and I saw my material performed before a well-dressed, paying audience for the first time. There was so much to do at college that if I didn't like an activity, I simply moved on to the next one.

I didn't let the summers slow me down, and I signed on as a counselor at Camp Onibar in Pennsylvania. After helping stage an all-camp production of *The Song of Hiawatha*, I thought I had found my destiny in musical theater. The fact that I couldn't read music or carry a tune didn't stop me. I saw that if you had the right words and music it was possible to move an audience emotionally with fifty nonactors, even if they were dressed as ears of corn. That certainly wasn't boring. (One of those ears of corn, my longtime friend Ira Glick, is now a professor of psychiatry at Stanford University.) The wonderful excitement that came with trying something new at college and camp outweighed my fear of falling flat on my face in real life.

I didn't always feel this cavalier toward failure and embarrassment. Growing up I wasted a lot of time being afraid and embarrassed over the smallest things and thinking I was near death from my allergies and ailments. When I was eight, I over-heard a doctor tell my parents that if we didn't move to Arizona right away, I would surely die. When we didn't move, I was certain my days were numbered.

However, my attitude changed after an incident when I was a teenager and went to a fancy birthday party for a girl in New Rochelle. Her parents served hamburgers smothered in mustard. All the other kids could eat mustard except me, so I made believe I could even though it provokes one of my worst allergies. I ate a hamburger and immediately felt an attack coming on. I didn't want to be embarrassed in front of the other kids, so I hid my attack until I could be alone in the privacy of my own home. When the party was over, the parents lined up in the girl's circular driveway to pick up their children. I made it to my parents' car, but then it happened—I got sick out the car window and was caught in the glare of all the other cars' headlights. Everybody saw me, and at that moment I wanted to die. I thought I would never be able to face my friends again. After that, however, nothing seemed quite so embarrassing ever again. I'd learned an important lesson: You can't really die of embarrassment. It just feels fatal.

In college I continued to daydream and it constantly got me into trouble. I accidentally set a teacher's desk on fire with a ciga-rette. I slept through a final exam because my band, The Holden Caulfield Trio, played a late-night gig in Chicago. (We gave our band a literary name to try to attract a smarter bar crowd than the usual drunks who threw things at bands.) As proofreader and night editor at *The Daily Northwestern* newspaper, I let the word "part-nership" run as "fartnership" in a sports story headline. Through it all, I learned how to meet deadlines and how to perform rather than crumble under deadline pressure. Even if I still needed to work at getting all the facts straight, I did learn how to sit down, write something, and finish it. Somehow, I knew this closure skill would be an asset no matter what profession I fell into later.

Cultivating confidence and learning not to be afraid of failure or embarrassment are very easy to talk about, but doing them is another story. I can best illustrate this with an example from many years later. In 1977, when I had already produced nine television

series and *Happy Days* and *Laverne & Shirley* were still big hits
for ABC on Tuesday nights, I got a call from Michael Eisner, who
was then the head of Paramount. He said, "Garry, help us out.
We're short on new programs to show the network in New York.
We are stuck. Will you please come up with another TV series?"

My first response was to say no way. Television is the only art
form in the history of the world where if you're doing one project
well and it's a hit they ask you to do another one at the exact same
time. However, I ended up doing it because of my son.

Several months earlier, Robin Williams had appeared in an
episode of *Happy Days* as Mork from Ork. The idea for the
episode came about shortly after *Star Wars* was released in 1977.
My two little girls were loyal *Happy Days* fans, but my son, whose
biggest disappointment as a child was that I had nothing whatsoever to do with *Star Wars*, didn't like *Happy Days*.

"What would make you watch the show?" I asked eight-year-
old Scott as he sat in his room playing with his menagerie of *Star
Wars* dolls.

"If it had a space alien on it," he said.

"A space alien? But *Happy Days* is a realistic show about the
1950s. Kids back then liked race car derbies and milk shakes, not
aliens from other planets."

"Well, Richie could have a dream," said the eight-year-old
mind.

Scott was absolutely right. Richie *could* have a dream and
that's what I told the *Happy Days* writing staff the next day. It
happened to be a time when we were running out of worthy adver-
saries for Fonzie to fight each week, and a space alien seemed like
a suitable opponent. If introducing an alien on *Happy Days* would
make my son watch the show, it also might attract a whole new
audience of young people.

While the idea for the show came about in a convoluted way,
there was nothing confusing about the audience's response to
Mork from Ork: When Robin came out to take his curtain call that
night after the filming of *Happy Days*, all three hundred people in
the studio audience gave him a standing ovation. There was no
doubt in their minds that he had the potential to become a star.
This prompted me to bring up the character when Eisner started

pressuring me about a new series. "Okay, I've got this alien that I could possibly do something with."

Before I knew it, he had me on a conference call with a bunch of ABC executives in New York. The only one I knew was Marcy Carsey, who was familiar with Mork's *Happy Days* episode, so I talked directly to her. I also suspected that Carsey and Eisner were the only two who actually watched my shows; the others just watched the ratings.

"Marcy, do you remember Mork? How about a show about an alien who visits Earth, observes life here, and reports back his findings to his planet? We could call it the *Mork Chronicles*," I said.

Another man came on the line and said, "That's not a good title. No one will know what 'chronicles' means."

"Sir, there are only two of us talking right now. Which one of us doesn't know what 'chronicles' means?" I said with minimum sarcasm.

Another voice interrupted. "The show should have a title that kids and zoos can name their animals after."

I paused for a moment and tried to remind myself that many network executives also come from an alien planet.

Although this comment might seem like it came from left field, I knew what they meant. When viewers start naming their animals after a show or the star, you know you have a hit. There were a lot of dogs named Fonzie walking around then.

"How about Mork and Melissa?" I said. "Mork and Marlo? Mork and Mindy?"

"That's good, Mork and Mindy," said the animal person.

"Where does Mork land?" asked another voice.

Whenever I go on a location shoot, I like to have a member of my family nearby to make me feel more comfortable. At the time, my niece was going to college in Boulder, Colorado.

"Mork lands in Boulder," I said, figuring if we had to shoot some location scenes in Colorado my niece Penny Lee could make me a safe sandwich. And as far as I knew, Norman Lear, Aaron Spelling, and Grant Tinker had no dibs on Boulder that year.

"Who will play Mindy?"

They were asking me too many detailed questions about a show I had just made up. Even if I had wanted to shrug off the idea I couldn't: Eisner was sitting beside me on the couch, prodding me to come up with more ideas. I remembered Pam Dawber, an actress I had seen in an unsold pilot about a young nun called *Sister Terry*. Although I thought the pilot didn't work, Pam was great and Marcy knew her work. I blurted her name out.

"Pam Dawber will play Mindy," I said.

Before I knew it, Marcy Carsey, whose name was reminiscent of Matt Batts', together with the dynamic and totally fearless Paramount TV president Gary Nardino, literally took some silent footage from *Sister Terry* (a few choice scenes of Pam without the nun's habit) and spliced it together with some film from Robin's appearance on *Happy Days*. That was it. For a total cost of sixty-three dollars and change, they made a pilot. A show was born. Pretty impressive considering that at the time pilots were running around $400,000 apiece.

After I pitched *Mork & Mindy* to the network, I went on vacation with my wife, Barbara, to a resort in St. John. The resort had one telephone and it was hanging from a tree. One day as I was lying on the beach listening to the waves, a member of the hotel staff came running over and said I had a phone call. I ran to the tree. It was a jubilant Gary Nardino. He said the studio had sold *Mork & Mindy* to ABC and it would air on Thursday nights. I ran back to my wife on the beach.

"Honey, I've sold another show," I said.

"What's it about this time?" she asked.

"I'm not sure," I mumbled.

Another example that show business is not an exact science: The series was rated number one in 1979.

I began to feel that if you are not totally afraid of failure, if fear doesn't paralyze you, and if you can work under pressure, then you've got a shot. *Mork & Mindy*, a hit show made up during a ten-minute phone conversation, also launched the careers of Robin Williams and Pam Dawber, who read about her new job in the trades and asked her agent, "When did I audition for this show?" Of course, I could have made a complete fool of myself, but this time I was lucky. I have failed with dozens of other pilots and shows, including the unfortunate *Me and the Chimp* (a family comedy that now runs on educational television under the heading "Let This Be a Lesson to You") and a Vegas show-girl sitcom called *Blansky's Beauties*, which I tried to make five different ways and failed with each one. The important thing was that every time I was ready for failure and, though I didn't enjoy it, I got up the next day and tried to think of another show. It's okay to fail; just don't give people time to contemplate your failures. I subscribe to the words of Samuel Beckett, "I try. I fail. Fail better."

College taught me to think fast on deadline, and the army continued that basic training. After graduating from Northwestern in 1956, I enlisted in the army with my childhood friend Martin Garbus. At first, I was assigned to a unit on Long Island and lived at home. After a few months I applied to be transferred to a foreign base so I could finally move out of my parents' house. I selected Germany as my first choice because I pictured myself eating a warm piece of strudel in a Berlin café with a voluptuous woman named Helga by my side, neither of which I was allergic to. I didn't get my first choice. Or my second. Or my third. I got Seoul, South Korea, known for being one of the worst posts in the army in 1956. No Helga. No strudel. No Berlin café. Just a cantankerous seventy-year-old Asian woman dishing out rice in a little hut.

In Seoul, I worked for the American Forces Korea Network as a writer and sound editor and helped edit the radio broadcasts. On my first day I was told to delete a few minutes from the broadcast because it was too long for our time slot. I discovered a very long Korean song at the end of the tape, so I simply lopped off a few seconds from the middle of that and spliced the tape back together. I didn't think anybody would notice. Unfortunately, the song I had edited turned out to be the South Korean national anthem and my abbreviated version was heard by thousands of Koreans. Having offended an entire nation, I feared I would be court-martialed, or worse—sent to work on the radio station at our base on the 38th parallel. However, because it was only my first day, the major simply reprimanded me. The experience, however, made me realize that there is such a thing as thinking *too* fast on your feet.

I was able to gain back some respect during a broadcast of the

Academy Awards. We were relaying the show for our troops, but the North Koreans were intermittently jamming the airwaves and ruining Bob Hope's opening monologue. Despite the omissions, I could tell from the punch lines what the straight lines had been and vice versa. So I quickly found a soldier who could do a passable Bob Hope imitation. Then I spliced together the monologue with the soldier's imitation so it made sense. My co-workers were stunned. They thought I was clairvoyant. They didn't understand that it didn't take a comedy genius to figure out punch lines, particularly of Hope jokes. I did it fast. They were impressed and we all got to hear the Academy Awards. My superiors were surprised and one said, "That idiot who cut the national anthem in half seems to have a flair for comedy."

I didn't perform my other duties as a soldier with the same élan. I couldn't shoot very well. I was never the first one up the rope. I couldn't load my gun blindfolded, being barely able to do it with my eyes open. The one thing I *could* do well was shoot a gun while resting on my stomach, possibly because I spent so much time in bed as a child. Clearly, I was not cut out to be a soldier. Instead, I had to find ways to get around my flaws. Most people make the mistake of trying to beat down their flaws or deny them altogether. I've always found it's best to say, "Here are my flaws. Now I have to find something I'm good at. What tools do I have that will make me stand out?" Don't use your flaws as an excuse to quit. Move forward or sideways.

Growing up I always had good hands. Not the kind of nimble hands capable of building a model airplane out of balsa wood, but fast hands that could play the drums or catch a ball. In the army I turned to music and sports to help set me apart from the pack. On the twenty-one-day voyage from Tacoma, Washington, to Seoul, I brought along my snare drum and cymbal and, after I conquered my seasickness, I got together with a few guys and formed a band. When we played for the new recruits on the top deck of the U.S.S. *Freeman* and they applauded and cheered us, it was the first time I remember thinking, "I'm successful at something. They're clapping for the band and I'm a member."

Once we got to Korea, I turned to sports: I was the only soldier in my barracks to try out for and make the basketball team. Even though I wasn't the greatest player, I made up for it with hustle. My spot on the team allowed me to be whisked off like a dignitary to a game, even if we were in the middle of a complicated maneuver. When I wasn't shooting baskets, I looked for other activities and stumbled into an army talent contest where I did a stand-up routine. I got up, told a few jokes, and they laughed. I was still frightened and shy, but both emotions proved to be great motivators for me in the army. I figured I could either let them push me around or I could try to demonstrate a unique talent and possibly get sent to a special place. In 1958, I did a comedy act called the Heartburns and with my partner, Jim Anglisano, we were winners in the Far East All-Army Entertainment Contest. Then I was flown back to the States to compete in the grand finals of the All-Army Entertainment Contest in Fort Belvoir, Virginia. After getting third place, I had such a short time left in the army that they released me instead of sending me back to Korea. I'm convinced that if I hadn't found a way to set myself apart from the other soldiers, I might still be in Seoul trying to figure out how to take my gun apart.

I consider myself a late bloomer and always envied those people who stood out in high school, because I didn't. Life is one struggle after another to try to find out where you can excel in a new arena. The first time I directed an episode of *The Odd Couple*, we were on location in New York City when a man came up to me near the food truck one day at lunch and asked me to get him a bowl of chicken noodle soup. He mistook me for a member of the catering staff instead of the director of the show. I got the man his soup, but the next day I was determined to change my image: I started wearing a cowboy hat, which I wore for the rest of the shoot. At least that way people could point to me and say, "The director is the one in the hat." (Later *Happy Days* director Jerry Paris told me that a director also should wear a red sweater so the actors know where to look.)

In show business, setting yourself apart from the group is essential when starting out, especially when the competition is fierce and your résumé is sitting at the bottom of a pile of junk mail. But this doesn't mean laboring over what color paper to print your résumé on. Save the discussion about paper and raised lettering for when you're ordering wedding invitations; you don't have time to worry about whether your role in *Jesus Christ Superstar* or your lighting credit from *West Side Story* would look better on ecru or heavy bond paper. Just try to tailor the résumé to whomever you're sending it and get it in the mail.

A young man once sent me his résumé written on a basketball after I had mentioned in an article that I loved sports. I immediately brought him in for an interview. Another time, a writer named Karyl Geld sent me a tank filled with fish as a thank-you for reading her script. I forgot a lot of other writers but never "the girl who sent the fish." Most people get mail every morning that aggravates them. If you can send them something that won't piss them off, then you already have an advantage.

In show business, and most businesses, if you can somehow differentiate your résumé from the others in the stack, then they'll remember your name. It's not necessarily that there are people out there better than you, but there are just so *many* people out there altogether. When film editor Priscilla Nedd-Friendly was starting out, she posted a big sign on a bulletin board at the American Film Institute that said WILL EDIT ANYTHING.

Everybody has his own approach; you have to find one that's comfortable for you. Marion Ross once told me that she always wears a red dress to an audition to set herself apart. Robin Williams auditioned for the part of Mork while standing on his head. When I first interviewed Julia Roberts, she told me that when she was little she and her sister used to dress up and play *Laverne & Shirley*. She wore an "L" on her sweater even though her name was Julia. I once knew two writers who always dressed in matching black outfits when they went to pitch a script. Clothing is a quick cheap way to set yourself apart.

For an actor, the point is to do something, anything, that will make you memorable and make the director or producer comfortable, *not* the other way around. Most actors don't understand this; they think it's the director's job to make them feel at ease. Wrong. It's the actor's job during an audition to make the director or producer so comfortable that they won't worry about risking money on the actor. If you can make them feel secure, then you'll get the job.

My problem when I was starting out was that I wasn't very good at promoting myself, so I found ambitious partners who were. Fred Freeman, my first partner, whom I met at Northwestern, was well read, highly motivated, and had a flair for satire. At first, I was afraid of everyone and Fred was afraid of no one. He designed the strategy that helped catapult our careers from young joke writers in New York City to sitcom story writers in Hollywood. Fred taught me that instead of becoming complacent about the current job, keep one eye on the next job to see if you'll like it better.

My second partner, Jerry Belson, a master of cynicism who was known as the "Kafka of Comedy," started his career in Hollywood writing Daffy Duck cartoons. In the mid-1960s, when Jerry and I were writing half-hour television scripts for sitcoms, he would draw cartoons relevant to the story on the cover of each script envelope before we submitted it to a studio. People started remembering us. "Oh, those are the two guys who draw cartoons on their script envelopes." This story may sound rather insignificant today when Hollywood is known for its superstar agents and pushy entertainment lawyers, but I think the goal of a creative person should remain the same: Get your work noticed.

The need to set yourself apart never ends. Even today I am constantly looking for imaginative ways to clinch a deal. In 1992, I was mounting a Los Angeles production of *Wrong Turn at Lungfish* and trying to get George C. Scott to play the lead. From the moment the negotiations started, I could tell things were not going well. George was reluctant to lock into the project. A barrage of meetings, letters, and faxes followed, but both sides appeared unwilling to bend on issues of money and time. I decided to ignore the agents and lawyers and go the unconventional route. Since I wasn't getting through to George on one level, I would appeal to something more personal.

I did some research and found out that two of his favorite things in life are chess and the Detroit Tigers. That gave me more than enough to work with. First, I sent George a letter stating that I would hire an intern, whom I had found by placing ads in the trades, to play chess with him backstage during the entire run of the play. His contract would include the clause "One chess partner on hand at all times." Second, I appealed to George's passion for the Detroit Tigers. I began signing all my correspondence to George with names of old Detroit Tiger ballplayers—"Sincerely, Hank Greenberg," "Fondly, Rudy York," and "Best Wishes, Dizzy Trout." A few weeks later, George signed the deal to star in the play.

Opportunities, particularly for writers, don't happen overnight. You have to make them happen. After I was released from the army in 1958, I thought it was finally time to put my journalism degree to work. I applied to The *New York Times* as a copyboy, but they told me they only liked Ivy League graduates. I insisted I could get coffee just as fast as any Harvard kid, but they didn't buy it. I ended up at the *Daily News*.

My job consisted of running around sharpening pencils, fixing typewriters, getting research from the library, carrying copy from one reporter's desk to another's, and being on call when anyone needed something to eat, drink, or be cleaned up. One reporter used to blow his nose into copy paper and leave it on his desk; needless to say, cleaning off his desk was not for the weak of stomach crowd.

One night I was given the plum assignment of accompanying a photographer on a story about a man who had committed suicide by hanging himself from a tree down by the Hudson River. On the way to take the picture, we got delayed because the photographer stopped for a drink. By the time we arrived, the police had already taken the dead man down from the tree. Desperate to get a picture, the photographer pleaded with the police to put the man back up in the noose—and they did! Only, in their haste the police picked up the man's hat from the ground and placed it on his head, making it an even better photo opportunity than what had originally occurred.

The photograph ended up in the *Daily News* and later earned the photographer a prestigious award. But the incident, although rather comical, simply confused me. Staging the photograph was against every rule I had learned in journalism school. I began to question my own ethics and journalism as a profession. The rules were clearly black and white in college and the army, but the real world seemed to be gray. And it wasn't even a definitive shade of gray.

I worked during the day as a copyboy and at night Fred Freeman and I wrote jokes for a couple of housewives from Long Island, the only ones who answered our ad in the newspaper. They wanted to sound witty at garden club meetings and some even harbored secret aspirations of becoming professional entertainers. We'd have them fill out a questionnaire telling us a little about themselves and then write up a routine. The material we wrote for them was certainly not an exercise in comedy brilliance, but they were just starting out and so were we.

While working at the *Daily News* I became friends with a reporter named Robert Sylvester, who wrote "Dream Street," a column laced with gossip and humorous tales of Broadway. One day I mustered up the courage to submit a few of my jokes to Sylvester for his column. He didn't use anything the first time, but he also didn't put me down, which encouraged me to try again. After a few more tries, he started using my material and placing my name (sometimes spelled wrong) in his column. "It was Gerry Marshall's story about the two lady tourists in Paris. One tells the other: 'You know, I've been here two weeks and haven't been to the Louvre yet.' And the other woman replies, 'Well, maybe it's the water.'" Sylvester eventually got the spelling down as he began to rely on me more and more when he needed to fill space in his column.

Sylvester taught me a lot, including the odd theory that illness is a stepping-stone for advancement in the newspaper business: If someone gets sick, then somebody has to do that job. If you get a chance to learn a new job while someone is sick, it will only be to your advantage. Whenever anyone looked pale I volunteered to learn a new job.

I was proud of my contributions to "Dream Street," but my parents were baffled by my professional progress. "This is what you're doing with your journalism degree?" my father would say. Or, "You spent four years in college and all you do is write jokes?" My mother was always asking me, "But, Garry, what do I tell the neighbors, the butcher, the baker, and the guy who runs the gas station? What do I tell them *you do for a living*?" I said, "Tell them I work for the CIA on a secret project in Arizona and you can't say any more about it. It's top secret. Or tell them I'm on assignment with the Peace Corps. In Peru." The key to survival between the ages of twenty-one and twenty-six is teaching your parents how to lie. You have to make up what you're doing for others while you're trying to figure out what you really want to do.

I told people I was an acrobat. I considered myself a writer, but whenever you tell people you're a writer they invariably ask, "What have you written?" When you haven't written anything significant, it's embarrassing. To say I was a copyboy by day and a freelance comedy writer by night was boring. So at cocktail parties or other get-togethers, Fred and I would say we were high-wire acrobats with the circus and that our third partner, the guy who caught us, was in the hospital. We thought this would account for the fact that we seemed to be out of work. Better to be perceived as out-of-work acrobats than out-of-work writers.

When I wasn't at parties lying, I played the drums in several bands and made a brief attempt at being a nightclub comedian. My stand-up act in the army had gone over so well that I thought it might be something to pursue. But I quickly discovered that people preferred to buy my material rather than hear me deliver it. Guys would come up to me after my show and instead of saying "Congratulations," they would say, "You know that contact lens routine? How much do you want for it? I can deliver it better."

When we started, the material Fred and I wrote was lousy or only appealed to fringe comedians. The first real money we ever made as comedy writers was from the entertainer Christine Jorgensen, who had undergone a sex change operation from "he" to "she." Christine paid us fifty dollars for three pages of jokes. When people asked me what it was like to write for her, I would say, "Loved him, hated her," or "Her delivery was good and his was only fair."

Thanks to the help of fellow writer Saul Turteltaub, our next job was writing for Shari Lewis and her delightful menagerie of puppets that included Charlie Horse, Hush Puppy, and the infamous Lamb Chop. We wrote sketches featuring sound effects, pantomimes, and gentle children's insult humor such as, "Make like a drum and beat it" or "Make like an ostrich and go bury your

head." Shari was very sweet to work with, but Lamb Chop was a
pain in the ass. Shari would give us a compliment, but then Lamb
Chop would curl up his little nose and say, "These four jokes are
flat boys. Punch 'em up!" One afternoon when Fred and I were
leaving Shari's office, Fred just snapped and said, "That's it! I've
had it. I don't want a career writing for a piece of cloth!" I had to
agree; it was time to move on.

The hard part about starting out is that you're always, unreal-
istically, waiting for the big break, the one that will set you on your
way. Too often you're hoping to get discovered at the legendary
Schwab's counter or fantasizing about selling a spec script for two
million dollars. The reality is that Schwab's drugstore in
Hollywood was torn down years ago, and most people don't make
millions for writing their first script. The real breaks are smaller,
but don't overlook them. Ours didn't come in the shape of a
Lamb Chop, but instead in the form of a bizarre tale involving a
broken elevator. Fred and I were with an old army friend of mine
named Charlie the trumpet player. We were waiting for the elevator, an old-fashioned kind with a round piece of glass in the
center where you could see who was in it. The elevator was always
messed up and sometimes when you pressed the down button, it
wouldn't stop on your floor. So there we were, standing in the hall
of my building, when the elevator went flying by with a guy
inside. Charlie yelled, "That was Mutt!" and went running down
the stairs.

Fred and I quickly followed. It turned out that inside was
Charlie's friend Muttle Tickner, who not only dated a girl in our
building but also worked for the theatrical personal management
firm Berger, Ross & Steinman. A week later we went to Mutt's
office and he introduced us to comedian Phil Foster, who would
become our first mentor (and whom I would later be able to pay
back by casting him in *Laverne & Shirley*). Lightning had struck
and Fred and I were ready for it: We started cranking out jokes for
Phil Foster.

Luck usually plays a role in most breaks. If you're in the right
place at the right time with enough talent to get noticed, you've got
a shot. Follow your passion. Follow the elevator. And keep going.

Everyone starting out in show business should have a mentor, preferably someone who is not a relative because most young people don't trust their relatives, and with good reason. When I was five years old and sickly, I had to take several aspirin a day, but I was rarely near a water fountain. My mother, knowing I worshiped drummers, told me that all bass drummers in marching bands took aspirin without water and that I should too. I believed her and started doing the same. That fall I went to Macy's Thanksgiving Day Parade and when I saw a band coming, I raced up and marched beside the bass drummer and said in my five-year-old voice, "I take aspirin without water just like you!" The guy looked at me like I was crazy and walked away, almost hitting me in the head with his bass drum.

Since I couldn't always trust my relatives when I was young, my first mentor was Phil Foster. He was the first professional comedian who told Fred Freeman and me that we had talent. He also relished the fact that we were cheap. Phil introduced us to other comedians, who also liked that we were cheap and were amused by our naïveté. We had business cards that carried our slogan: 100% VIRGIN MATERIAL. However, most of the comics didn't have much money, so they would buy us a bowl of soup, give us a new tie or whatever they had access to as payment for jokes. Even Phil was sometimes short on cash and would take us to baseball games instead of paying us. It didn't really matter. We were working writers and to be reimbursed in food wasn't the worst thing that could have happened to two guys who were hungry.

While Phil was very supportive of our career, others were not so kind. Be prepared at all times for rejection, even after you break in. One night I was backstage at Jack Silverman's International Nightclub in New York City. I nervously handed a page of jokes I had written for a famous veteran comedian. He read my jokes without laughing or even cracking a smile, removed a silver monogrammed cigarette lighter from his coat pocket, and set my page of jokes on fire. He then very nonchalantly tossed the burning page into a small metal trash can and walked away. Unable to speak, I simply stood there staring at the can as the bright red flames turned my jokes into ashes. It was my first flaming rejection.

I went home that night to my apartment feeling like quitting the business. Fred and I talked about the rejection, and we decided that it was too easy to get depressed and feel sorry for ourselves. Instead, we made a pact: We would devote one half hour of each day to self-pity. We pledged to sit in our cold fifth-floor apartment for thirty minutes each day and say things like "No one will hire me. I will never work. I will fail. I am sad." However, at *all* other times, we had to maintain an air of supreme self-confidence.

Just because you have a desire to succeed doesn't always mean you can move forward all the time. Sometimes you have to take two steps back before taking three steps forward.

In the early 1960s, Phil Foster introduced Fred and me to comedian Joey Bishop, who worked in the clubs and often appeared as a guest host on *The Tonight Show*, at that time called *The Jack Paar Show*. When we heard that Joey might be interested in buying some freelance material, we went to see him. I handed him my Northwestern diploma as a way to introduce myself; I thought it would impress him. He examined the front of the diploma, turned it over, then said, "There are no jokes on here. Take it home and write jokes in the white spaces and then bring it back to me."

And so Fred and I wrote material for Joey, who eventually helped us get a staff job writing for Jack Paar and other guest hosts. Our first joke used on the show by Joey was "The traffic was so heavy, I drove from Manhattan to Long Island in neutral." Not a gigantic laugh, but we were in heaven. It was the best job I had ever had in my life. The hours were great, 3 P.M. to 8 P.M., with Fridays off; the pay was good, $300 a week; and I was learning so much from the show's staff writers. The one drawback was my parents: The show only ran the writers' credits once a week and even then it was difficult for my parents to be proud of my work.

"What exactly do you do on the show?" my mother would ask.

"Did you hear that, Ma? I wrote that duck joke," I said.

"What should I tell my friends?" she asked.

"Tell them I'm a lawyer," I said.

After we had been writing for a few months, *The Jack Paar Show* raised our salary to $400 a week. Bingo! The next day a man knocked at our door and said, "Hi, I'm Frank Cooper. Are you boys going to be seeking representation?" We didn't know what that meant. After Mr. Cooper explained that he was an agent, we signed a deal with him. People are always worried about finding an agent, but my philosophy is that once you get a job worth representing, the agents will find you. Of course, it's hard to get that first job without an agent but once you do, you're set. Most people starting out spend too much time worrying about agents and too little time worrying about writing something that will sell. Sending your work out to stars and production companies is often easier than getting representation.

I loved working for Jack Paar and could have stayed in New York and written for him for the rest of my life. But Fred, always more ambitious than me, had different ideas. In the summer of 1961, Joey Bishop moved to Hollywood to star in his own television series. Joey called a few months later and asked us to come to Hollywood and write for his show. Fred said it was time for us to move on and Jack Paar graciously agreed to let us out of our contract.

The good part was that we were free to move because neither of us had wives or children. The bad part was that we had just been given our raise. I already had abandoned my job at the *Daily News*, where I worked 8 A.M. to 4 P.M. for $68 a week, following my first byline on a story about a stamp collector. The story was so boring my father fell asleep while reading it. To move to California to work on the *The Joey Bishop Show* we would have to take a cut in pay to $200 a week. My first instinct was to say, "Hey, wait a minute. Isn't this a step back for us?" Fred convinced me that the cut in pay was worth the chance to learn how to write television scripts. Thinking it would be easier to follow our dreams in sneakers while we were young rather than in slippers when we were old, we headed for California on the eve of my twenty-seventh birthday.

On *The Joey Bishop Show* we met a writer named Milt Josefsberg, who would become my second mentor. Milt taught me that even in Hollywood it was important not to put all of your jokes in one basket. After writing for Jack Benny for seventeen years, Milt was out of work for the next *six years*. I couldn't imagine being out of work for six days, let alone six years, so I quickly learned to diversify to protect myself.

Once I was getting work as a sitcom writer, I tried other forms such as drama, movie scripts, and variety shows. Then I branched out into other areas such as directing and producing. I figured that if someone didn't hire me as a sitcom writer, then he could hire me as something else. Eventually, I earned enough credits to join the Writers Guild, Screen Actors Guild, Directors Guild, Producers Guild, the local musicians union, and every other professional entertainment group that would let me in. If I could have gotten a card in the cameramen's union, I would have done that, too. I soon discovered that the key to being versatile was not telling anyone. I repeat, don't tell anyone you're versatile.

Nobody wants a field goal kicker who says, "I can also catch passes in the end zone." He'll think you're not concentrating on kicking. At first most employers don't want a Renaissance man; they want an expert. So you must get in the door under one banner and then once you're in, you can unveil your versatility. Once they love you as a field goal kicker and can't live without you, *then* say, "I'm not kicking anymore unless you let me play flanker back, too."

When I was in high school, my dad had an advertising account with the American Medical Association and during his best year he made $80,000. He was proud of the fact that he often played golf and ate dinner at fancy restaurants with the head of the AMA. However, one year a new man became the head of the AMA and my dad lost his job. Just like that. This bothered me. I didn't understand why my dad lost his job just because someone else changed positions. Things didn't work that way in my mother's world because she was her own boss. No one could fire her or push her aside because she ran her own dance studio. I took my mother's approach.

Looking back on my dad's career, I decided to live by a different philosophy. My father was from the Willy Loman school: If you are well liked, they will hire you. I took the opposite approach. I wasn't going to wear expensive suits, dine at fancy restaurants, or schmooze over cocktails with clients. If I did that, then how could they evaluate my talent? I only wanted people to judge me on my work, not on how much they liked me or how well I spoke or dressed. I wanted people to say, "Garry is not exactly the type you would want to have over to your house. He's not the kind of guy you would want to take to lunch. But he delivers the goods, so hire him."

Chapter Two

Learning from the Old Comics Despite the Yelling

Pain Plus Time Equals Humor

"The premise is soap and shampoo. Write a routine about buying soap and shampoo."

"Okay." Fred Freeman and I nodded in agreement.

"You know, how they come in so many different shapes, sizes, colors, and smells that it's impossible for me to make a decision. You got it?"

"Yes," we agreed.

"Good, because I was up very late last night doing a club date in the Catskills, so I'm gonna go take a nap. Wake me when it's funny," said Phil Foster as he got up from the couch in his Englewood, New Jersey, home and headed for his den.

Huddled together in his living room, Fred and I would then try to come up with material for Phil's nightclub act that would please him. It had to be good enough to wake up a tired, cranky man from his much-deserved nap. We were scared to death at first. How did we really know when a joke was funny? Would it be funny only to us and nobody else? What if we woke up Phil and he didn't find it funny? Would he get mad? Would he yell? Or worse, would he fire us?

"I had to buy a new shampoo. I had so much dandruff that a man came up to me and asked if he could ski on my shoulders."

"I bought something new. It's called soap on a rope. In case you're depressed, you can hang yourself in the shower."

"I'm selling a new shampoo for bald men. It's called a wash cloth. Is that funny? Should we wake him up?"

Sometimes we wanted to sneak out of his house, get on a bus, and go home. But that would be admitting we weren't funny because we never woke him up. After a few naps, we decided that our opinion had to count for something, or else how could we possibly make a living at comedy writing? What Phil was really saying was wake me when *you* think it's funny, and we had to make a decision right or wrong.

After Fred and I graduated from Northwestern and started writing material for other comedians in the early 1960s in New York, we realized that we really had no idea how to write for these men. They were older, from a different generation, and many had been doing stand-up comedy all their lives. It wasn't enough to stay in our apartment and devote hours to sitting in front of our typewriters conjuring up jokes about traffic jams and the weather. We had to spend time with the comedians, listen to their rhythm, and learn from their experience.

In 1960, Phil Foster hired us to write for his NBC radio show called *Monitor*. He paid us $150 a week, but more important than the money was that Phil let us go with him to the Stage Delicatessen. The restaurant was a New York hangout for popular comedians and those hoping to become popular comedians. We would walk into the deli and find famous nightclub and Catskills comics like Jack Carter, Jack E. Leonard, Shecky Greene, Buddy Hackett, Red Buttons, Allan Kent, Lenny Kent, Gene Baylos, Bob Melvin, and Joey Bishop sitting around eating and working on their stand-up routines. When you're used to writing material for Long Island housewives and testy puppets, just eating in a roomful of talented comics is like a dream come true.

We met these comics at a time when television was beginning

to eclipse the popularity of the Manhattan nightclub scene, and most comics were cleaning up their acts to try to get on television. While a few had appeared on *The Ed Sullivan Show*, many of them were still vying for their first big TV break. The problem was that their club routines were often too dirty, or full of jokes about drinking booze like Joe E. Lewis's "This morning I woke up at the crack of ice," which didn't work on television. Some comics were able to clean up their acts, but others, like B. S. Pully and Joe E. Lewis, never were able to make the transition very successfully.

So the Stage Deli was a place full of comics looking for new, hip, clean, commercial material that would play well on television. Because of our association with Phil, the comics let us participate in a comic ritual called "Check, please." This is how it went: A comedian would let you sit at his table while he was eating. Over a pastrami on rye or corned beef sandwich, he would listen to a few of your jokes. If the comedian didn't like your material, he would raise his hand and call out to the waiter, "Check, please." This was your sign that the meeting was over and you should move on to the next table. However, if the comedian liked your jokes, he would invite you to order a bowl of soup or a sandwich and stick around for a while to pitch him more material. On a bad day, a writer might come home depressed and say "I got three 'Check, pleases.'" But we learned from them.

Buddy Hackett held up a matchbook and said, "What jokes can you do about this?" I pitched a few about the advertisement on the outside of the matchbook, then a few behavior jokes about trying to light a match with one hand to impress a girl.

"That's good," Hackett said, "but the trick is not only to think about the exterior of the subject like the cover and the matches, but also remember the interior and the lit match. See the flame burn. Part is yellow with blue around it and as it burns the tip twists, turns, tilts, and then droops to one side like a small penis. You must think not only about what matches do, but what they're made of, too."

I never forgot from then on to examine a comedy subject from all sides: What it looks like. What it smells like. What it tastes like. Years later I wrote a joke that went "My wife's cooking is like sucking a burnt match."

The trick to writing a page of jokes on any subject is to look on the outside for the obvious and then the inside for the more obscure.

Working for these comedians, whom I had grown up watching on *The Ed Sullivan Show, Your Show of Shows,* and later on *The Jack Paar Show,* had its good days and bad. When comics wanted material they would very often throw a tantrum to get it. We were taught that this was the way nightclub comics worked. They were nervous and high strung, particularly before a show, so they would yell at their writers until they got enough good material to choose from. They would scream loud and hard right in your face and as they were doing this you would be thinking of new jokes.

The rules were very clear: Writers were peons. Most comics wanted their audience to believe that they wrote their own material. To maintain the illusion, Jackie Gleason didn't even talk to his writers, but communicated only through his head writer. There was a rumor that when it came time for Bob Hope to pay his writers, he would stand at the top of a high staircase, with his writers at the bottom, and then drop their checks one by one so they'd float down from the top. This was demeaning, but the checks were always good.

Even though some were often vulgar, dirty, mean, and misogynistic, comics all seemed to understand what it took to get up in front of an audience and deliver material that made a roomful of people laugh. They knew what type of stuff was worth trying and that's what Fred and I wanted to learn to do. It *is* possible to think and even pitch a bunch of new jokes while someone is yelling in your face.

Just when I thought I understood how to write a good line, Phil Foster headed in a different direction. He was one of the first comedians to break out of the traditional one-line joke format and venture into personal narratives. He would talk about his wife, his childhood, politics—anything he could put his personal spin on. Through his tales of family and friends, Phil taught us that the best way to write comedy was to view everyday life with a comic eye. He encouraged us to abandon our sophomoric gag humor and

said, "Look at people and pick up on their mistakes and inade-
quacies. Watch human behavior. Telling the truth about people
will make them laugh." (Phil pronounced "truth" like "troot" and
made people laugh just by speaking.) Whatever you do, said Phil,
don't just use your imagination. A comedy writer who just uses his
imagination will be selling shoes in a week.

Phil's style was the beginning of a new comedy era in which
comics would let audiences into their homes. They weren't just
guys standing onstage in a suit. They had wives, friends, and children. After Phil performed, people would come up from the audience and tell him, "My father did that same thing" or "I have the
same problem with my kid." Fred and I realized how powerful this
kind of humor could be and started looking inward for commen-
tary on everyday life. When we did something stupid or embarrassing in real life, we'd put it right into a routine.

During my brief journey into stand-up comedy, I did a routine
about my first job in the garment industry as a fox-face stuffer
who shoved pieces of cardboard into the faces of women's fox
stoles. My story about this job, which really didn't happen to me
but to my childhood friend Harvey Keenan, made audiences laugh
back then and still does today when I repeat it at lectures. Phil said
that people would laugh about human trials and tribulations and
he was right.

One of Phil's strengths was delivering an odd sound in just the
right tone that could make an audience burst out laughing. When
I was writing for Phil and would get stuck, I'd always think about
funny sounds to help me come up with material. I once wrote an
entire routine for him on the difference between football players'
names in the 1960s compared with those in the 1940s and 1950s.
"Players in the forties used to have real names like Bulldog Turner,
Bronko Nagurski, and Ken Strong. Today players have names like
Rosie Greer, Dante Laveill, and Y. A. Tittle. 'Hey, Y.A.!' What kind
of name is that for a football player?" The routine became one of
Phil's signature pieces and showed me what an important role
sound played in comedy writing. (Even today's comedians use
sound to their advantage. Laurie Metcalf, Robin Williams, Julie
Kavner, and Goldie Hawn all have a range of voices and sounds
that enhance their performances. Just a simple guttural whine

from Laurie Metcalf playing the sister on *Roseanne* will make the
audience laugh.)

Writing for Phil pushed Fred and me to try our hand at making
a roomful of people laugh, rather than just one guy at a bar. Phil
insisted we write humor that appealed to the mainstream. He didn't
want off-beat material with references to Greenwich Village hangouts or existential authors that only the band could understand (like
the kinds of jokes I had done when I did stand-up). Phil wanted
material everyone could understand, such as "My wife is so polite,
if someone lets her make a left turn she doesn't wave, she sends a
thank-you note." Appealing to the mainstream to Phil was the key
to becoming a successful comedian in the commercial world.

Of course, not all successful comedians were appealing to the
mainstream. Entertainers like Herb Shriner and Lord Buckley
(one of Robin Williams's comic idols) were doing cerebral humor.
While old-time comics like Milton Berle weren't happy until the
audience fell off their chairs laughing, Buckley wanted the audience to laugh inside themselves, a smaller and more acute internal
laugh. Perhaps the most famous cerebral comic at the time was
Woody Allen. These comics aimed away from the mainstream and
found their own successful niche.

Years later my writing partner Jerry Belson wrote a joke and I
said, "But Jerry, that's only going to make four people laugh." He
said, "That's more than enough for me." Even though we had
decided to write comedy for mainstream audiences, in every script
we'd put in a couple of jokes that were off-beat or that only a few
people would understand. In the first draft of our screenplay *The
Grasshopper*, we wrote a joke about Siamese twins who were race-
car drivers from Indiana. They longed to race in London so the
other one would get a chance to drive.

In addition to cerebral comedy, the 1950s and early 1960s saw
the beginning of improvisation. Mike Nichols and Elaine May
invented entire casts of characters onstage right before the audience's eyes. Their comedy was almost an extension of the cerebral
approach: They would take a concept, character, or prop and
experiment with it to see where it would take them. Fanny

Keenan, my friend Harvey's mother, who lived in the Bronx, once went to the Catskills to see an evening of comedian improvisations. When she came home I asked her how she enjoyed it. She said, "For the price I paid, they should have practiced."

Joey Bishop's style was low key, very clean, and appealed to a family audience. We liked working for Joey because he was very nurturing to us, almost like a father figure (and he certainly had a better sense of humor than my own father). The highlight of writing for Joey was the night we stayed up and pitched jokes for a speech for President John F. Kennedy.

While many of the other comics yelled onstage, sweated, and pounded out their material, Joey was different. He didn't want audiences to hear his act. He wanted them to *overhear* his material. He wanted material he could present in a casual, cute way that looked like he had just made it up: "I once got on a bus in Chicago and said to the driver, 'Do you go to the Loop?' The bus driver said 'No. I go beep beep.'"

Jack Paar, on the other hand, didn't want to be perceived as a comedian at all. He thought of himself more as a personality. Fred and I had to switch gears for Jack because rather than jokes with punch lines, Jack wanted us to write remarks and stories that were funny all by themselves. He taught us how to write natural dialogue so that it didn't sound like it had been written, a skill that helped me later in my career. However, he also wanted to maintain the illusion that he thought of the stories all by himself. One night after the show, Fred and I were standing in the hallway with the four other writers. Jack saw us and came running over and said, "You guys shouldn't bunch up! Spread out or else it looks like I have too many writers! I'm supposed to be ad-libbing."

Whenever Fred and I needed material for the opening monologue on *The Jack Paar Show*, we'd check out a newspaper and try to spin off jokes. (This is how I sold a joke to *Reader's Digest* in November 1965 for $25. I saw an article in the newspaper about a new pill that made people stop craving nicotine. I wrote, "While waiting for an elevator in an office building, I overheard one executive ask another: 'Say, could I bum another stop-smoking pill?'") But some days there wasn't any news suitable for jokes. When we were starved for material and pressed for time, I would turn to my secret comedy weapon, Fanny Keenan. Fanny had something amusing to say about almost everything, and I could get material just from talking to her.

"Mrs. Keenan, do you like violence on television?"

"Yes, I do," she said.

"Why?" I asked.

"Better to see it on TV than look out the window."

"Fanny, are you going to vote for president?"

"No," she said.

"No? Don't you care who's president of the United States?" I asked.

"Why? Does he ever call me?"

The comics not only taught us where to find humor, but they also taught us how to recognize inappropriate jokes. While there are no steadfast rules in the ever-changing comedy business, we knew when a comedian missed the mark. When Joey Bishop was working the gritty Manhattan nightclub scene, part of his act was to throw his hat into the air and let it fall to the floor. Then he would say, "For what they're paying me, I don't catch hats." People laughed. Later, when Joey moved his act to Vegas and played in some of the big hotels and glitzy nightclubs, he did the same joke and it didn't get a laugh because now he *was* being paid well. We kept begging him to take the hat joke out because the audience just didn't believe it. He wouldn't give it up and we never knew if it was because of sentimentality or insecurity.

When Penny applied to the University of New Mexico to go to college, my mother said, "Good. You'll be close to home."

"But Mom, New Mexico is clear across the country out west," said Penny.

"Really? I thought all the 'news' were together."

"The 'news'?"

"You know, New York, New Jersey, New Hampshire, and New Mexico."

That's a true story but if you told it in a nightclub, most audiences probably wouldn't buy a mother with such a geography gap. You have to edit the unbelievable.

Fred and I also learned to watch out for dated material or silly puns like "It must be raining cats and dogs outside because I just stepped in a poodle." Those kinds of jokes were too easy while others were too cruel. Some comedians got into trouble when they told the truth, thinking it would be funny, but in the end it turned out to hurt someone.

As much as I've tried over the years not to write or tell any jokes that would hurt other people, I nonetheless have. One night I was on the dais at a roast with top television executive turned independent producer Gary Nardino, a heavyset man. An impressive list of television executives attended the affair. I also sat on the dais with Barbara Walters and Burt Reynolds, and when it was my turn to get up, I said, "It's nice we all get to talk to Barbara Walters. I just saw Gary Nardino go over to Barbara and say, 'Hey, are you gonna eat the rest of that pie?'" The joke got a big laugh. Afterward, Gary came over to me and said, "You did fat jokes in front of all these important people? How could you?" I did the joke at the expense of Gary and I was wrong. Aside from the fact that Gary was a positive and influential force on my career there are times you should resist the temptation to get a big laugh involving anybody.

That same evening I also did a joke about Fred Silverman, who was then the head of NBC. At the time NBC's biggest actor was child star Gary Coleman of *Diff'rent Strokes* and I said, "Fred Silverman was supposed to be here tonight, but he had to play miniature golf with Gary Coleman." The audience responded with a bigger, more comfortable laugh because I was mocking Fred's image as a typical network executive rather than attacking him personally like I had done with the pie joke.

Another time I was at an event honoring Jack Klugman and Tony Randall's agent, Abbey Greshler, a man with the whitest skin you've ever seen, skin so pale he looked forty years older than he really was. In the course of the evening I said, "Abbey is going to open a chain of tanning salons." The audience laughed and I thought the joke was tasteful. But later in the program I added, "After the show, we're all going over to Abbey's house to watch his liver spots move around." That joke went too far and I was sorry that I pushed it. Sometimes you have to make a few mistakes until you learn what is funny and what is simply cruel.

•   •   •

Hurting other people with your humor is one thing, but hurting yourself is entirely another matter and much more acceptable. One of the best things about comedy is that you can turn your own painful experiences into laughs. The master of this was comedian Lenny Bruce.

One winter Fred and I went down to Copa City in Miami Beach to write for comedian Alan Gale. Unfortunately, shortly after we arrived, Alan's show closed, so we were out of a job. It was a terrible time in my life. I had no job, no future, and the lovely cocktail waitress whom I was dating told me one night she was gay.

However, the gay girl turned out to be a good friend and helped me get a job as a drummer for Lenny Bruce's back-up band. I would sit onstage playing in the trio that performed in between his sets and listen to Lenny's act night after night, but I never got to know him well. He was usually stoned and whenever I handed him a joke, he forgot it. One time between engagements, when Lenny had gone back east, I heard the club manager talking on the phone with Lenny's agent. Lenny wanted the club to wire his $5,000 advance to the YMCA in Philadelphia. I couldn't believe that such a great comedian was living at the YMCA.

I realized that people who have perfect-looking outsides don't always have perfectly matching insides. But Lenny was still a comic genius to me. His philosophy—pain plus time equals humor—made sense to me. I realized I didn't have to search for material anymore. I could simply look back on my life and collect my most painful experiences, with allergies, parents, whatever.

Robert Frost wrote, "No tears in the writer, no tears in the reader." The trick for the comic is to find those tears and transform them into material. Everybody has had at least a dozen, if not hundreds, of terrible, painful experiences they can turn into comedy. Comedians share their painful stories onstage while most people keep them hidden. I think this type of humor works well because everybody can relate to it; people like to hear about other people's embarrassing situations. They laugh either because it happened to them or because it didn't. Either way, the comedian wins. On the other hand, in *Crimes and Misdemeanors*, Woody

Allen kind of makes fun of it with a pompous TV producer named Lester, played by Alan Alda, who says lines like "Comedy is tragedy plus time. Tragedy plus time. The night Lincoln was shot you couldn't joke about it . . . Now time has gone by and now it's fair game."

Today I think part of the problem with comedy is that we've become numb to pain. Network and cable television news programs have brought such a steady stream of death and destruction into people's homes that it's difficult to turn it into humor. Somebody did a line about raising money for prison charities by having O. J. Simpson and Heidi Fleiss appear in a stage production of *Love Letters*, but it's not very funny because there's so much pain involved. The world is so politically correct these days that comedians have to be careful what they joke about. The safest bet is to stick with yourself: Berating yourself is an acceptable and very popular road to humor today. The drawback is that with so many people berating themselves it's hard to find any heroes.

When we came to Hollywood, many of the sitcoms were staffed with former radio writers and we said to ourselves, "Hey, we can write one-liners much better and faster than these old guys. No problem." But there *was* a problem: Writing comedy in Hollywood wasn't about writing jokes or one-liners or gags.

Sitcom writing was about stories with characters who became entangled in different situations each week. We had to write character jokes and abandon the regular jokes we had been writing in New York. (A regular joke is, "A man goes in to a psychiatrist and asks two questions: One, 'Can I possibly be in love with an elephant?' The psychiatrist says, 'No.' Then question two, 'Do you know where I can get rid of a large engagement ring?'" A character joke, which we soon learned was much more difficult to write, might go, "A boy calls his mother in New York and she says, 'I haven't eaten in twenty-one days.' The boy says, 'Mom, why not?' She says, 'In case you called I didn't want to have food in my mouth.'")

We joined the staff of *The Joey Bishop Show* thinking we had perfected a trade. However, we quickly saw we had to learn a whole new trade and write humor as part of a sitcom story while fighting our reputation as gagsmiths and shtickticians. At first I resisted. "What do you mean story? We write big jokes." But we soon realized that big jokes only found a home in nightclubs and television variety shows, neither of which paid residuals. The goal in Hollywood was to write for a show that paid residuals so you could get checks years later at the home for old comedy writers.

Fred and I were lucky because we arrived in Hollywood when people like Sheldon Leonard and Danny Thomas had the patience and energy to teach young one-line joke writers how to write full scripts. They surrounded us with veteran writers like Milt Josefsberg, Harry Crane, Fred Fox, Izzy Elinson, Jack Elinson, and producer Marvin Marx, who shared their years of comedy writing experience.

Our first script for *The Joey Bishop Show* (and the first sitcom script we ever wrote) was called "Penguins Three" and starred Joey, Abby Dalton, and Joe Besser. In the script we wrote a scene that was inspired by my wife: One day when I was trying to write she was using an oil can to fix an appliance, and I kept hearing this "click, click, click" noise. Finally I said, "Honey, if you don't stop that soon I'm going to break into a flamenco dance." Fred and I used that bit in "Penguins Three." We were learning to weave everyday life into the sitcom format.

During the second season, Joey had to juggle guest stars to boost the ratings while developing new script ideas and sometimes the pressure of the show got too much for him to handle. One day we were all in a room pitching story ideas, and Fred and Joey started fighting about the script. Fred, a well-read man who was writing plays in his spare time, said to Joey, "The *protagonist* wouldn't do that!" This put Joey's teeth on edge and he grabbed Fred by the shirt collar. I grabbed Joey, Joey's brother grabbed me, and it was a tableau of hostility.

Joey always thought Fred was using big words to make fun of him. Joey said, "If you don't like it here, then get out!" And Fred said, "Fine. I will." Fred said I could stay if I wanted to, but this was it for him; he was getting out. Until that point I had always allowed Fred to make most of the important decisions for our career. He even did most of the speaking for us because I was still inhibited by my heavy Bronx accent. But it was time for me to make a decision on my own. Later that night I said, "I want to stay," trying to hide my fear as I watched the only partner I'd ever known walk out the door.

I felt bad for not sticking with Fred and leaving, but I thought Joey was right. Not about grabbing Fred, but about wanting to do things his way. When we used to write for Phil Foster's radio show *Monitor*, he would say, "Garry, when you get your own show you do it that way. This is my show and we do it my way." I truly believed that this was Joey's show and that he should be able to do what he wanted. He worked thirty years in dirty, smoky nightclubs to get that show and it wasn't up to us to tell him how to change it. I wouldn't even have been in Hollywood if Joey hadn't brought me out to write for his series.

When Fred quit he didn't have much money saved. So we wrote a few scripts together, handed them in to Joey with only my name on the title page, and split the money. However, that didn't last very long because Fred soon moved back to New York and got a good job on Jackie Gleason's *Magazine of the Air Show*. Around the same time, Milt Josefsberg was hired as the new head writer and script consultant on *The Joey Bishop Show*. Milt, who had one glass eye from an old bow-and-arrow accident (he announced that he could wink but not blink), helped me get through a rough time in which I struggled to write without Fred. Whenever a writing team breaks up, the industry always wonders which one was the real writer. I felt we both were.

Milt was a wonderful teacher. He didn't just say *make* it funnier; he actually showed me *how*. He gave me specific criticisms, wrote elaborate notes on ways to improve the dialogue, and shared credit with me on the show every six weeks. It read "script consultant Garry Marshall." Milt taught me a valuable lesson: Share your credit when credit is due. (The Writers Guild didn't have the definitive ruling then in deciding which writers should get credit as it does today.) He didn't have to share credit with me, but

Milt was one of the few writers in Hollywood who didn't let his ego get in the way of fairness.

While I was learning how to write scripts I also found that I had another thing going for me: No matter what disaster happened on the set, I believed I could find a way to fix it. Call this fearless optimism or naïveté, but I always thought I could find a way to make a deficit an asset or an enemy a friend and maybe save a dollar. Many writers working on their first series try to come up with these great ideas to *make* the producers money. I've found that it's equally impressive for a new writer to show them how to *save* money on an idea the producers already have and are dying to do.

One day on *The Joey Bishop Show*, Joey started ranting and raving around the set because the show was four minutes too short.

"We're through," he said. "We're going to lose all the money. It's over. This episode is history. You can't hand in an episode that's four minutes short and we can't afford to shoot more on this one."

I figured out a way to fix the show pretty fast. In those days you could insert a public service announcement, so I added a one-minute Red Cross commercial, which made us look philanthropic and left us with only three minutes to fill. The show was about Joey and some friends who got stuck in a log cabin in the rain, so I got a three-minute film clip of a plain old cabin in the rain from the producers of *Bonanza*. We inserted the cabin footage in the middle of our show and then wrote three minutes of comic dialogue for Joey and two friends to say voice-over the shot about how their vacation was ruined because they were trapped in the rain. This started my reputation as Mr. Fix It.

Each year *The Joey Bishop Show* completed its final episode in April and we didn't start work again until July. In March 1963, I married Barbara Sue Wells, a nurse from Cincinnati whom I had met through my roommate, Tom Kuhn, and was immediately faced with two months of unemployment. Not exactly a newlywed's dream, but I didn't really have a choice so I started taking on freelance jobs.

Cool guy from Yonkers: my childhood friend Pete Wagner, one of the inspirations for Fonzie on *Happy Days*. Here he was pretending to be Marlon Brando in *The Wild One*.

After Ronny and I showed no promise for careers in dance, my mother put all of her hopes on Penny. Even when Penny was the star of *Laverne & Shirley*, my mother would say, "So, when are they gonna let you dance?"

While playing for the Bronx Falcons, I dreamed of playing for the Yankees, but most of the time I ended up catching a cold instead of the ball.

A little girl, playing ball in the streets of the Bronx, who would some day grow up to be the director of *Big, Awakenings,* and *A League of Their Own.*

With my sister Ronny at a Northwestern University formal. She ran with a very refined crowd while I spent time with the bohemians, but at certain dances we hung out together because we were a very good jitterbug team.

Hoping to meet Northwestern University girls, I played the drums in my fraternity band, the ATO Combo, with brothers Otto Bauer, Chuck Urban, and Jack Morossy.

Trying not to do too much damage at my post in the army's Seoul, South Korea, radio station, AFKN.

1965: sharing offices at 8277 Sunset Boulevard with struggling comedy writers. *Clockwise from top right:* Carl Kleinschmitt, Arnold Margolin, Jim Parker, Dale McRaven, Jerry Belson, and me. We gather together in the same spot every five years to take another photo.

1970: same group, same spot. Finally working. Who do you think has changed the most between 1965 and 1970?

On *The Jack Paar Show*, Fred Freeman and I wrote for a segment featuring children's letters from camp, and Jack praised us for our ability to get behind the mind of a seven-year-old.

In New York City with my first writing partner, Fred Freeman, and comedian Phil Foster, the first employer who paid us in food.

With director Jerry Paris and partner Jerry Belson on the set of *Evil Roy Slade*, the project that Jerry and I loved the most but that audiences understood the least.

Partner Fred Freeman and me backstage with comedian-actor-mentor Joey Bishop, the man who later gave us two plane tickets to come to Hollywood, which we cashed in for bus tickets so we'd have a down payment to rent an apartment.

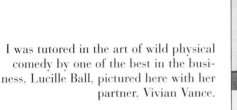

I was tutored in the art of wild physical comedy by one of the best in the business, Lucille Ball, pictured here with her partner, Vivian Vance.

Acting in the army flashback episode of
The Dick Van Dyke Show with Rob and Laura Petrie.

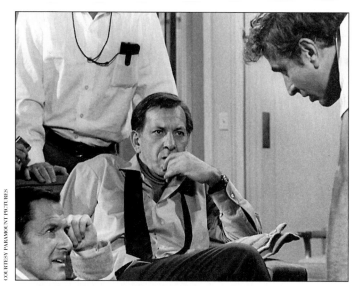

Directing Tony Randall and Jack Klugman. Jack looks very serious because he was waiting for the Santa Anita race-track results.

On the stage of *The Odd Couple* with Jack Klugman and Tony Randall, two men whose talent and professionalism set my standard for what a sitcom should be like.

Jack Klugman and Tony Randall complained
that two *Odd Couple* writers, Lowell Ganz and Mark Rothman, were
dressing too sloppy. The first day of the new season this is how they came
to work. However, nobody mentioned haircuts. Here's some of
The Odd Couple producing and writing staff. *Left to right, standing:*
Jack Klugman, Lowell Ganz, Mark Rothman, Tony Randall, Tony Marshall,
and Marty Nadler; *left to right, kneeling:* me, Harvey Miller,
Frank Buxton, and David Duclon.

Doing it our way:
striking a defiant pose
with Jack Klugman,
Jerry Belson, and
Tony Randall during
The Odd Couple amid
fights against censor-
ship and network
meddling.

Standing backstage at *The Joey Bishop Show* with Milton Berle, whose show had been the hit at eight o'clock Tuesday night during the 1950s. *Happy Days* was the eight o'clock Tuesday night hit of the 1970s.

With my writing partner, daughter Lori at age six, thinking about this book but waiting until she was old enough to reach the computer.

With Phil Foster and Red Buttons, another very funny boy from the Bronx.

I wrote material for Corbett Monica, Rip Taylor, Guy Marks, Dave Ketchum, and Bob Melvin, but my steadiest client was a comedian named Vaughn Meader, known for his imitation of John F. Kennedy. Meader paid me a $150 retainer and I wrote jokes for him every week. He appeared in nightclubs across the country, so I would mail jokes to wherever he was staying. (Later when I teamed up with Jerry Belson we also wrote material for Meader until Kennedy's assassination brought his stand-up career to an abrupt and irreversible halt. When Belson found out about Kennedy's death, he said in his unspeakable manner, "Shit! That means we're not going to get paid!" We were able to find other work, but Meader wasn't as lucky.)

Writing at home was a shock for me. I went from writing for comics who would yell in my face until I gave them a joke right away to writing alone in a room where nobody cared when I finished. I would procrastinate, often until three o'clock in the morning, if I had a deadline the next day. I found out that the main post office in Los Angeles stayed open all night. When I finished writing, I would take my material there to mail it to wherever the comic was performing. I had learned to write solo but, unfortunately, I still wasn't very good at driving alone. In the middle of the night my then-pregnant wife would have to put on her bathrobe and drive me, chain-smoking and biting my nails, to the post office.

While the work was often steady, the money as a freelance nightclub writer was not. I hadn't come all that far from the days in New York when I used to work for soup and sandwiches at the Stage Deli. Some comedians in Hollywood and Vegas preferred to pay me in trade instead of cash, either because they didn't have the money or because they didn't want to admit they hired writers at all.

One year when I wrote some material for Lenny Kent's Vegas act he gave me Alpaca sweaters. When I wrote jokes for the annual Baskin-Robbins employee party, I got gallons of ice cream. Another comic gave me appliances because his brother owned a kitchen store. Since Barbara and I had just gotten married, getting an electric knife and a hot plate wasn't so bad. However, one day my wife asked, "Sweetheart, do you think we can pay the rent with a blender?"

• • •

In December 1963, my wife and I had our first baby, Lori, and I thought it was about time that I got serious about my writing career. Writing jokes for nightclub comics around the country wasn't exactly the stable, I-have-to-support-a-family-now kind of job I thought I should have (and Barbara couldn't drive me to the post office in the middle of the night anymore because she had to stay at home with the baby). I had had enough of the late nights and now I wanted to be more like Danny Thomas. He was the first comedian I had ever met who seemed able to balance his work life and home life. Most of the other comedians I knew were anxious, paranoid guys who lived for their work and tried to avoid their shaky marriages and disgruntled kids by running off to nightclubs on the road. Danny was different.

Danny was a comedian, a TV executive, and a warm family man who made time to raise money for charity. He was the first person I saw in show business who hired his relatives and children. (Daughter Marlo Thomas appeared on *The Joey Bishop Show.*) His philosophy was that nepotism was not only okay, but essential, particularly when you were in trouble. Danny said, "When your back is up against a wall, the best person to turn to is blood."

He showed me that you could have a life and still be a success in show business. That's what I wanted. I decided that the quickest way I could add some balance was to find a new writing partner so I wouldn't have to do all the work and would have time for my family.

Finding a writing partner is difficult and tricky because you not only have to match writing styles, but also egos. You have to try a few on for size before you get the one that fits. I had tried out some with little success, when one day I literally ran into my new partner on the Desilu lot. His name was Jerry Belson and he was the younger brother of Gordon Belson, whom I had worked with on the radio station in Korea in the army. Gordon was proud of his brother's material, and had played me a tape of his brother's stand-up routine. I recognized it as an old bit by Jack Carter. Even though the jokes were borrowed ("I was walking in the jungle through the muck and the mire and I said hello Muck, hello Meyer"), I could tell from Jerry's delivery that he was funny and had perfect comedy timing.

When I found out that Jerry was an amateur magician, I was sure we would make a perfect team. I have a theory that all good male comedy writers were once either magicians or drummers (Woody Allen was a magician; Bill Cosby a drummer). Women comedy writers usually have talkative, crazy mothers. Since I was a drummer, it was perfect that Jerry was a magician.

Jerry wasn't working as a scriptwriter or doing magic when we met. He was writing cartoons for Dell Publishing, fixing typewriters, and working in a shoe store to pay his rent. We started talking and decided to try writing a script together for *The Danny Thomas Show*. A few weeks later, Sheldon Leonard, who had heard I was looking for a new writing partner, called me into his office. He suggested that I pair up with a talented young comedy writer named Jerry Belson. Jerry and I pretended that it was all Sheldon's idea and didn't tell him until years later that we already knew each other. It's always better to let a producer think he came up with the great idea.

So Jerry and I teamed up and my career moved permanently from dark nightclubs into the studio sound stages full of lights and cameras. Television writing paid better and didn't seem to place as much pressure on a writer as churning out jokes for comics did. Somehow, listening to a sitcom actor whine about his lines didn't pack the same punch as when a nightclub comic screamed, spat, and anguished in your face. If it hadn't been for the comics who trained me, however, I never would have been able to write so prolifically or so effectively for television.

Stand-up is one of the most difficult professions and one of the toughest kinds of comedy writing because there's so much at stake. You can call a comic many things but never a coward. In all the surveys I've ever seen, the thing that frightens people most, far ahead of shark attack, snakebite, and walking down a dark alley, is getting up in front of an audience and speaking. Night after night comics get up onstage all alone with just a microphone and take a chance, knowing that if his line misses, a comic faces a mean wave of silence with his mouth drying, brow sweating, and legs shaking. There is no way out. A stand-up comedian stands alone. No help. No hiding. No safety net. I know because I've been there. It's terrifying. That's why the first stand-up comedians were court jesters who usually were deformed: Nobody else wanted the job.

Chapter Three

Writing for Television and Making a Fortune

Oh My God, We've Killed Lucy!

Sometimes the best road to success is to do what other people hate to do. The first time Jerry and I went to the set of *The Danny Thomas Show* we asked the guys on staff what characters on the show did they hate to write for the most. We posed this as a sort of get-to-know-you question rather than as the strategic career maneuver it really was. Everybody loved writing for Danny and Uncle Tonoose, but we discovered that the majority of the writers had an aversion to writing scripts for Rusty and Linda, Danny's two little kids on the show. They were minor characters and the writers figured that writing for Rusty Hamer and Angela Cartwright wouldn't help them get other jobs. Jerry and I decided that we would write scripts for the kids because that's what was needed. If you write what a show needs, then you have a better shot.

We knew we didn't have the experience to compete with the show's veteran writers; instead, we had to set ourselves apart from the pack. A television show, particularly one that has been on for a few years, is extremely difficult to break into because the staff writers know the characters much better than you do. They've lived with them longer. Probably most of the situations you can think up for these characters have already been done or at least thought up by someone else on staff, so you have to do it a little differently. A mistake many young writers make is that they write the *main* characters *too* differently. Nobody wants to hear your brand-new version of Lucy or Seinfeld. Proust said that "the voyage of discovery is not always in seeking new landscapes but in having new eyes." You might look for a problem the series has that you can help. On *The Danny Thomas Show*, we had found it: the kids.

The first script Jerry and I wrote was called "Linda's Crush." In the episode, Linda falls in love with a little boy in her class named Wendell Henderson. As a sign of her undying devotion to Wendell, Linda begins secretly scraping the dried mud off her boyfriend's baseball cleats and saving the dirt in her scrapbook. When Danny discovers the scrapbook, he sits Linda down and, while brushing the dirt from the scrapbook off his pants, teaches her how not to be obsessed with boys. This was known in sitcoms as the father-daughter poignant moment scene. The producers of the show loved the story because they had to do one script that featured the kids. With that one script we had gone from being just another comedy writing team to "those two guys who can write well for the kids who our staff doesn't want to write for anyway."

A few months later, our accountant told Jerry and me that we were writing too many scripts to remain freelancers. The fact that we even had an accountant made us think our days as starving comedy writers were over. He suggested that we form our own corporation and write scripts under that banner. Jerry and I decided to call our company Wendell Henderson, Inc., in honor of the character in our first script. From that moment on, the words "Wendell Henderson" appeared on everything we wrote together. We would go on to become one of the busiest freelance comedy writing teams of the 1960s and it all started with some dirt in a scrapbook.

•   •   •

Jerry and I were an odd pair. He had been an overweight little boy from El Centro, California, who was always the last one picked when the baseball team chose sides. I had been a sickly little boy who always got hit in the head with the ball. He now had long hair and wore Nehru suits with a chestful of love beads. I had short hair, wore dark conservative suits, and was too thin from allergies and the two packs of Larks I polished off each day.

One year I took Jerry home to the Bronx to meet my mom. He had hair past his neck, a full scraggly beard, and wore one of his usual hippie outfits including gold chains with satanic emblems. We went down to the basement where my mom taught her dance classes and she introduced us to several of her friends. One of the little old Bronx ladies asked, "Which one is your son?" When my mother pointed at me the lady looked at Belson and said, "Thank God!" Belson felt that was the worst he'd ever been insulted.

Even though we didn't look alike, what Jerry and I had in common was our stamina and determination to try to write above the crowd. Most young comedy writers in those days didn't want to write for the shows like *Father Knows Best* and *Ozzie and Harriet* because they weren't punchy enough. We wanted to write for shows like *The Phil Silvers Show* with Sergeant Bilko, which was the watershed for most sitcom writers. It showed us that the humor we were writing for the stand-up comedians could actually be adapted for a television series. When Sergeant Bilko went off the air in 1959, we had to reconsider our writing goals. The new targets became Danny Thomas, Lucille Ball, and Dick Van Dyke. These comedians were doing more than just making people laugh one night a week; they were changing the face of television comedy with their physical, visual, and thoughtful humor.

Jerry and I wrote our TV scripts at a rented Sunset Boulevard office, complete with a pool and water volleyball net to combat bouts with writers' block. We shared the office with comedy writers Carl Kleinschmitt, Dale McRaven, Arnold Margolin, and Jim Parker. All four men would later write and produce for such shows as *The Dick Van Dyke Show*; *Love, American Style*; *The Odd Couple*; and *Mork & Mindy*.

We swam and played volleyball during the day, then wrote late into the night, smoking lots of cigarettes (all varieties, legal and otherwise) and ordering in coffee and take-out food to keep us awake. When we weren't at the office, our hangouts were Nate 'n' Al's deli in Beverly Hills or the coffeeshop at the Sunset Marquis Hotel where we would meet up with other writers and comedians. Jerry and I worked well as writing partners, which was helpful because we spent more time together than most people spend in a marriage.

Aside from his bleeding ulcer attacks that often drove him to the hospital, Jerry is best known for his cynicism. When he saw a new house my sister Penny had bought, he said, "What a lovely place to live if life were worth living." When he heard that *Hollywood Squares* regular Wally Cox had died, he said, "Fell out of his box?" When told about a ninety-eight-year-old woman who had died in an accident, he said, "Skiing?" Those were typical Belsonisms. Perhaps my favorite was the remark he made after helping me in and out of cars for weeks with my full-length cast from a basketball injury. One day he mumbled, "Now I know how Eleanor Roosevelt felt."

Jerry believed that as long as a joke was funny you could say whatever you wanted. I, however, always worried about the audience's taking offense. Jerry would deliver a joke in front of ten people and eight would laugh and two would cry. I then spent the rest of the evening consoling the two people who had cried while Jerry took the eight laughers out for drinks. He was never afraid to say the unspeakable.

Some comedy teams write head to head on each scene of a script but Jerry and I worked a bit differently. First we would pitch the entire outline of a script and break it down scene by scene. Then we would go off on our own and one would do the first scene, the other the second, and so on. Very often we'd write our separate parts at home and then bring them into the office the next day to exchange them.

The exchange was the hardest part. The first time I handed Jerry one of my scenes, he said, "This is shit." I said, "You can't say that. You have to explain why, and you have to be nicer about it." Half the battle of writing with a partner is learning how to be sensitive. Insulting your partner will get you nowhere. We learned how to say things like "We could do better here" or "Maybe this would work better here." You can learn to take criticism, but it's harder to learn how to *give* it. You want to make comments that will inspire another writer, not depress him.

After Jerry and I exchanged our scenes, we would rewrite the whole script. A half-hour script took us two to three weeks to complete. We'd give it to our typist, Ragan Marlowe, when it was finished and if she didn't like it, with typical insecurity we'd throw it in the pool and start again. After we finished a script we became very vulnerable and found that it helped to hire secretaries who could type and laugh at the same time.

Writing together was fun but sometimes lonely, so every few weeks we would write a big disco or nightclub scene into one of our scripts. This way we would have an excuse to visit the set because there'd be a big party. It was our way to meet people without drawing too much attention to ourselves. There would be girls and food, and the director would say, "Oh, look, the writers came for a visit."

In 1964, Jerry Belson and I wrote thirty-one television scripts, which broke the freelance record for the number of scripts written by one team for *different* shows in a year. Our credits that year included five scripts for *The Joey Bishop Show;* two for *Gomer Pyle, U.S.M.C.;* five for *The Lucy Show;* three for *The Bill Dana Show;* nine for *The Dick Van Dyke Show;* one for *Chrysler Theatre;* a pilot called *Hank;* a Danny Thomas special; three for *The Danny Thomas Show;* and one for *I Spy.*

The more shows we wrote for, the more offers we got. It wasn't that we were writing so much better than the other writers; we were just writing from a different angle. This was one of my first insights into the way show business worked: No producer wants to hear a writer say, "I can do as good as that." They want to hear him say, "I can do *better* than that." Jerry and I tried to do better than that. We were never happy when someone said our script was "fine." We knew they didn't pay much money for "fine."

There were only two times that Jerry and I quit jobs. The first was *I Spy* in 1965 over a script we had written called "No Return on Damaged Merchandise." The plot involved the Russians trading a captured American fighter pilot for a double agent. At the end of our script, Robert Culp was chasing a Russian spy who had just killed two people. When Culp caught up with the spy, the two began to fight and just as the spy was about to kill Culp, Bill Cosby came to the rescue and shot the Russian.

Jerry and I went to a meeting of network executives and producers for notes on the script.

"Cosby can't shoot the Russian," said a network executive.

"Why not?" we asked.

It seemed like a strange response. After all, the Russian had just gunned down two innocent people and was about to make Culp his third victim.

"Have Culp shoot him instead. Cosby can't do it."

We were stumped. After the meeting, we approached Sheldon Leonard, one of the producers on the series, and asked him what was going on. I sensed there was another agenda behind all of this. Sheldon was very honest and said, "The network doesn't want to see a black man kill a white man. They don't like it." So Jerry and I quit. We thought they were wrong. I don't think the network or the producers were too upset to see us go. They had other writers who could tailor material for the show better than we could.

The second time we walked off a job was on a series called *Many Happy Returns*, about a man who worked at the complaint desk of a department store. Shortly after we handed in our script, one of the producers called us into his office for a meeting.

"Boys, I have a problem. This script is not 'schmunny.'"

"Excuse me?" I asked.

"All television is based on 'schmaltz' and 'funny' and that equals 'schmunny.' And remember, 'schmunny' makes money. What makes a show a hit is 'schmunny!' I want you boys to take this script back and write some more 'schmunny' into it."

We left. We made no money writing "schmunny."

In the mid-1960s we had several offers to take steady sitcom staff positions and while the stability was tempting, we turned them all down. Jerry and I found that we could make more money (about $50,000 a year per person) writing freelance and enjoying various shows as opposed to joining the staff of one show. Eventually, we got so much freelance work that we had to start turning down some of the jobs. That was the case with *The Lucy Show*.

We had been writing for Lucille Ball for about a year when we started to write for *The Dick Van Dyke Show*. At the time the thrill of writing verbal comedy for Van Dyke interested us more than Lucy's physical comedy, so we let our association with Lucy slack off. Then one day we got a visit from Lucy's producer and head writer, Milt Josefsberg, who had recently left his job on *The Joey Bishop Show* to join Lucy.

"Listen Milt, Jerry and I are writing sophisticated stuff for Dick Van Dyke now and we don't want to write that slapstick stuff for Lucy," I said. "We really don't have time this year. If you're stuck, maybe we could squeeze in one or two scripts."

"Garry, I don't need a favor. I want to do *you* a favor," Milt said. "I'm not talking about just another show. I'm talking about an insurance policy."

Milt put his arm around my shoulder.

"I heard that you and your wife have a child," he said quietly.

"Yes. Our daughter, Lori, is almost one," I said.

"Well, Garry, let me tell you something. If you come write for Lucy, I guarantee it will pay for your daughter's college education. Writing a Lucy script is like an insurance policy."

There was no doubt in Milt's mind that *The Lucy Show* was going to run forever. His words really struck a nerve in that I-want-to-be-a-good-dad side of me and I reconsidered our writing plans. After talking it over with Jerry, we decided that we would *make* the time to write for Lucy. Sure enough, Milt's words proved to be prophetic. The money and residual checks from the scripts we wrote from 1964 to 1966 helped pay for Lori's college tuition from 1982 to 1986 and is still trickling in. It was the best insurance policy I ever took out and it taught me a valuable lesson: Don't be such a big shot.

A major part of writing for television is learning to tailor the scripts for the actors. One of the advantages of writing for a show that has been on the air awhile is that the characters and their reactions are already built in; you just have to create new situations. Of course, the negative side is that unless you created the show yourself, you have to write for characters someone else cre-

ated, which was what we were doing. Characters like Danny
Williams, Lucy Carmichael, and Rob Petrie were already defined.
We had to tailor our words to fit into their mouths. You have to
understand the characters and the format of the show before you
even put your first page into the typewriter. Most new writers
screw up here.

On *The Lucy Show*, the producers continued to receive scripts
from people that featured Desi Arnaz, even though he hadn't been
on the show in three years. Those writers hadn't done their homework and their submissions were quickly dumped in the trash can.
To write for Lucy, you had to create situations that would show off
her talent for physical comedy. The pain plus time equals humor
equation regarding my life wasn't a perfect fit here because Lucy
was a woman.

Instead, I searched for stories from my mother's life because
Mom and Lucy were very similar. They were both independent,
strong-willed women who had a quirky, klutzy side to them that
could be very funny. I tried to remember some of the amusing stories my mother had told me as a child.

She was knitting a sweater for my father one day when they
got into a terrible argument. She was so mad at him that she
decided to knit the sweater for our dog, Blackie, instead. Jerry and
I turned that story into a Lucy episode called "Lucy and the
Sweater." In the script, it was Lucy's boyfriend Frank's birthday
and she was knitting him a sweater, but she made it too large. She
tried to shrink it in the washing machine, but it grew too small.
When she gave it to him anyway she expected disappointment, but
he mistook it as a present for his dog named Lightning.

FRANK

Why, Lucy, that's wonderful!

LUCY

It is?

FRANK

Yes . . . Who else would think of knitting a sweater for
Lightning.

Another story involved my godmother, Rita Levy, who some-times taught dance class with my mother in the basement of our Bronx apartment building. Rita once went on a date with a marine who had just come back from a combat zone. He told her that he was still suffering from battle fatigue and that whenever he dozed off and someone woke him up suddenly, he would become violent. Rita and the marine went out to dinner anyway and when they came back he fell asleep in her lap. She was too afraid to wake him up for fear he would get violent, so she just sat there with his head in her lap until dawn.

Using Rita's story as the starting point, Jerry and I wrote a script called "Lucy and the Sleeping Beauty" in which Lucy went on a date with a similar marine. In the episode he tells Lucy about his sleeping problem: "I was a commando during the war and learned karate. Whenever somebody wakes me suddenly, I blank out and swing." They go out on a date and when they come back to her house, he falls asleep in Lucy's lap. At first she remains as still as a stone, but after a few seconds she realizes she has to go to the bathroom. She tries to wiggle out from underneath him without waking him up, but suddenly he leaps into the air, assumes a karate position, and chops down her kitchen door.

Aside from *The Lucy Show,* one of the shows that most com-edy writers wanted to write for was *The Dick Van Dyke Show.* Not only was it a well-respected comedy with great actors and gifted writers like Bill Persky and Sam Denoff, but it was also important to us because of the show's group of multitalented producers and directors: Carl Reiner, Sheldon Leonard, and Jerry Paris. Carl, a hyper, bright, and funny man who often talked with his hands, could write, produce, act, direct, and change his toupee all with-out missing a beat. Sheldon, who began his career playing gang-sters in films and on any given day could still convince you that he had a gun in his pocket, was a real-life gentleman as well as a wiz-ard of a television creator, producer, and innovator. And finally, Jerry Paris, who played Jerry the dentist on the show and directed many of the episodes, was a fearless optimist who could force you to buy a box of his daughter's Girl Scout cookies, get the best table at Hollywood's most popular restaurant, and direct a half-hour sitcom all at the same time. For us, these were the Renaissance men of television.

We were dying to write for *The Dick Van Dyke Show*, but Carl Reiner wasn't exactly rushing to hire us. He knew we freelanced for a lot of the comedians in Vegas and had pretty much written us off as gagsmiths and joke writers who couldn't write characters. Carl was looking for playwrights, but since we showed some initiative he said he would take a chance if we were willing to master story structure.

Jerry and I set out to write for *The Dick Van Dyke Show* and prove to Carl that we were professionals. On one of the first scripts we proved we weren't. In the script Laura and Rob Petrie were going to a black-tie event. During a scene in which they were getting dressed for the party, we wrote a stage direction that said, "Rob puts his cummerbund on funny." Shortly after we handed in the script, Carl called us into his office.

"What does this mean?" he said, pointing to our line of stage direction.

"You know, Dick does something funny, some physical comedy, when he puts on the cummerbund," I said.

"No. Dick doesn't do it funny unless you write it funny," said Carl. "The studio gate guard could write 'Dick puts his cummerbund on funny.' From you guys we need more. You know why? Because that's why we pay you money."

Needless to say, from that moment on Jerry and I took great pains to write out even the smallest bits of physical humor for the leading characters. Later we learned that a good writer will also write physical jokes for the supporting characters as well. By writing for *The Dick Van Dyke Show*, we learned how to write the detailed visual and physical humor that would help set us further apart from many other writers. Legendary humorist Harry Crane used to say, "Show me an idea man and I'll show you a fraud." An idea man is not a writer. To be a scriptwriter you have to come up with ways to execute your ideas on paper both verbally and visually.

•   •   •

There are many different kinds of comedy, and when we were writing for television each show had its own style. On *The Dick Van Dyke Show* the goal was to start with a funny incident—as we did in an episode called "Talk to the Snail" in which Dick worked for a puppeteer—and see where the incident would lead.

With Lucy it was the opposite; we pitched the ending first. The framework for *The Lucy Show* was to write a broad physical comic last scene for her (as we did in an episode called "Lucy, the Good Skate" in which she attends a formal dance on roller skates) and then write a script that would motivate her to that ending scene. Lucy's physical comedy was at its strongest when she got stuck in some place that she shouldn't be. As writers, our job was to get her into a jam so the audience could watch her wiggle out. While nailing a Van Dyke script could take up to three weeks to write, a Lucy script took about two weeks after you had beaten the premise. Once she had the roller skates on, you didn't have to write too many lines.

Unfortunately, when they shot our script for "Lucy, the Good Skate," things didn't go exactly as planned. The premise was that Lucy met a handsome salesman in a sporting goods store, bought a pair of roller skates with all the accessories just so she could keep talking to him, and then spent the rest of the afternoon roller-skating. (Quite a chauvinistic plot today, but this was 1964.) That evening she had plans to go to a fancy country club dance, but when it came time to get dressed she couldn't get her skates off because her feet were too swollen. She did the only thing she could: Put her long evening gown on over her roller skates.

At the dance a tuxedoed doorman announced each guest as she arrived. When he said "Lucy Carmichael," she was supposed to start forward, lose her balance, come whizzing through the door on her skates, zoom past the startled reception line, shoot underneath a buffet table (which was to be lifted up just in time by two waiters), come flying out the other side, grab on to a pillar to stop herself, swing around it a few times, and finally flop down in a chair.

During rehearsal the two waiters lifted up the buffet table too late and Lucy crashed into it. When I saw her hit the ground I said, "Oh my God, Jerry, we've killed Lucy!" Fortunately, they took her to the emergency room and it turned out to be only a sprain.

The next day we went back to the set to apologize to Lucy and were surprised to find that she wasn't mad at us at all.

"No, no," she said. "You guys keep writing it funny and I'll keep doing it."

Lucy kicked off her 1964 season with that episode and even wrote us a personal thank-you note for the script.

Once you had the basic framework of a sitcom series mastered, there were other formulas to help you develop the tone. Danny Thomas introduced us to a concept called the "treacle cutter," designed to diffuse excessive sentiment in a scene. On each episode of *The Danny Thomas Show*, the writers would give Danny, or one of the other series regulars, a sequence of lines that were very wise and sentimental. However, just before it became unbearably sappy, Danny would say a zinger or harsh joke and surprise the audience with a completely unsentimental line.

In an episode that Jerry and I wrote called "Pupa Loves Rusty," Danny and his family befriend a young Italian singer named Pupa, and in the last scene they receive a letter from her mother. Danny's wife, Kathy, reads the letter aloud.

KATHY

This is sweet . . . She writes that the grocer is translating this letter into English for her . . . Listen to this part, Danny . . . (READS) Pupa called and told me about the wonderful party you gave for her and about all the wonderful American boys and girls. She is happy and that makes me happy. I thank you for all you're doing for her and you are in my prayers every night . . . (BRUSHING HER EYES) . . . She's such a nice woman . . . the letter makes me want to cry.
DANNY IS BRUSHING AWAY A TEAR, TOO, AS HE LOOKS AT
ANOTHER OPEN LETTER IN HIS HAND.

DANNY

So does this one, honey.

KATHY

What's that?

DANNY

The phone bill!
FADE OUT.

I liked the treacle cutter technique, and later when I had my
own shows, I tried to do warm, feel-good scenes, especially on
Happy Days. But I always remembered to cut the scenes to ease
the sentiment. Lowell Ganz and I even used a treacle cutter when
we wrote our play *Wrong Turn at Lungfish*. In the scene where
Ravenswaal, the blind professor, talks about death, he says to his
volunteer reader, Anita:

RAVENSWAAL

Do you know what Beethoven said when he was dying?

ANITA

No . . .

RAVENSWAAL

He said . . . "In heaven I will hear." (SHE SMILES.) Of course,
by that time, he was probably insane . . . but who knows?

Another favorite formula of sitcom producers was the "stuck-
inna" plot, in which the main characters would get "stuck in"
something because it helped reduce the number of sets and kept
production costs down. These stories might find characters stuck
in a bath tub, a basement, an attic, a bus, or anything that would
be conducive to physical humor. Jerry and I wrote a two-part *Dick
Van Dyke* episode called "8½" in which Dick and Mary got stuck
in an elevator and were held up by a thief played by Don Rickles.

The episode was nominated for a Writers Guild award, which goes to show you that just because an episode is cheap productionwise, it's not always without merit.

Sometimes you can improve an entire scene with just a touch of physical humor. We were on the set of *The Dick Van Dyke Show* one day watching a scene we had written in which Dick and Mary were in the kitchen having an argument while she cooked chocolate pudding. The scene was flat, and we were struggling to think of some major way to fix it. We were considering changing the dialogue, having Mary cry, or making Dick lose his temper. But suddenly, in the middle of our discussion, Carl Reiner rose out of his seat and slowly walked into the set.

"The spoon is too big," he said calmly.

"What?" we said, all looking up at him. What was he talking about?

"If you give Mary a smaller spoon, then every time she walks over to yell at Dick, the spoon will fall into the chocolate pudding pot," said Carl. "She'll have to fish it out each time. Her hands will get sticky and she'll become more agitated. It'll be funnier."

Sure enough. Just by changing the size of the spoon, the scene came alive. Carl showed us that with one deft directing stroke, you could improve an entire scene without changing a word. We were beginning to put the pieces together and slowly maturing as comedy writers.

One of the tricks was to not only write special behavior for your characters but also repeat it each week. Getting laughs with quirky behavior, whether it was Carol Burnett pulling her ear, Mary Tyler Moore crying "Oooohhh Roooobb!" or Fonzie saying "Heeeey," was crucial to making a sitcom pop off the screen. Behavior was what actors liked to act and directors liked to direct. The challenge was for the writers to get it down on the page.

Behavior doesn't come across as funny, however, unless it's done by likable characters. Movie stars are people you are willing to sit in the dark to watch. Theater actors are people you are willing to pay forty-five dollars to go see. But television characters are people you must be willing to invite into your living room with the lights on and even if you're wearing your pajamas and having a bad hair day.

Once you have the characters and their natural funny behavior, you have to find a story for them. To come up with stories on *The Dick Van Dyke Show*, Carl encouraged us to take incidents from our personal lives and turn them into scripts. As Phil had taught us to do it with jokes and routines, Carl was now taking it to the next level—stories and scenes. After all, the show itself was based on Carl's experience as a writer for Sid Caesar's *Your Show of Shows*. However, our pitching sessions on the show didn't involve a group of guys swapping snappy one-liners, but a roomful of men with sad faces. We would relate the most horrifying and embarrassing moments from our childhood and adult lives and then try to weave them into a plot for the show. As Samuel Beckett said, "Nothing is funnier than unhappiness."

One day when it was my turn to share a painful memory, I remembered something that had happened when I was nine years old. I had gone to the beach with my mother and was the brunt of one of her many jokes. When I took off my shirt, she said, "Garry, you have so many moles on your back that if you connected them with a pen, I bet they would form a picture like in the connect-a-dot game." Of course, at the age of nine and newly aware of girls, such a remark totally devastated me. I didn't take my shirt off at the beach for the next two summers.

Albert Brooks's father also told jokes at Albert's expense. When he was little, his family would be eating dinner in a nice restaurant and his father would suddenly tap his water glass with a fork and address the other diners: "Ladies and gentlemen," he would say to the room of strangers, "I'd like to make an announcement. My son will not eat his spinach. It's perfectly good spinach and he is refusing to eat it. How many of you ate your spinach this evening?" Everyone would laugh except Albert. While acting on *Murphy Brown*, Candice Bergen told me that when she was young her father, Edgar, used to embarrass her in restaurants by pulling potato chips from her ears and sneezing ice cubes from his nose. That's the way my mother worked: Her humor was very funny but always at someone else's expense. Albert, Candice, and I have all found good use for our embarrassing childhood memories. Belson and I turned the mole story into a script for *The Dick Van Dyke Show*.

In the episode, called "Odd but True," Rob Petrie falls asleep on the living-room couch with his shirt off. His son comes into the room, connects the moles on sleeping Rob's back with a marking pen, and, lo and behold, it forms a picture of the Liberty Bell. Rob then goes to *Ripley's Believe It or Not* and auditions his belled back for them. Jerry and I had always wanted to write a script that featured what we imagined was the bizarre and funny "waiting room" of Ripley's: What must it be like? Do those people actually talk to each other? In the end, the episode worked so well because it came from my own painful experience.

As our writing developed, I tried to look at life with a comic eye as Phil Foster had taught me. One day in Los Angeles, I was in a park playing softball on a team called the Third Avenue El and went to get a drink. I needed to take an allergy pill but found a little boy drinking at the fountain. I popped the pill into my mouth, hoping that the boy would be done drinking soon. But the kid was taking forever. He had finished drinking, but had stayed to fool around with the waterspout. Frustrated, I thought to myself, this could only be worse if I had an aspirin under my tongue. It would have already started to dissolve and I would have that horrible medicinal chalk taste in my mouth. I remembered that moment in a *Van Dyke* story meeting and we wrote it into an episode. It was easy for anyone to relate to this bit of physical comedy that could be conveyed to the audience without a single line of dialogue, and Dick did it brilliantly.

While I stole from my own life, I also stole from my wife's. Jerry and I liked writing *Van Dyke* episodes featuring Mary Tyler Moore and my wife provided us with plenty of material to choose from. Sometimes when Jerry and I worked late we would sleep over at the office. One night when I was planning to sleep over, I changed my mind and came home without bothering to call because it was late. When I opened the front door to my house, I toppled over a pyramid of Campbell's soup cans. Barbara came running out of the bedroom in her nightgown.

"Get out! Get out! I'll call the police! I have a gun!" she said.

"Honey, that's not a gun. You're holding a coat hanger."

"Garry, I thought you were a burglar."

"What are these soup cans doing here?"

"When you're not coming home, I barricade the front door."

"Why?"

"Look, I'm home alone with the baby. If a burglar breaks in I'd like to have a little advance warning. So I pile soup cans up. It's my own security system."

The next day Jerry and I outlined an episode where Mary did the same thing on the show. After a while, Barbara started noticing her material, including conversations we had had in bed. We'd be watching a television show I had written for and she'd suddenly turn to me in shock.

"You told them *that?*"

"Well," I said, "I didn't exactly mention your name."

"Who else would you be in bed with?"

Eventually, I had to cut a deal with my wife. Any time she could find Mary doing something from her life, I had to give her money. The more Jerry and I wrote for the *Van Dyke* show, the more my wife's fortune grew.

When you had a story idea for *Van Dyke*, you had to pitch it to the producers and other writers before you could write the script. Some writers used to be so afraid, they would literally throw up before they had to pitch a story out loud. Pitching was usually painfully difficult for me because I felt my Bronx accent was a handicap; it made me sound like a hoodlum from the neighborhood rather than the clever, articulate writer I wanted to be. I forced myself to try, and Jerry and I would often practice pitching into a mirror.

I was always looking for advice on how to improve my pitching and Harry Crane taught me a simple, effective lesson: *Use swear words.* "Curse a lot," he said. If you pepper your pitch with swear words, it keeps the producers awake and adds some spice to your narrative. A traditional pitch on *The Dick Van Dyke Show* might be:

Rob's boss, Alan Brady, gets angry and fires the whole writing staff including Rob Petrie. Rob has to get a job at a women's shoe store.

By using Harry's method, a pitch to Carl would turn into this:

The son of a bitch Alan Brady gets pissed and fires the whole goddamned writing staff. Rob is out on his ass and has to get a job at a fucking shoe store and wait on a bunch of bitchy women. Isn't that funny, Carl? Dick as a fuckin' shoe clerk?

After three years of writing for other people's television shows, Jerry announced one day after water volleyball that it was time to start writing for our own characters. Around the same time my new agent, Joel Cohen, said, "Boys, see these residual checks? If you get this much money writing for other people's shows, imagine what you could get if you created your own show?" With those two thoughts in mind, Jerry and I set out to create our own show.

As usual, I had been pretty content just to write for other people's series, but Jerry, always the more ambitious partner, said it was time to strike out on our own. In 1965, we sold our first pilot to NBC and Warner Bros. The show was called *Hank* and chronicled the life of a boy who masqueraded as a college student and managed to get an education for free. It never even made a ripple in the ratings and was yanked off the air after only one season.

The first show we could call our own was *Hey Landlord!*, which we sold to NBC in 1966. It was a sitcom about a guy named Woody who had inherited a New York brownstone and shared an apartment with his roommate, Chuck, an aspiring comedian. The show followed Woody, a naïve midwestern transplant, and his struggle to balance the responsibilities of being a landlord.

One night while Jerry and I were pitching story ideas for *Hey Landlord!* we had a strange conversation.

"Hey, Jerry," I said, "why don't we write an episode where Chuck finds out he's adopted?"

"Huh?" said Jerry.

"You know, like your brother, Gordon."

"Gordon?"

"Like how he found out in the army that he was adopted."

"Gordon is adopted?" Jerry said, shocked.

"Yeah."

"I can't believe it."

"Didn't you know?"

"My brother Gordon is adopted? Really?"

As it turned out Gordon was from Jerry's mother's first marriage and when he discovered he was adopted, he didn't tell Jerry. I knew about it only because I was in Korea with Gordon when he found out from some army clearance papers. There I was trying to launch a television series and I ended up spilling the beans on a well-guarded Belson family secret.

Despite some revealing and terrific scriptwriting sessions, appearances by up and coming actors (Sally Field, Richard Dreyfuss, Rob Reiner), one of the most talented writing staffs around (James Brooks, Harvey Miller, and Chuck Shyer), fine directors (John Rich and Jerry Paris), and an impressive list of producers (Lee Rich, Sheldon Leonard, and Bruce Johnson with Quincy Jones writing the music), *Hey Landlord!* quickly went into the toilet, as they say. The series was canceled after one season and went out at ninety-ninth in the Nielsen ratings. We had learned an important lesson: We really had no idea how to run a television series, so we went into movies.

After a two-year unsuccessful attempt at screenwriting with two screenplays filmed and two failures, Jerry and I came back to television determined to create another show of our own and get it right. In the meantime, we made a living freelancing for other people's shows, including *Love, American Style*, which was run by our friends Arnold Margolin and Jim Parker. Whenever one of our friends wanted a script—we called this "loyalty work"—we would pitch in and write one. However, we didn't want everybody in town to know about our freelance jobs. Hollywood has always been very image conscious and even writers have to keep up pretenses. So to protect our successful, upwardly mobile image, we invented two noms de plume: Jerry was Tawasaki Kwai, I was Samuro Mitsubi, and we became the comedy writing team of Kwai-Mitsubi.

At the time, there were no well-known Japanese comedy writers in Hollywood and we hoped that the names might start a buzz in studio commissaries across the city with people turning to each other in line for their hamburgers and saying, "Do you know Kwai? How about Mitsubi? Has anyone ever seen them?" The names proved to be a great cover and allowed us to write scripts anonymously and even take on the occasional job of directing episodes of *Love, American Style.* Sometimes you have to go backward, but just don't advertise it. We all go backward now and then and you have to learn how to do it gracefully and quietly.

I wasn't so graceful or so quiet the night I brought home the tuba. I wrote an episode of *Love, American Style* called "Love and the Tuba," which starred Annette Funicello and Frankie Avalon. In the episode, which I also directed, I wanted the two actors to get stuck inside a tuba. I needed to make sure the trick would work, so Paramount loaned me a tuba from the prop department. I lugged it home and my wife and I put on bathing suits and put the tuba around our waists at the same time. Unfortunately, our dog then, Cindy, saw us inside the tuba and she thought it was attacking us. She started barking, pawing, and biting at the tuba trying to get it off us. It was a mess, but directing the episode turned out to be much smoother than the rehearsal. There was no dog.

In terms of being producer, head writer, and running a sitcom, everything finally came together for us when we adapted Neil Simon's *The Odd Couple* for television. We were able to take what we had learned about story structure and physical and visual comedy and teach it to other people. Critics felt *The Odd Couple* was well written week after week, and the first episode was just as funny as the last episode. That kind of consistency is rare in a television show, especially one that ran for five years. The credit goes to Tony Randall and Jack Klugman as much as it does to the men and women who sat around a table pitching stories for Oscar and Felix.

It was during *The Odd Couple* that many women broke into network comedy writing. Susan Harris, Karyl Geld, Susan Silver, and Iris Rainer Dart were some of the women who spent time at *The Odd Couple* writing table. The first full-time female writer on our show was named Marilyn Suzanne Miller. We were always looking for new writers and one day James Brooks, who was then producing *The Mary Tyler Moore Show*, sent me a script written by a young woman from a little town called Monroeville, Pennsylvania.

Jim said that his writing staff was full but that the woman wrote very funny dialogue. He knew I was looking for some new writers and thought she might be right for *The Odd Couple.*

The first time I called Marilyn, her mother answered the phone.

"Hello, this is Garry Marshall from Hollywood. I would like to talk to Marilyn Suzanne about coming out here for a job."

"Who is this? Are you crazy? Is this one of those crank phone calls?" her mother yelled.

"No, really. I produce *The Odd Couple.* Here's my number at Paramount Studios. Call me back and see," I said. "Okay?"

"Leave my daughter alone." Click.

A few minutes later I called back and after some coaxing, she let me talk to her daughter, who was only twenty-one years old and worked as a cashier at the local May Company. As it turned out, Marilyn hadn't even told her mother she had submitted a script to James Brooks. It was a shot in the dark that paid off when we flew Marilyn out to California to write for *The Odd Couple.* Later she became one of the head writers on *Saturday Night Live.* It just goes to show you that talented writers still get discovered, even in Monroeville, Pennsylvania.

I was always on the lookout for a good writer. As Carl, Sheldon, and Danny had done before me, I started searching for people with strong comedy writing backgrounds whom I could teach story structure to. You can't teach funny but you can teach structure. The second year of *The Odd Couple,* Jack Klugman and Tony Randall handed me a script written by Lowell Ganz and Mark Rothman, two young writers from New York looking to break into television. Jack and Tony said they got the script from a limousine driver.

As it turned out, Mark's father was a limousine driver who shuttled guests back and forth to *The Mike Douglas Show.* One night he learned that he would be driving Tony and Jack the next morning. He told Mark and Lowell and they stayed up all night writing an episode for *The Odd Couple.* The next day when the limousine came to a stoplight, Mark's dad turned around and handed the script to Tony and Jack. They had to take it; they were afraid if they didn't he'd throw them out of the car. So they came back to L.A. and gave the script to me. The script showed a lot of potential, so I called Lowell and Mark and said that if they ever came to Hollywood they would have an entry-level job with me. They came.

Unfortunately, shortly after they arrived I had to fire them. It happened to be a very combative season among the staff because I was away much of the time in Hawaii shooting a new Brian Keith show called *The Little People*. When I came back from Hawaii, Jack and Tony were very upset that the scripts weren't good enough and I agreed. So we fired the whole writing staff. Mark and Lowell got caught in the crossfire. I never forgot them because I felt they had potential and they weren't afraid of rewriting. When the dust settled, I invited them back to the studio to hang around the show again.

Lowell, a man with the peculiar talent of being able to tell you instantly how many letters there are in any word (you say "onomatopoeia" and without any hesitation he says "twelve"), was an awkward, lanky guy whom Billy Crystal later described as a man who never had a tan while Mark was a tall, talkative type with a passion for humor and the Las Vegas gambling tables. Most of all, they were funny. After they were fired from the show, they didn't have enough money to go back to New York, so they were forced to live in their car. The main thing was that they never gave up writing.

They submitted another script about income taxes, which demonstrated their new understanding of story structure, and I again hired them. They had learned one of the most important lessons of television writing: If a show is strong only in its gags, it will usually fail. An audience needs a story or structure to follow. A strong narrative or unique situation is a half-hour show's basis and serves as a clothesline upon which to string the humor. Then the characters can discuss situations as on *Murphy Brown*, *Seinfeld*, or *Mad About You* and not just look like they are telling jokes. The dialogue is character driven or situation driven instead of unmotivated.

The other key to a half-hour series is a main character. The early sitcoms starred comics like Danny Thomas, Bill Dana, Jim Nabors, Andy Griffith, and Joey Bishop who had honed their characters in nightclubs for years before moving to television. Today we have a similar situation except finally many star women comedians. Series like *Ellen, Seinfeld, Grace Under Fire,* and *Home Improvement* have the benefit of stand-up comedians who spent years before the show developing their characters on the road, and their hard work shows in high ratings.

Sometimes, however, a good, strong script and a great cast don't guarantee success, which was the case with the pilot for *Happy Days.*

During *The Odd Couple* run, Michael Eisner, then an ABC executive, came to me with the idea for a new series. He said he and Paramount development executive Tom Miller recently had been stuck in a New Jersey airport during a snow storm when they came up with the idea to find a new sitcom along the lines of the *I Remember Mama* series. I knew the show, which was about a Norwegian family in the 1930s with characters named Lars and Nels, but I didn't know how to write for guys named Lars and Nels. However, I did understand what they were going for: nostalgia. So instead of a Norwegian family in the 1930s, I came up with an American family living in the 1950s.

I pitched the show to my partner, Jerry, a man who detested living through the 1950s and was appalled I wanted to make a whole show about it, and he passed. Jerry had grown tired of the television grind and after writing more than one hundred sitcom episodes together I decided to go out on my own. He went on to write such wonderful, edgy films as *Smile* and *The End.*

We didn't exactly call it quits; we just took a break so I could pursue my new idea. While we always did joint projects under our Wendell Henderson, Inc., banner, we decided that when we did separate projects, Jerry's would be under Wendell Productions and mine would be under Henderson Productions (which it remains today).

I took my concept for a nostalgic sitcom in the 1950s and joined forces with Tom Miller and Eddie Milkis, two ambitious, young, talented television executives who had a great thing in common—they both liked my work. The original title of our show was *Cool,* but early test audiences thought it was a series about Eskimos who might have smoked. So Tom renamed the show

Happy Days, and we set it in Milwaukee where he had grown up. (Belson said that if he had stuck around, he would have called the show "Not So Happy Days." He was most comfortable in the 1960s and was still mourning the passing of the decade.)

We chose to set the show in Milwaukee because we figured that if we ever had to go on location, we could stay at Tom's parents' house. (Not only would they give us food, but his father also owned a dry cleaners, so we were assured of clean clothing.) We shot the pilot—about the first family in a neighborhood to get a television set—and called the episode "New Family in Town." It starred Ron Howard. We sent it off to ABC and waited for the verdict.

When ABC called back, they told us nobody cared about the 1950s. Although Eisner was disappointed, he said the network wanted to go in another direction and thanks but no thanks. Paramount ended up pawning the pilot off to *Love, American Style* to make some of its money back. Renamed "Love and the Happy Day," the show appeared in February 1972.

Then the pilot was placed high on a shelf somewhere at ABC where I thought it would remain to gather dust with my other unsold pilots. Many of these I wrote with Jerry Belson, including such classics as "Crazy Castle," a satire on a royal family living during the Crusades (there was a guy with a long beard who was hanging from shackles in a dungeon. He looked like he'd been there for fifty years, and he was softly singing to himself, "I did it my way"); "The Murdocks and the McClays," about two feuding hillbilly families; "Uncle Lefty," about a left-handed gangster and his young niece; and "The Recruiters," a military sitcom about new recruits that Jerry and I were stupid enough to write and try to sell during the height of the Vietnam War. We were writing about men happily going into military service while the world outside was burning draft cards. We learned a great lesson: When you're creating work for the mainstream, look out the god-damned window.

However, *Happy Days* wasn't destined to remain on that shelf for long. Around the same time, director George Lucas had started production on *American Graffiti*. Fred Roos, an old friend from Korea, was casting the film and asked to see *Happy Days*. He said George wanted to see Ron Howard play a character from the fifties. George took one look at Ron's performance as Richie Cunningham, with his honest fifties face and freckled I-still-look-like-Opie innocence, and cast him in *Graffiti*. When the film was released in 1973, it became a big hit and ushered in a nostalgic era in film and television. Then one day an executive at ABC said, "Don't we have something gathering dust on our shelf that takes place in the 1950s?" Michael Eisner said, "Yes we do." Nostalgia was suddenly hot and my pilot was given a second life.

Television is all about money and safety. The network wouldn't take a risk on my show until they knew it had a good chance of making some money. It took the success of *American Graffiti* coupled with the popularity of the Broadway musical *Grease* for most television executives to finally say, "Hey, that's a good idea. Let's do the fifties. We're safe. If it's derivative, we won't lose our jobs." So when someone else comes up with an idea similar to yours, relax. It might help you, particularly in television.

To hear someone say about a show "They ad-libbed the whole episode" is really a compliment to the writing staff. It meant they were able to write lines and make them roll out of the characters' mouths with such ease that it seemed like an ad-lib. When the writing on a sitcom is really working, you can achieve the same effect: It doesn't look like writing at all, which happened during the first season of *Mork & Mindy*.

When the series started, the rumor was that we didn't have any writers. "Robin Williams improvised it all," they said. Well, that wasn't the case. I know because I paid the ten people (nine members of the Writers Guild and Robin) to write the scripts. The reason that the show worked well the first season (I say "first season" because after that the writing was never as strong) was that the writers gave Robin a story structure or clothesline to hang his ad-libs on. The writing was conducive to his kind of comedy, the physical, hip, topical humor that set him apart from the rest. Mork represented your typical fish out of water. Each week people tuned in to see what zany thing he was going to discover about Earth so he could report back to Orson. It was a simple format, but made the most of Robin's talent. Yes, he ad-libbed, but he ad-libbed in character and many of the roads for his lines had already been paved by the writers.

Writing for Robin was very similar to writing for the veteran comics. Robin didn't want you to come in with a cut-and-dried list of lines for a show. He would start on Monday, play with the props, do jokes about the set, and see where they took him. He would pitch ideas with the writers, bounce jokes off the producers, and by Friday the cameras and the studio audience came in and we shot the show. Sometimes Robin and the producers would argue over what was working and what wasn't. The studio audience would act as the referee: If they laughed, the joke stayed in.

Working with improvisation does have its drawbacks for writers. Robin would love a line or bit on Monday, but by Friday he would be tired of it and want a new one to replace it. This process exhausted the writers and forced us to look for new writers to replenish the staff each season. *Mork & Mindy* wasn't such a picnic for the other actors, either, because they rarely got the same cue from Robin twice. Everybody learned to adapt because they all loved Robin. He was one of the good guys and still is. The press, however, blew Robin's improvising out of proportion with headlines like ROBIN WILLIAMS AD-LIBS WHOLE SHOW—DOES HIS THING. One morning the cast arrived for the Monday reading and the writers sent down a script full of blank pages with a cover sheet that read, "Robin does his thing." Robin laughed and said, "Hey, guys, you know I didn't tell the press that." The writers then gave him the real script.

The writing staff worked very hard to make *Mork & Mindy* competitive with other comedies. To start a buzz about the show, they had Mork do quirky things such as drinking orange juice with his finger. At breakfast a parent might say to her child, "Johnny, why are you drinking your orange juice with your finger?" and Johnny would say, "Because Mork does it this way." Then the parent would tune in to *Mork & Mindy* to see what the kid was watching, and we'd get another viewer.

Television is a visual medium and people get bored quickly. If an actor came through a door carrying nothing, I would always ask my writers, "Where's the ax?" This meant you had to give all of the actors things to do with their hands, something odd to wear, or something new to hold. After a while even the casts on my shows would start anticipating the big physical comedy if the verbal comedy wasn't working. On *The Odd Couple*, Jack Klugman would turn to Tony Randall and say, "You'd better say the lines well or Garry will make you wear a funny hat."

Since the actors on *Happy Days* weren't trained in broad physical comedy as they were on *Mork & Mindy* and *Laverne & Shirley*, we emphasized small visual not physical humor. One of our most well-received episodes was the show where Fonzie got his library card, which was given credit for boosting U.S. library card applications by 500 percent. We didn't just have Fonzie stand in the middle of the set and say, "Go get a library card." Preaching rarely works. You have to do it with fun and entertainment: He got trapped in a sorority house and had to wear one of the girl's dresses so he wouldn't get caught. Only on American television could a man wearing a dress inspire millions of people to rush to the nearest library.

The Odd Couple was also a show that benefited from small visual humor. While the verbal humor was sophisticated, I was always looking for ways to make the show more visually appealing. In one episode, Oscar was writing his column and he didn't want to be disturbed. He refused to open the door when Murray the Cop, played by Al Molinaro, stopped by. During the rehearsal, I saw that the scene lacked something. I tried to think back to my days on *The Dick Van Dyke Show* and wondered how Carl Reiner might fix the scene.

After a few minutes, I got my answer. I told the propman to cut a peephole in the front door of Oscar's apartment. Then I told Al that when Tony opened the peephole, he should stick his nose through the hole. (Al's large nose was a constant source of material.) We rehearsed the scene again and the actors played it with the same dialogue. But with Al's nose sitting in the peephole throughout the scene, it suddenly came alive.

Producers and studios love writers who can fix scenes, especially if it saves them money. My biggest financial save was a ten-thousand-dollar line I wrote in an episode of *Happy Days* when Fonzie served on jury duty. Our production designer had built the required courtroom, but with Arnold's restaurant and the

Cunningham living room already built on the stage, it would have cost an additional ten thousand dollars to build a "jury room" set on another sound stage. I said I'd figure out a cheaper way. Right before the judge gave his deliberation orders to the jurors, I had a painter come in with a ladder, paint brush, and paint can and tell the judge that the jury room was being painted. The judge said, "Okay, the jury will stay here and we'll leave." With that one line, the audience accepted the jury in the courtroom and we came in ten thousand dollars under budget for the week.

In Hollywood when you can save people money, they usually make you a producer, and that's exactly what happened to me. I started writing less, producing more, and found it necessary to leave the scriptwriting to the new writers. While my shows were on the air, I was never able to turn my writer's mind off completely. Whenever something bad happened in my life, I tried to put it into one of my shows. I figured as long as I was in pain, maybe there would be a way of sharing it with others and making a living at the same time.

When I tore my Achilles tendon, so did Oscar. When I had a sinus infection, so did Felix. When I had surgery to repair a torn knee cartilage, so did Fonzie. When I was on a family vacation and our car broke down in a town called Atascadero, California, I created Pinky Tuscadero out of boredom while waiting for the auto club. When Debbie Reynolds lent my family her house in Palm Springs and one of my kids accidentally broke an expensive marble chess piece, I had Laverne break an ear off a priceless statue during a society party. I was afraid of the dark as a child, so Mork was afraid of the dark as an alien. When I recalled my sometimes unpleasant days in the army reserve, Oscar and Felix got nostalgic too and we did army shows. I was just doing what the comics had taught me to do: not relying on my imagination but relying on my daily life.

While Robin Williams and Lucille Ball were masters of single-person physical comedy, I think Laverne and Shirley showed that two people could do it together. I took everything I had learned about writing big, robust, broad comedy from Lucy and taught it to my sister Penny and Cindy Williams. Whether they were dressed as Christmas elves in a toy store, tied together at a fat farm, or learning to fly an airplane beside an unconscious pilot, Laverne and Shirley were reinventing what physical comedy was all about.

The writers on *Laverne & Shirley* had to work hard to make sure that the comedy was *equal* because Penny and Cindy were so competitive. Whenever one got more jokes than the other, they would fight. I would give Penny a funny bit to do while making a bed and then Cindy would want something better. I would give Cindy something funny to do with a prop and then Penny would want something better. Despite their often petty desires to outperform each other, neither Penny nor Cindy was ever afraid to try something new. Many actresses in television shy away from physical comedy because it might mess up their hair or make them look foolish. Penny and Cindy were willing to try anything, no matter what the risk, for a big laugh.

While most people love watching physical and visual comedy, most critics hate it. They think it's too easy. Laverne and Shirley did the pratfalls and Bea Arthur won the praise. Critics would rather tout Archie Bunker's latest insults than Laverne and Shirley's latest adventure sneaking into a pool hall to erase their names from a men's room wall. Today, *Roseanne* is breaking new sitcom ground in an unsophisticated blue-collar series, but she's mostly noticed by the exploitation press, rarely the critics and awards shows.

Despite the critics, I think writing physical comedy is the hardest. When it's done well, it's also the most rewarding for me because it makes everybody laugh. It has the strength to reach out and simply knock down any age, language, economic, or cultural barriers that stand in its way. Shakespeare pioneered physical comedy and his plays are still on the air.

Stephen Sondheim once said, "It is better to write *funny* than *clever* because when you write clever it's only enjoyed by clever people. Funny is enjoyed by all." Many foreign audiences simply don't understand the humor of Bob Hope, David Letterman, and Woody Allen, but people are laughing all over the world at the work of Charlie Chaplin and Lucille Ball, and even Laverne and

Shirley, because it doesn't have to be translated. Even the wild success of Jim Carrey's movies today is a testament to the lure of physical humor.

One day James Brooks, who was producing *Taxi* at the time, came to visit me on the set of *Laverne & Shirley*. We were shooting a scene in which the girls got jobs as extras on a horror movie. He watched as they were lifted ten feet in the air by a giant monster reptile claw that placed them screaming into a nest. After we shot the scene, Brooks turned to me and said, "I can't believe that we're in the same business."

The truth is you can do any kind of situation comedy on television you want as long as you can find someone to buy it. Mark Twain said that man is the only animal that laughs and the rest of the animal kingdom is not in on the joke. If Twain had been forced to sell comedy to a network, I think he would have said the rest of the animal kingdom and a few network executives.

Writing for Film and Theater and Not Making a Fortune

I'm Trying to Be Artistic and They're Eating Chicken

The first screenplay that Jerry Belson and I ever wrote together we lost somewhere in Europe. We didn't just misplace it. We lost it forever.

The idea to write a screenplay came about when we were still freelancing in the 1960s. Jerry decided that given our rising popularity as TV writers, the time was ripe for us to break into film. I, of course, would have been content to stay put in television, but I admired Jerry's determination and decided to go along for the ride. I was reminded once again that one of my greatest talents was my ability to choose an ambitious writing partner.

It was 1965. We rented an office above the Troubadour night-club on Santa Monica Boulevard, where we devoted our weekends to teaching ourselves how to write a screenplay and watching famous folk singers take drugs in the alley behind the club. The office wasn't furnished, so we brought in some of our own patio furniture from home, which we used to sit on and occasionally sleep on.

For about four weekends in a row, we would say good-bye to our wives and children and lock ourselves in the office and work on our screenplay. Finally, after a last-push, three-day, round-the-clock weekend marathon, with breaks only to eat take-out food on the wicker table and take quick naps on the lawn chairs, we completed our first screenplay, titled *Ciao*. It was the story of a famous Italian actor who comes to America to star in a film, but has a terrible time fitting in to the Hollywood scene because he doesn't speak English.

Our plan was to get the script to Marcello Mastroianni. We knew films were mostly about packaging and we thought that if Mastroianni liked the script and wanted to play the lead, he would have the clout to get the film made. At the time, Jerry was married to a woman from Sweden and he traveled to Europe several times a year to visit her relatives. On one of those trips, Jerry took our screenplay with him and planned to stop in Italy to give it to Mastroianni.

Unfortunately, Jerry lost the script. He was never quite sure where he lost it, perhaps in a taxicab or a crowded airport, but the reality was very clear: We didn't have a copy. It was before the days of a Xerox machine in every office and we had only the original. So our initial plans to break into film were lost somewhere in Europe. You may wonder how two men who proved to be so incompetent could ever have made it. The young make mistakes. Never again did we have fewer than five copies of a script.

Even though we lost our first script, we had gained a rough understanding of how to write a screenplay. For television comedy we had learned to string together a lot of conflicting, funny, and energetic sentences that could fit in a character's mouth and be said quickly. Screenplay writing, on the other hand, seemed to involve building a story with vivid images, askew glances, and sparse dialogue that shouldn't be rushed. While characters in sitcoms get the point across with fast jokes, characters in films often do it with long looks.

Learning to be concise in screenplay writing can make the difference between getting your script read or not. Something big and exciting better happen in the first fifteen pages of a screenplay or most producers won't bother to read farther. When considering a script, the first thing many studio executives do is quickly flip their thumb across the edge of a script to see what color the pages are. If the pages are gray and filled with thick dialogue and tedious description, then they throw the script in the slush pile for some intern to read. If the pages are covered with wide-open white spaces, then they take a closer look. This might seem rather callous, but in film it's the short, tight dialogue that tells the story.

We didn't give up just because we didn't sell our first screenplay. J. F. Lawton wrote something like twelve unproduced screenplays before he sold *Pretty Woman*. This doesn't mean that every screenwriter is destined for financial success. You just have to believe that the more you write, the greater the chances are that you can write something that will sell.

If I had to break it down, in general a freelance writer's chances probably go like this: The chance of selling an original television pilot script today is almost zero because networks and studios care about who's running and starring in a show, not the writing or the idea. The chance of selling a TV script to an existing sitcom is 10 percent while the chance of selling a screenplay to a studio is probably 25 percent. I'm not saying a studio executive will make your movie, but he might buy the script. In the movies a good script is a good script and a freelance writer has a shot.

"Show us an example of your screenplay work, Mr. Belson, Mr. Marshall," a prospective employer asked.

"Sorry, we lost it," we said.

It's difficult to get a job when you have nothing to show for your work, but Jerry and I were lucky. Another opportunity did come along shortly after we lost *Ciao*. We became involved with a new film company called National General Pictures that was producing its first film based on Muriel Resnik's novel *The Girl in the Turquoise Bikini*. Betting on our reputation as television writers, National General hired us to write the screenplay for Debbie Reynolds. We also signed a deal to produce the film, which was to be called *How Sweet It Is*. Jerry and I were only novice screenplay writers and had no idea how to produce a film, but my agent, Joel Cohen, sold us to National General. This was their first film too.

How Sweet It Is, directed by our old *Dick Van Dyke* friend Jerry Paris, was a romantic comedy centered around the European escapades of a married couple and their teenage son. James Garner played the husband, a photographer hired to accompany a group of girls on a summer tour of Europe; wife Debbie Reynolds tagged along to rekindle the romance in their marriage. With big stars and an up and coming studio behind us, Jerry and I felt we had finally gotten our big break into the movie business.

How Sweet It Is was meant to be a fun, *Pillow Talk*-style movie (originally conceived for the quintessentially perky Doris Day, but she dropped out) but unfortunately our movie came out about ten years too late. It probably would have been a big hit in the 1950s, but it came out in 1968 and drew a lukewarm response from critics and audiences. Timing is crucial. Even good writing can't save a movie that's released at the wrong time.

A bad title can hurt a film as much as bad timing and we had that too. The title *How Sweet It Is* was misleading. Many fans went down to their local theater expecting to see Jackie Gleason, because "How sweet it is" was his catch phrase. When they realized that Gleason wasn't in the film, people said, "That's it. Gleason isn't in this. I'm going home."

The Flamingo Kid was a coming-of-age story set at a country club that featured Matt Dillon and a gin game where the players yelled the phrase "Sweet Ginger Brown" when they won. This story was originally called *Sweet Ginger Brown* but we dropped the title after test audiences thought the movie was about an Atlanta girl on the run from the Klan. I wish I had changed the title to *Stand by Me,* but back then I didn't *understand* how just the right song could fuel the popularity of a movie by embedding it in people's minds. Rob Reiner, who directed the movie *Stand by Me,* understood and had a hit.

Pretty Woman was originally called *Three Thousand,* because that's the amount of money the prostitute gets paid in the film. Test audiences given the premise and the title said they thought *Three Thousand* was a movie about prostitutes from the moon who had orgasms in orbit. No matter what title you finally choose, some critics are going to mock you: "'Nothing in Common' should be called 'Nothing in This Movie,'" "'Pretty Woman' is pretty awful," or "'Overboard' should have thrown the script overboard."

Despite the bad title and mixed reviews we received for *How Sweet It Is*, I came away from 1967 with a coproducer and coscreenwriting credit, an offer from National General to write another movie, and a second child, a baby girl named Kathleen. My wife's due date happened to be the week we were scheduled to go out and shoot on a cruise ship for seven days. As one of the producers, I was supposed to go on the cruise (and was looking forward to it), but I was worried that I would get stuck on the ship and my wife would go into labor. So I stayed at home instead. When the ship came back to port the following week, sure enough, my wife still hadn't gone into labor. Sometimes you have to make choices: Movies happen every day. Babies are born only once. In 1969, my wife and I had our third child, a son named Scott. For him, I missed a softball playoff game.

That year I also learned that sometimes great ideas cost too much. National General gave Jerry and me the green light to write a script loosely based on our proposal to explore the devastating physical and emotional effects Hollywood had on young actresses. During our years writing for television, we were constantly shocked when we met beautiful eighteen- and nineteen-year-old actresses auditioning for shows whom we'd see again two or three years later and they'd look fifty years old.

We combined our concept with a book called *Passing of Evil* by Mark McShane, which National General already owned, and called it *The Grasshopper*. (We chose the title to mean a girl who jumped from man to man. The test audience thought it was about an insect or a drink. In this case, we didn't care.) Jerry and I wrote the first draft and it turned out to be among the best things we ever wrote. One of the first people we sent the script to was Jack Klugman because we wanted him to play a pivotal role. As it turned out, Jack had previous commitments and couldn't do the movie.

However, a year later when we approached him to do *The Odd Couple,* he said that *Days of Wine and Roses* and the first draft of

The Grasshopper were the best screenplays he had ever read. Unfortunately, the first draft of *The Grasshopper* was never made into a movie because National General said it was too expensive. (It took place in London, Los Angeles, New York, Vegas, and had seventy-five speaking parts.)

For a screenwriter starting out, the last thing he wants to worry about is a budget. However, if your goal is to get produced, you have to try. What does this mean? Try not to have exotic locations, a cast of thousands, or elaborate sets that are used only once. Studios love a writer who can find a way to cut a budget so it just bleeds but doesn't die.

We wrote a second draft of *The Grasshopper* that was less expensive, but in our minds not quite as good. It was the story of a nineteen-year-old girl named Christine Adams, played by newcomer Jacqueline Bisset, who runs away from her home in Canada to become an actress and live with her boyfriend, who is a bank teller in Los Angeles. On the way to L.A., Christine gets side-tracked and becomes mesmerized by the glitz and glamour of Las Vegas, and then heads for Hollywood to seek her fame and fortune. She eventually gives up everything to return to Vegas, where she becomes a show girl and falls in love with an ex-athlete, played by Jim Brown. By the end of the film, Christine is a twenty-two-year-old burned-out call girl. It was one of my few unhappy endings.

Writing and producing *The Grasshopper* was far more difficult than *How Sweet It Is*. There were so many more characters, locations, and musical production numbers to worry about, even in the revised script. One hot night in July, Jerry and I were camped out in a hotel room in Las Vegas rewriting some pages for the next day's shooting. As we outlined a production number featuring topless Vegas show girls, the *Apollo 11* astronauts took man's first walk on the moon. We stopped to watch the historic pictures flicker across the television screen. Then Jerry turned to me and said, "It was easier to do that than to make this movie."

When *The Grasshopper* was released in 1970, the reviews were mediocre. It was in the days before video sales, so when a movie didn't perform well at the box office, it went straight to the drive-in theaters, which is where *The Grasshopper* made a beeline. When you're older it's easier to ignore bad reviews but when you're a young writer, bad reviews look like they were designed to ruin your career. No one understood what we were trying to say in the film. We thought we wrote a dramatic, sensitive love story between a white woman and a black man but the studio sold it as a sexy exploitation film. Audiences and critics simply dismissed it as a self-indulgent dirty picture, but I never gave up hoping that the film would someday find an audience.

In 1979, *The Grasshopper* was honored by Filmex under the title "Unappreciated American Films" and more than two thousand people showed up.

For writers, screenplays can elicit passion or frustration, and Jerry and I were in the second camp. After the tepid response to *How Sweet It Is* and *The Grasshopper*, we decided to abandon our screenwriting career, and nobody seemed to care. We got involved in writing and producing our own television shows and didn't have the time or desire to write for film. Instead, when we had time, we decided to write a play.

The theater had been my mother's first love. When I was small she used to take me and my two sisters out of school on rainy Wednesday afternoons and we would all go see a Broadway matinee. It had to be raining because she knew that in bad weather people turned in tickets and we could get a deal. We always had to sit in the balcony because she said that if you sat in the back of the theater, you could see two shows for the price of one front-row orchestra seat. It wasn't that she was being thrifty; she just loved the theater so much, even from the balcony.

As my mother introduced us to the wonderful musicals of Broadway, I grew to love the theater, too. In the late 1950s, I would put on my army uniform and stand outside the Broadway theaters hoping an usher would take pity on me and let me in for free. Sometimes, they'd let me in during the second act. I saw a lot of second acts, which left me a little confused about the plots but not about how much I loved the theater.

Unfortunately, the theater is probably the hardest way to make a living. The phrase "starving artist" seemed to be invented to define the plight of a young playwright. An aspiring novelist, unproduced screenwriter, and spec sitcom writer all seem to have a greater chance of getting a paycheck than a playwright. Maybe poets have the worst slot, but they get accolades after they're dead. When I was younger, I was afraid of becoming an "artist" because I thought it meant you had to live in a small, cold, cockroach-infested flat in the Village with no food. I thought with my illnesses and allergies, I would die as an artist. It was only after I had some financial security that I felt confident enough to venture into playwriting.

Neil Simon once said that "words are not interchangeable." There is a difference between the right word and the wrong one. If you believe that, then *don't* write for television or the movies; stick to the theater. The theater is one of the few places where words are still totally respected and preserved, and definitely the last place where long speeches are allowed.

In television, everyone was always telling me to write shorter. They would say, "The actor can't learn that many words" or "We don't have enough time for that many words." In film they would say, "Let's cut the dialogue and do it with a look or a glance." But the theater not only welcomed long speeches, but also protected them against the whims of poorly trained actors or shrinking budgets. Once I realized that I wanted to write for the theater, I had to make time for it. I had a family to support and television still paid the best so it was my top priority. But during hiatus from my TV shows or in between my movies, I would work on plays.

What I like about writing a play is that you can write about what you want and take as long as you want to write it. No one is breathing down your neck telling you what to write. You don't have any studio executives providing you with "creative input" on the characters. If something goes wrong while you're writing, you have the power to fix it. In movies, once you start shooting, it's too expensive to make substantial changes and in television there isn't enough time to make the changes. In a play, until you get someone to produce it, the time is your own. Noël Coward said that you have to keep popping out of a different hole. After television and film, I looked to the theater as my next hole. And it was quite a deep one from which I still haven't managed to crawl out.

•   •   •

If you find something that you like to write, I think it's important to surround yourself with people who have similar writing interests. In 1962, I joined a playwriting workshop with Lajos Egri, author of the popular how-to book *The Art of Dramatic Writing*. Fred Freeman had taken one of his classes in New York and recommended it. I took the class in Los Angeles for more than a year and dedicated most of my Friday nights to completing my playwriting assignments. Then on Saturday mornings, I met with a group of aspiring playwrights and listened to the Hungarian-born Mr. Egri share his wisdom about the theater. A low point in the class was the day Lajos revealed to me that his dream was to write a sitcom. I was astonished. Why would this talented veteran of the theater want to write for television? Money, of course. He had a script for *The Flintstones* that never sold.

My dream was to write a play, so I asked him what he thought made plays work. Lajos said that a play is like an orange: When you first hold it in your hand, you see just the tough skin. But when you begin to peel it, you start to see the different pieces, with the membrane and the seeds and finally the center. Then when you pull the fruit apart, the center collapses and it no longer resembles an orange at all. That simple analogy gave me some idea to start with: A play begins as one thing but ends up looking like something else. In other books there are different theories, but this is the approach I decided to try.

I had written my first play in the early 1960s shortly after Jerry Belson and I had turned in our record-breaking thirty-one television scripts in one year. It was a time when I was totally burned out as a writer and started to realize that if I didn't take a break soon, I would run naked through the audience of some sitcom and be put away. I worried that I might have lost the ability to write alone. I had become so dependent on having a partner that I needed to see if I still had my own voice.

To mentally give myself a break I needed to physically separate myself from Hollywood as well. So I temporarily moved with my wife and daughter to Palm Springs. Over the next six months I wrote a play called *Shelves*, which dealt with the first burst of feminism. The play was inspired by my mother and set in the 1960s in the Bronx. It told the story of a fifty-year-old housewife named Harriet Keenan and what it was like for her to watch the introduction of feminism into our culture and realize that she was too old to participate or really benefit. When I finished the first draft of my play, we packed our bags and headed back to Los Angeles because I had to make a living again. Every time I told anyone in Hollywood that I had a play they asked, "Can it be a movie? Or can it be a TV series?"

In 1974, I had my second brush with the theater. Producer Michael Kidd hired me to come to New York as a script doctor on his Broadway revival of *Good News* starring Alice Faye. I had to leave my wife and kids for a month, but I knew chances like this didn't come along very often, so I headed east. It was a brief but exciting job featuring music and dancers; my mother was thrilled. My first Broadway credit read "Additional Dialogue by."

In 1978, I finally got my shot with *Shelves* because I went out of town. The play was produced at the Pheasant Run Playhouse, located in the Chicago suburb of St. Charles, with *Happy Days* mom, the charming Marion Ross, in the lead. It was a dinner theater and people ate pieces of chicken and beef while watching my play. While the chewing was annoying, the experience was rewarding: I had finally written a play and I had gotten it produced.

One thing I learned from my experience with *Shelves:* It's best to be a playwright with a dollar, which I had from TV. In the audience there was a small table for two in the way of one of the stage entrances where the actors had to enter from a bedroom. I asked the theater owner to move the table. He refused because he said he made money from the diners at the table each night.

"How much money?" I asked.

"About a hundred dollars a night," said the theater owner.

"One table at a hundred dollars per night, six nights a week. Fine. I'll give you six hundred dollars a week to move that table so my actors can get on and off the stage," I said.

"It's a deal," he said.

For the run of the play, I paid six hundred dollars a week for him to keep a table and two chairs in a closet. That is art.

•   •   •

I've always felt that to write a believable play you have to write about what you know. Jerry Belson disagreed. In TV he used to say "What? All the *Mr. Ed* writers actually had talking horses?" I said but this is a play.

"I can write about a crying kid in a shack in China. I know what the kid is thinking. I don't have to be there."

"Well, I can't," I said. "So for our play, let's find something we both know."

After some discussion, Jerry and I decided to write a play about something we knew very well—the old comedians who had been our writing teachers and mentors. In between television projects, movies, and sometimes on our lunch hour, we wrote *The Roast.* Our play was about a famous comic named Phil Alexander whose stag roast for Humanitarian of the Year Award is ruined when his young protégé reveals a dark secret from his past. The play explored the dual lives that many comedians live—part bitter comic, part benevolent philanthropist—and the ethical dilemma that presents itself when these two lives come into conflict. The play had a lot of dirty jokes, strong financial backing, and a heavyweight cast.

Unfortunately, Jerry and I were very naïve playwrights and we set our sights on Broadway right away. That was our first mistake. Today it's common for plays to start outside of New York and gain momentum, but back then we had eyes only for Broadway. We got Paramount to back the play, along with Carl Reiner to direct and Rob Reiner and Peter Boyle to star. Our previews in Boston were met with a barrage of bad reviews but we ignored them. That was our second mistake. Third was that we underestimated the power of the New York critics.

In April 1980, *The Roast* opened at the Winter Garden Theatre and the reviews weren't just bad; they were terrible. Sitting in Sardi's restaurant with my family and friends on opening night I had to tell my children what bad reviews the play had gotten. My ten-year-old son said, "But Dad, they laughed so hard." They had, but that wasn't enough.

Frank Rich of The *New York Times* wrote, "In writing for the stage, Mr. Belson and Mr. Marshall have not been able to abandon the rigid disciplines of sitcom writing; they write well in short takes, but do not know how to develop characters, themes or drama over the long haul. It must be frustrating for them, and it is certainly frustrating for the audience."

The Roast lasted three nights. I knew the play had some problems, but many of the critics seemed to be saying that television writers had no place in the theater. They were saying, "Go back to Hollywood. Write a silly sitcom. But don't stick around here." I realized for the first time what I had been secretly feeling all along—that the writing game had a hierarchy and it went like this: television writers at the bottom, screenwriters in the middle, and playwrights on the top. The great irony is that financially the order is reversed.

There were other problems with *The Roast*. Two people who write a play, or any project, must agree on an ending. Jerry and I never did agree on an ending and so it was no wonder that the audience came away confused. What we both agreed on was that the strongest asset of *The Roast*, and perhaps the best comedy writing of our career, was the middle twenty minutes of the play when the drama took place in between the comedians' nightclub acts.

It's hard to predict what will last on Broadway. When *The Roast* closed, Jerry and I watched as a crane took down our marquee and replaced it with a big black sign that said CATS.

"A musical about pussy cats?" asked Jerry.

"It won't last, either," we agreed.

More than fifteen years later, *Cats* is still playing at the Winter Garden.

When a project turns out badly you have to find your own way of dealing with it. I have a lot of trouble mentally letting go, particularly when a project fails. I tend to play it over and over in my head, trying to find the key that would have made it better. In his autobiography, Marvin Hamlisch wrote that there are only really two ways to destroy a show: to overwork a bad idea or to take a good idea and do it badly, which I believe was the problem with *The Roast*. We fell short in our execution, not our creation.

In terms of my writing career, the closing of *The Roast* was my lowest creative moment. But I knew from sports that I had to find a way to overcome my adversity. In baseball when you strike out or make an error, sometimes you get so upset you carry it around with you for days or weeks. The key is to learn how to shake it off.

That's the same attitude you should take when a creative project flops. Some people have a flop and then don't write again for years. I didn't want to be one of those people.

I packed my bags and went on the road to lecture to college students. Lecturing always cheers me up and helps me put my life back in perspective, especially when I go to my alma mater, Northwestern University. The school reminds me of what I once was and what I still have the potential to become. Northwestern also has always represented a place where it was okay for me to fail.

My dream was to work in the industry for five decades. As I started my third decade, I was a failed playwright but one with TV shows on the air, giving me a steady salary and residuals. A nest egg is a good thing to have when you are writing plays. It also reminded me of why I always go on strike with the Writers Guild and carry a picket sign.

Just because you don't find success as a writer in one area, this shouldn't prevent you from finding it somewhere else. Writing can take a person many places and it took me into directing. After *The Roast*, I began directing movies and started spending more of my time behind the camera than behind the typewriter. I have always considered myself a writer first, however, and even when I started directing in 1981, I continued to write and rewrite scenes and dialogue for my movies.

I don't "write" like a director; I "direct" like a writer. Richard Gere once said that I was a good director because I could provide an actor with fifteen possible ways to say a line. That seems to be why studios hire me to direct a movie. It's not because I can shoot a scene with a large army and thousands of extras; I like small casts. It's not because I can supervise pyrotechnics; explosions make me nervous. It's not because I can direct high shots; I'm afraid of heights and if a shot is too high for me, the crew takes a Polaroid and reports back. People hire me to direct because I can fix a bad script, execute a good one, and handle the actors in character-driven projects.

When I directed my first film, *Young Doctors in Love*, I worked with the writers on the script every day, typing pages in my trailer in between scenes. I also was hiding in my trailer because I was scared of directing. When I'm directing, I try to use my writer's mind to remain focused on the story. People are running around dealing with wardrobe, makeup, and catering trucks and I have to stay focused on the story. I always felt that was my main job: to tell a good story.

However, I don't storyboard. I don't lay out each day's shots, and I don't always follow the dozens of other so-called rules of directing. I improvise as I go along while always remembering to protect the structure of the story and script and the integrity of the characters. Every character must want something and the main character must want the most noble thing of all. There must be constant heat and tension that puts the main character's future in jeopardy until the end of the film. Those were the major rules that guided me on each film I directed.

In movies, actors like to have something to do with their hands just like in television. During *Overboard*, I gave Kurt Russell walnuts to play with in one scene. From then on whenever I saw Kurt standing too still in a scene I would call the propman and say, "Get Kurt the walnuts!" This was my code for "Somebody better get Kurt a prop fast." It became such a running joke on the set that the last day of the shoot, Kurt gave me a silver walnut from Tiffany.

There are some actors who can't pour water and talk at the same time. My advice to you is don't hire these actors for an important part. Sometimes you get lucky and the props can come from the actors themselves. On *Frankie and Johnny*, one of the first questions I asked Michelle Pfeiffer and Al Pacino was, "So, fine actors, tell me about your lives." I wanted to know their hobbies, interests, and quirks so I could put them into the film to enhance their characters.

It's much more difficult to teach actors new hobbies. In *A League of Their Own*, Penny hired coaches to teach the actresses how to play softball. One player almost broke her nose, Penny's daughter, Tracy, was badly bruised sliding, and almost all of them ended up with bumps and scrapes from the experience, even Madonna, who had bleeding hands from batting practice.

Michelle Pfeiffer told me she likes to bowl, so in *Frankie and Johnny*, we wrote in a scene at a bowling alley. I also like to ask an actor what things he thinks his character might carry around in his pockets. Then I have wardrobe put some of these items in the pockets of his costume. You'll notice that most Garry Marshall movies usually have actors with bulging pockets.

Before I sat down with Al Pacino, I knew about his love of Shakespeare and his altruism toward actors and esoteric projects, but what he told me was that he also had a passion for handball. We were able to work handball right into *Frankie and Johnny* when we placed a small rubber ball in his character's pocket. Throughout the film, whenever it was appropriate, Johnny would play with his rubber ball. Adding details like this to a film is an easy way to enhance a character without hurting the dialogue.

There are various ways for a screenwriter to create a project. He can be paid to adapt a story from another medium, like a book, play, or newspaper article. He can be hired to write a script based on an idea that a studio has purchased or developed. Or he can sit down and write an original screenplay on "spec" ("speculation," meaning no money) or by pitching an idea to a studio or production company and getting some money up front. No matter what road a screenwriter takes, he's always looking for new material. New scenes. New moments. Something odd or unique. Something amusing. Something that's never been seen before on screen.

You can never be sure when an idea is going to come up. One day while I was relaxing I watched a TV documentary on the life of the conductor Arturo Toscanini, and it described his travels around the world giving concerts. During his tour he would often have dinner with members from the local chamber of commerce. At one such dinner, a man clearly uncomfortable with small talk said to Toscanini, "Sometimes I eat my entire meal with my salad fork." Toscanini was startled at such a statement and stared at the man with a puzzled look on his face. It was such a wonderful moment that I quickly made a note of it. Later, in *Nothing in Common*, I used the line in the scene when ad executive Tom Hanks first meets the airline owner played by Barry Corbin. After Barry said the line, Tom topped it off by answering, "And, sir, when you ate the whole meal with your salad fork, did that include the soup?"

During preproduction on *Pretty Woman*, I was looking for set dressing to define Julia Roberts's apartment. I was in a friend's house and noticed something odd in his teenage daughter's bedroom. Attached to the mirror above her bureau there was a collection of headless old boyfriend photos. She told me that whenever she breaks up with a boyfriend, or vice versa, she takes revenge by cutting the boy's head out of her photos. However, she would leave her own head and body perfectly intact. In the opening scenes of *Pretty Woman*, there are several pictures of Julia with headless boys stuck in the mirror above her bureau. Whenever you visit people's houses always ask to see their children's rooms. The other rooms always sparkle because the parents want to impress you, but the children don't give a damn. The comedy is in the kids' rooms.

When writing for film, write specifically. A scene written in the original script of *Nothing in Common* called for Tom Hanks's character to come back from a vacation and waltz into his advertising office "with a word for everyone." But there were no words written for this "waltz." I wondered what kinds of words? To which co-workers? To a secretary? How many words? Why? With what kind of attitude? The screenwriters should have come up with ten different lines for the actor to say and the director to choose from. Instead, Tom and I had to stop, sit down, and make up lines for the "waltz."

The biggest lesson a screenwriter can learn is how to master a rewrite of his own script, or someone else's, and make the changes a studio wants without destroying the story. It's like a football game: If you think of writing an original screenplay as "offensive" creativity, then rewriting is all about "defensive" creativity.

There are some screenwriters who are great on offense while others excel only at defense. The greatest screenwriters—and the ones who are in demand—are those who can handle both kinds of creativity. The problem I've found is that young writers usually change too much in a rewrite and old writers often don't change enough. What writers should remember is to read a first draft or rewrite twice, not once but *twice*, before handing it in. First, read it for pacing and plot, and then read it a second time to see if there are good parts for the stars, because that's exactly how the stars are going to read it.

When Disney first sent me the script for *Pretty Woman*, it was a dark tale about a cold and heartless corporate raider and a drug-addicted prostitute who had been hooking for six years. The relationship ended with the raider's giving the prostitute three thousand dollars and knocking her to the ground. Vivian then screamed, "Go to hell! I hate you! I hate your money! I hate it!" as he drove away, leaving her in the gutter where he found her.

Initially, the darkness of the script and its sexuality appealed to me as a director because I hadn't done anything like it before. But what bothered me about the script was that it didn't make me care about either of the characters. Neither of them generated much sympathy and I rooted for no one.

When I told my thoughts to Jeffrey Katzenberg, who was then at Disney, he said, "It's not our type of film, either. That's why we want you to supervise the rewrite and lighten it up." The instructions for the rewrite came in cryptic Hollywood shorthand: If the gritty, British call-girl film *Mona Lisa* was a two and *My Fair Lady* and *Cinderella* were tens, then Disney wanted me to make *Pretty Woman* an eight. I told them I would deliver a six or seven and I would do it with laughs.

We had five different writers on *Pretty Woman* and the first to attempt the rewrite was the original screenwriter, J. F. Lawton. Even after Lawton took a stab, the studio still felt that the script needed more work. Our approach to the film was to make it the story of two people from totally different backgrounds united in a fairy tale. In all the rewrites, the part of Vivian, the prostitute, came quite easily. It was the character of the businessman, Edward Lewis, that presented the most problems. Only Barbara Benedek, the sole woman writer in the group, got the voice of Edward down by creating a Donald Trump-style executive with a vulnerable side.

On most films there are dozens of rewrites, which usually end up offending the original writer, and *Pretty Woman* was no exception. J. F. Lawton became disillusioned about the movie-making process and its propensity for changing a writer's words. Well, unfortunately, that's the way the movie business works. There have been advancements for all groups—production designers, editors, and directors—but in most cases writers still have the least amount of clout, particularly when it comes to protecting their words on film.

There has never been a screenwriter's contract with the provision "The writer's words in this movie can't be changed." That phrase is reserved for the world of the playwright. The only power a screenwriter has is the prerogative to take his name off a script, and some screenwriters do go this route. But movies are all about rewriting. Those who can do it get the jobs and those who can't move on to something else.

In 1981, the year after our play *The Roast* bombed on Broadway, I found myself back in New York with my wife. We were staying at the Elysee Hotel and had come to town to eat well and catch up on the latest plays on Broadway. I was hoping that the trip would make me relax so I could figure out what it was I wanted to do next with my life. I had come to a stage in my career when it was time to take stock.

I was successful in television with shows still on the air, but I had gone as far as I could, or wanted to. I had to make a change in my career, but after getting burned so badly on Broadway, I had little interest in going back to the theater; and the theater had even less interest in me. Instead, I had started to think about making the move into film directing.

Then one afternoon I was resting on the bed at the Elysee and couldn't find my allergy pills. (Whenever I fly, the plane's recycled air always screws up my sinuses and I need to take pills for relief.) I thought the medicine bottle might have fallen off the side table and slipped underneath the bed. So I crouched down on my hands and knees to take a look. I spotted a pill bottle and reached out to grab it, but when I looked at the empty bottle I realized that it wasn't mine.

It was a prescription for Valium made out to Tennessee Williams. The playwright was a frequent guest at the hotel and, as we would soon find out, he usually stayed in our room; we later discovered some of his famous string ties in a drawer. Being a superstitious writer who pays close attention to signs, I took this as an omen: Maybe I shouldn't give up on the theater after all. The day we closed *The Roast* was the day I stopped thinking about writing plays. The day I found the pill bottle I went back. I decided that in addition to trying to break into film directing, the 1980s would also be a time for me to write another play.

One of the credos I live by is that no matter what you write, never throw anything away. After writing with Jerry Belson for more than ten years, I teamed up with Lowell Ganz, who started out with me on *The Odd Couple* and later produced *Happy Days* and *Laverne & Shirley*. Our first project was the screenplay for a blue-collar love story called *Cookies*. We finished the script but I hadn't directed a film yet and Lowell had not yet become one of Hollywood's premier comedy screenwriters, so we had zero clout in the film world. If the business is all about who you know, we knew no one in movies, so our screenplay went absolutely nowhere. It was time to move on to something else. We simply put the script away in a filing cabinet.

Several years later, Lowell and I decided to write a play together. We pitched several ideas but ironically kept coming back to one of the characters from *Cookies*. She was a tough, mean, street girl who volunteered to read to blind patients at a local hospital. The impetus for the character was my blind grandmother Nanny, whom I used to read to. In several scenes in the screenplay, the girl read to a blind professor who spoke in very long, intellectual narratives. Long speeches are death to good screenplay writing, so we tossed them out. When we thought about writing a play, these scenes came back to us as the best speeches.

If you want to write something badly enough, you'll make the time for it. Lowell and I met once a week for three years to write the play. There was no pressure. We would just write. We enjoyed ourselves because there were no studios, no producers, and no actors waiting for our script. We wrote a two-act, four-character comedy-drama called *Wrong Turn at Lungfish*. When writers reach their late forties or fifties, they usually deal with the theme of death. So this was our death play and we made it a comedy.

The odd title of the play refers to Darwin's theory of evolution (in which the lungfish plays a key role) and the evolution of a friendship between a blind, cranky professor and a secretary who reads to him in the hospital.

I promised myself that I wasn't going to make the same mistakes I had made with *The Roast*. It's always helpful to learn from your mistakes because then your mistakes seem worthwhile. Otherwise, one keeps calling himself a dope. We rushed on *The Roast*, but this time I took it slowly. We did rewrites, adjusted scenes, and I even directed the play, placing myself in a reasonable position to protect the writers' interpretations. The play was first workshopped and then produced at the prestigious Steppenwolf Theatre in Chicago, later at the Coronet Theatre in Los Angeles, and eventually at the Promenade Theatre Off-Broadway in New York with George C. Scott. Two characters from an unproduced movie screenplay wound up Off-Broadway making people laugh.

What has always fascinated me about the theater was that because it was live, almost anything could happen at any performance in any theater. When we were working together on the film version of his play *Frankie and Johnny*, Terrence McNally told me what had happened in a production in New Orleans.

Terrence watched in horror as the actress playing Frankie, the waitress, walked around stage during the entire first act without any clothes on. After the show Terrence went backstage to find the director and asked, "What happened? Why was Frankie nude?" The director pointed to the script and sure enough, Terrence had written in the stage directions that the play started with Frankie in bed naked, but he had forgotten to write that moments later Frankie puts her robe back on. In his defense, the director said, "I thought this was just one of those sophisticated chi-chi plays from New York."

The one problem I've discovered regarding the theater is that you usually have to work in New York. Whenever I worked on my plays I not only had to leave my family, but also, in the beginning, leave my television shows. After spending several months on *The Roast*, I returned to the set of *Mork & Mindy*.

When I opened the stage door, a guard with a gun stopped me and said, "Sorry, no visitors allowed." From behind me my secretary was waving and mouthing the words "This is Garry Marshall and this is his show." That's what you get for wanting to write for television and the theater.

Despite its drawbacks, I think every writer should try a play. I've written only three and judging from my reviews I'm certainly no expert, but I know the joy that writing for the theater has given me. Despite the mixed reviews, audiences showed up for *Lungfish* and laughed. For six straight months they filled the Off-Broadway theater (not a dinner theater) and it was a special thrill for me to see people enjoying and laughing at the play without having food in their mouths.

In 1994, I learned that *Lungfish* would be published by Samuel French, Inc., the premier play publisher. At the time I was directing my eighth movie, *Exit to Eden*, but I rushed to get the play ready for publication. As *Eden* technicians were setting up shots and costume designers were dressing men and women in leather and chains, I was hiding out in my trailer proofreading the play and working on fulfilling a dream.

Even though *Lungfish* didn't make a lot of money and I still got another bad review from Frank Rich (he moved to the Op-Ed page the following year), I was proud of the play that Lowell and I had written. Awards aside, a television writer dreams of big ratings. A screenwriter dreams of big box office receipts. And a playwright dreams that his play will run forever. When Samuel French published *Lungfish*, I knew the words we had written would last beyond the final curtain.

Chapter Five

Television Producing and the Use of Prayer

Charm Is the Family Business

When we started out in television, Jerry Belson and I spent a lot of time watching how other people did their jobs. We observed how Carl Reiner ran a writers' table consisting of ten writers and picked the best material from the group. We watched Jerry Paris direct a sitcom. We watched how Sheldon Leonard produced half a dozen of prime-time's top-rated sitcoms at virtually the same time. In the beginning, I was too busy trying to learn how to be a professional comedy writer to even consider if I wanted to try any of these other jobs. Everything changed for me one day when I had a conversation with Sheldon Leonard in 1964.

I had always liked Sheldon because he was the first executive I ever met who had a heavy New York accent like mine. His accent also proved to be an asset to his acting career (he often played gangsters). He was very patient and took the time to help me as a writer in TV. What I didn't expect was that he would open the door to another career for me. One day we were joking around, comparing accents, his thick Bronx to my nasal Bronx, when Sheldon said, "Kid, I like the way you talk. You could be a producer." Until then, people had always made fun of the way I spoke.

A television producer? Sheldon Leonard thought *I* could be a television producer? This was a man who would eventually sell an unprecedented seventeen pilots to the networks and he thought I could be a TV producer? I replayed our conversation in my head for several weeks until I finally got up the nerve to talk to Sheldon again.

"Sheldon, exactly how does a person *become* a television producer?" I asked.

"Say something," he said. "Always say something. Make a decision, right or wrong, because most of the people in show business are afraid to make a decision."

And that's pretty much how I became a television producer. In the sixties there were lots of good writers in television but not that many who could or wanted to handle the job of being a writer and a producer. I realized that's what would set us apart. Each time Jerry and I created a new show, we asked if we could produce it along with a technical producer. The studio gave it to us because they thought, "Hey, if we let them produce we can get them as writers and if we hire them as writers *and* producers we'll save a dollar."

There are very vague rules when it comes to who gets to be a producer and who doesn't. There is a Producers Guild but it doesn't have as strong a collective bargaining agreement as the Writers Guild, Directors Guild, or Screen Actors Guild. Fundamentally, a producer is defined by his responsibilities, which is why you see dozens of producers getting credit on television shows.

There are four different kinds of television producers. Sometimes they overlap, but the breakdown goes like this: The creative TV producer, often called the executive producer, is what I was—basically a writer and producer. People like Aaron Spelling, Douglas Cramer, Norman Lear, Diane English, and Susan Harris are all creative television producers. They can write or work with writers, cast, and come up with the entire concept of a television show, *and* they have the clout and track record to sell a sitcom to a network. Their biggest asset is the ability to write or work with the writers because most of the other kinds of producers don't have the respect from the writers or network to be able to do this. The nickname for this type of producer is the "show runner."

Tom Miller (*Full House, Perfect Strangers*) is a creative non-writer producer, which is sometimes called a visionary or mounting producer. He comes up with great production thoughts, casting ideas, guides the writers, and then, acting as the front man, he presents them to the network. This allowed Tom (and later with his talented partner Bob Boyett) to produce several different television series at once.

The line producer is the one who handles the nuts-and-bolts administrative side of a television show. He makes sure the budget is on target and that everybody gets his paycheck. He very often doesn't know what all the jokes are going to be each week (or even think the jokes are funny), but he definitely knows how much the show is going to cost. Line producer is a job I've never been able to do well, so I've always made it a point to surround myself with people who could. My sister Ronny Hallin, Bruce Johnson, Eddie Milkis, and my father, Tony Marshall, were line producers for me on several of my television shows.

The fourth type of producer is the one I call a friend of the court. This is a person who has received the producing credit on a TV show either because he is the manager of the star of the show (without him you won't get the star) or because he is related to someone on the show or at the network, and often has no experience. This job carries responsibility, but usually not the fear of being fired. All those who fall into the category of "Untalented Nepotism," such as friends, sycophants, and itinerant relatives, are qualified to be this kind of producer.

That's the way I see it. There are some producers who won't agree with me—so write me a letter.

During my twenty years as a television producer I created fourteen shows, and I'd have to say that with each one I was shooting for the mainstream. That's what I wanted to be—a prime-time television creator whose job it was to get the biggest share of the audience. You can't get big ratings if you create a show that is watched only by thirty people in Greenwich Village or Portland, Oregon, no matter how great it is. You need to have people across the country canceling plans, cutting dinners short, and hanging up the phone to tune in to your show. When I was growing up, everybody in my neighborhood stayed home on Tuesday nights at eight o'clock to watch Milton Berle. The streets were deserted. That was my barometer of what made a successful show.

Critics have knocked my shows for targeting society's lowest common denominator. I believe that television was, and still is, the only medium that can truly reach society's lowest common denominator and entertain those people who maybe can't afford a movie or a play. So why not reach them and do it well? When I produced a television show I didn't just roll out of bed each morning and say, "I'm going to make some rich, smart, and successful people laugh." I thought, "Let them get their own laughs. They have the money to pay for it." What I wanted to do was to make people laugh who had come off a hard day at work, maybe from a job as a waitress in a diner or as an assembly-line worker at a factory.

I wanted to be the Norman Rockwell of television. I don't know exactly when or why I adopted this philosophy. Maybe it was because I grew up in the Bronx. Or because I went to college in the Midwest. Or because I did not have a story-book family so I created my own on television. There was just something that made me want to produce sentimental, family-oriented television shows that appealed to the middle class. After seeing Penny's movie *Big*, Lowell Ganz said, "Well, charm is the family business." That's the way I felt about my television shows.

I wanted my shows to help balance all of the other negative images on television. One Tuesday night I was watching a news-magazine program about defective Pintos. Drivers were banging into things with these cars but instead of fender benders, the cars were blowing up and killing the passengers. When *Happy Days* came on next, I was relieved.

When I started producing for television, my three children were still young and I dreamed of creating shows I could watch with them. In those prevideo days, the entertainment options, other than reading, for parents with small children were limited to

Disney cartoons or nature movies in which a raccoon licked a duck for two hours. I thought there had to be some other form of entertainment parents could watch with their children without getting a headache or falling asleep.

It was definitely to my advantage that I took this family approach because nobody else was doing it. That's the key to television: Ideas are everywhere and if all you can come up with is just like what everyone else is doing, then why should they buy it from you? When I started to produce my television shows, the networks were buying most of their prime-time shows from four men: Norman Lear addressed issues like racism and feminism in the shows *All in the Family* and *Maude;* Grant Tinker depicted women in the work place on *The Mary Tyler Moore Show* and *Rhoda;* Aaron Spelling put a new tits-and-ass spin on crime shows by producing *Charlie's Angels;* and Lee Rich was reenacting life during the Depression with *The Waltons.*

The networks always buy shows from producers they can count on. That's the way it was then and that's the way it continues to be today. I decided that I could either whine and complain like a lot of the other people and say, "They only buy shows from those four guys," or I could *become* one of those four guys. I created feel-good sitcoms like *Happy Days, Laverne & Shirley,* and *Mork & Mindy* that gave people a sense of warmth and nostalgia. If television was the education of the American public, then my shows were recess.

My feeling is that to be a successful television producer—and probably a successful anything in the industry—you have to find out what it is that you do well and stick with it. What I did well was create television shows for a studio—Paramount. Unlike Lear, Tinker, Spelling, and Rich, who all became independent producers, I stayed with Paramount. Paramount bosses like Douglas Cramer, Gary Nardino, and Emmett Lavery gave me what I wanted: a basketball court on the lot, a malted milk machine in my office, and any title I wanted to have on the screen. Why I really stayed was to protect myself. I had a family I loved to spend time with. I didn't want to have the headaches that came with overseeing the finances and responsibility of my own production company.

I just wanted to put all my energy into creating and running my shows. I was like a painter represented by a well-respected gallery. All I wanted to do was get the paint on the canvas and let the studio worry about who to sell it to. I made money, but I didn't really need the power. My power was freedom. A man who runs a company that goes public can't always make it home in time for dinner or his son's T-ball practice. To me, I had the greatest power of all—the power to go home when I felt like it.

If on one of my shows an actor needed help with a scene or a writer was stuck on a rewrite, I would stay until 2 A.M. to work things out. Even on his busiest day, that's the way Sheldon Leonard used to work, too. He would put down everything to find the answer to a writing problem. But if someone on one of my shows complained about his salary or the size of his dressing room, then I pointed him in the direction of the Paramount administration building and I went off to make myself a chocolate malted. Some people said I was crazy to work with a studio but, honestly, the only thing that interested me was the creative product. The business side didn't frighten me; it bored me. I never saw a television actor deliver a better performance because he got a nicer dressing room than the rest of the cast.

While I avoided the business side of television, I couldn't shy away from the fact that I was the boss, and as the boss I had to take the blame when things went wrong. But I had had experience with taking blame: On *The Joey Bishop Show* whenever anything went wrong I would say, "My fault," just to move things along. Joey once said, "You're just saying that to move things along." And I said, "You're right." I started out as a boss on *The Odd Couple* overseeing the daily creative operations of the show. Eventually, I moved up to executive producer and just supervised the series, which meant I might not know what everyone had for lunch on each show but would hear when an actress threw her lunch at one of the writers.

I was not the kind of boss who spent a lot of time delegating responsibility or blaming others when things went wrong. I tried to be a hands-on manager whenever I could. Arnold Weber, the distinguished former president of Northwestern University and one of the most intellectual and erudite men I have ever met, described his work habits to me as "My ass; my hands!" Those are words I've always tried to work by. If you lose or something goes wrong, you should do it with your own hands.

Even when I had four shows on the air, I wasn't the kind of boss who would yell and scream a lot. I personally feel that screaming is an uncivilized waste of time and should be reserved for the sports field (where I scream loud and often). To remain sane as a television producer, you should find an alternative to screaming or you'll lose your voice during the first week on the job or end up with an ulcer. Michael Eisner said that I was the master of the "velvet threat" when dealing with studios, networks, or lawyers. I used a gentler method of getting my point across but it was heard loud and clear just the same.

Most of the time instead of screaming, I caused strange "accidents." Early on I learned how even small accidents could work to my advantage. Whenever we would screen a new show for the network, I would bring along my sister Ronny. If there was a particular joke or beat that wasn't working, I would signal Ronny (a chain-smoker) at the appropriate moment and she would knock an ashtray onto the floor. This would divert the executives' attention long enough for the joke to pass unnoticed.

Later I caused bigger accidents to buy myself some time. If a network executive demanded a show from me on Wednesday, very often a mysterious flood caused by a broken pipe would occur in the editing room, wetting the film on Tuesday, forcing the executive to push back his deadline. If it wasn't a flood, then a fire sprinkler might break or a valve would come loose, all of which was a mystery—except to me. I would call the editing room and say, "I hear a sprinkler just broke. I'm sure it'll be fixed in two days."

I kept a small wrench in my desk drawer just for the purpose of causing accidents when people rushed me too fast and I didn't want to be defiant. One year my shows had so many mishaps that an ABC executive called up Paramount and said, "Why do you have Garry working under such awful conditions? Things are always breaking over there."

•   •   •

When accidents couldn't solve a problem, I used a philosophy I developed called the Three Forks of Creativity: The first fork is instinct, the second experience, and the third analysis. Whenever I was faced with a big creative decision, I would turn to my three forks for help. Probably the first time I put the philosophy to the test was during the first season of *The Odd Couple*.

Like most new shows, *The Odd Couple* was previewed before a test audience. While the show received above-average results overall, some people were concerned about Felix's "manliness"; not Tony Randall's, but the way he was playing Felix. Comments ranged from "too effeminate" to "definite homosexual" to "that damn fag is too light in the loafers." Remember this was 1971, not a big year for political correctness. The testing organization recommended that we give Felix a serious girlfriend who would be out to "bed and wed" him so that viewers would not be confused about his sexuality.

I got out my Three Forks of Creativity and tried to decide what to do. *The Odd Couple* was my first hit and I didn't have much experience in television producing, so I couldn't rely on the experience fork. The comments from the research testing organization were mixed, so there really wasn't much to analyze. I went with my instinct, which was to leave the show exactly as it was. I basically ignored the research and went about my business. After talking to the other producers, we decided that to give Felix more than a casual girlfriend would conflict with the show's basic premise: *The Odd Couple* was about the relationship between two divorced men who were trying to live together, period. ABC boss Leonard Goldenson backed me.

Network executives hate it when you ignore research and they bugged us about it for the entire run of the show and blamed our decision for the show's less than impressive ratings. While *The Odd Couple* went on to achieve a quasi-immortal status in syndication, it was rarely in prime-time's top ten and struggled to stay on the air each of its five seasons. We were a constant disappointment to the executives at ABC, prompting one particular executive to write us a note declaring: "The ratings are not high because viewers think 'The Odd Couple' is about a couple of queers."

Shortly after the note arrived, each week we filmed additional scenes in which Jack and Tony would flat out hug and kiss. Then we would add those scenes to our dailies and send them to the executives at ABC just to aggravate them. That prank was rather indicative of the spirit on *The Odd Couple* and of my philosophy as a television producer: Let the network and the studio worry about the dressing rooms and let me worry about the show.

Sometimes I would find myself in a situation where even my Three Forks of Creativity couldn't save me. When all else failed, I would usually pray. I would pray to the television God (who looked very similar to the imaginative Fred Silverman in those days) to give me strength. In TV you can't pray to win; you just pray to survive. Mostly I would pray that no one on my shows would get sick because I hated having to recast a part. I once shot a pilot for *Barefoot in the Park* and one of the actors, an older man in his seventies, died. My partner then, Jerry Belson, blinded by the intensity of pilot season, got all upset and said, "Died? How could he die? We already shot the pilot and sent it to the network." Fortunately, the pilot didn't sell, and we didn't have to recast until a year later when we did the show with a black cast that included Scoey Mitchell and Nipsey Russell. The show ran a year.

Most of the time I would pray quietly to myself before I called the network to find out a show's ratings, and I probably wasn't the only one who prayed during the 1972 earthquake. I prayed for my family, for nobody to get hurt, and for *The Odd Couple* set to be left standing. The only time I have ever been *forced* to pray in television was when I shot my series *The Little People* (which starred Brian Keith as a pediatrician) in Hawaii. Before you can begin production on a show in the islands, the locals make a serious ritual and bless your show with a traditional Hawaiian luau ceremony. They even kill a pig and roast it right there in front of the cast and crew. I know another series where I wish I had roasted a chimp, but that probably wouldn't have gone over as well. Even prayer and St. Jude couldn't have helped *Me and the Chimp*.

Another pitfall of television is that the networks constantly try to fix shows that aren't broken. They'll move time slots just to kill a series on another network. They'll try to bump up a character's name to the title to capitalize on an actor's newfound fame (the reasoning behind the rumors that we were going to change the

Out on the town in the early 1970s with my wife, Barbara, sister Ronny, then brother-in-law, Rob Reiner, and sister Penny. You could almost call this the directors-to-be club.

All in the Marshall Family: My father Tony, sister Ronny, mother Marjorie, sister Penny, and me the night we all worked together on *Laverne & Shirley* in 1979.

Penny watched with pride as our mom tap danced in an episode of *Laverne & Shirley*.

Sitting on the steps of Paramount's Building G with my stars from three of the top-rated sitcoms of 1979. To hire these people today it would cost more than Building G. *From left to right:* Ron Howard, Cindy Williams, Robin Williams, Penny Marshall, Pam Dawber, and Henry Winkler.

In a 1977 *Laverne & Shirley* episode, they took a trip to Alice's Wonderland. *From left to right, back row:* David L. Lander, Michael McKean, Eddie Mekka, Phil Foster, and Betty Garrett; *front row:* Penny Marshall and Cindy Williams.

Jay Leno, Mark Harmon, Teri Garr, Carrie Fisher, and Anjelica Huston were just a few of the up and coming actors and friends who appeared in episodes of *Laverne & Shirley*. Here's the future host of *The Tonight Show* trying his hand at sitcom.

Happier days: The cast of *Laverne & Shirley* gathers for a reunion special in 1995 and ironically remembers the turbulent years on their sitcom rather fondly.

The woman in the background playing the piano in this episode of *Happy Days* is my mother, with stars Henry Winkler, Donny Most, Anson Williams, and Ron Howard.

The 150th episode of *Happy Days* startled the many critics who said it would be canceled after 13. At the party, director Jerry Paris and I flanked the cast. *From left to right:* Donny Most, Anson Williams, Tom Bosley, Erin Moran, Marion Ross, Henry Winkler, Ron Howard, Scott Baio, and Al Molinaro.

Great producers. Great cast. Great writers. Ninety-ninth in the ratings. *Hey Landlord!* was the first sitcom that Jerry Belson and I created and the producers included Sheldon Leonard, Lee Rich, and Ron Jacobs.

An early gangster role on *Hey Landlord!* in which I demonstrated with a cantaloupe how to crush a person's head. I always wanted to use this demonstration at a network meeting.

Directing former model turned comedy actress Pam Dawber, who learned she got the part on *Mork & Mindy* when she read it in the newspaper.

Under that hat and goggles is Robin Williams during an episode of *Mork & Mindy* when he roller-skated down the Rocky Mountains in Colorado . . . backward.

Magic was made the night Mork from Ork landed in Milwaukee. Here I'm trying to work out a scene in that *Happy Days* episode with Ron Howard, Robin Williams, and Henry Winkler in 1978.

Who are these people
from my career?

PHOTO BY GLORIA STEVENS

a

COURTESY PARAMOUNT PICTURES

b

c

The answers:
a) comedian Allan Kent, the waiter who
caught the snail in *Pretty Woman*;
b) actor Gavan O'Herlihy, who played
Richie's brother Chuck, on the first
season of *Happy Days*; and
c) actress Carole Ita White, who played
the rich snob Big Rosie Greenbaum on
Laverne & Shirley.

In 1980 with my dad and sisters Ronny and Penny at the ground-breaking ceremony for my mother's dance building at Northwestern University in Evanston, Illinois.

The peacemaker: My diplomacy on the basketball court would help me later in television and movies.

To relieve stress I play on the four-peat championship softball team, the Pacemakers. If you hit a home run, you get to take a nap.

One of the keys to directing movies is to get the right hat. This is what I chose for my first film. Not a hat often worn in the Bronx.

Good jobs, bad gums: Besides keeping a lot of people in show business working, Penny and I also keep a lot of dentists busy.

1983: accepting the National Association of Television Program Executives' Man of the Year Award from Jerry Lewis in Las Vegas.

name of *Happy Days* to *Fonzie's Place*). And they will not so discreetly try to take creative control of your series.

During the first year of *Happy Days*, I had to leave the show for two weeks to go to Hawaii to shoot the pilot for *The Little People*. While I was gone, *Happy Days* and Fonzie's clothing took a turn for the worse. When I left, Fonzie was wearing his classic outfit: a dark-brown leather jacket, a white cotton T-shirt, blue jeans, and heavy black motorcycle boots. The character was based on a childhood friend of mine from Yonkers named Pete Wagner, who was the coolest person and the only person I knew growing up who had a motorcycle.

Two weeks later, when I came back from Hawaii, I was shocked to find that Fonzie didn't even have a passing resemblance to Pete Wagner anymore. Fonzie was wearing a light-gray windbreaker, a red-and-blue–checkered button-down shirt with a collar, tan slacks, and penny loafers. He had gone from hoodlum to nerd in one week.

"No, no," I said. "This is all wrong. Fonzie is dressed just like Potsie. What happened to Fonzie's real clothes?"

I discovered that the network had orchestrated the wardrobe change because some executive (perhaps the same man who had written that sensitive *Odd Couple* note) found a hoodlum inappropriate for the eight o'clock time slot.

"But that's the show," I said. "It's about a nice boy named Richie who hangs out with a hoodlum. Fonzie is a hoodlum with a heart of gold."

I wanted to scream, "Put Fonzie back into his own clothes right now!" Because I don't yell, I had to figure out another way to go. I decided to write a memo that went like this:

Dear ABC Executives Involved with Happy Days:

We have a problem. Fonzie can't ride his motorcycle in the new clothes you've given him. The public knows that if he wore a light-weight jacket and a pair of flimsy loafers on his motorcycle he would either freeze (it can get very cold in Milwaukee) or break his ankle. He needs to wear authentic motorcycle clothing, such as a leather jacket

*and a pair of sturdy boots, for protection. If he is forced to
stay in his present clothing, the audience will worry about
Fonzie freezing to death or getting hurt rather than paying attention to the show (or the commercials in between
the show).*

ABC quickly responded, "Okay, he can wear those hoodlum
clothes only when he is with his motorcycle."

The next day I sent out a secret memo to the entire cast and
crew of *Happy Days* telling everyone that whenever Fonzie
appeared on screen, he had to be accompanied by his motorcycle.
For the rest of the season, we had Fonzie sitting on his bike, leaning on his bike, and standing near his bike in every episode. He
even pushed the bike into the Cunningham living room in one
episode because he was afraid of vandals. By the time the network
figured out what we were doing, Fonzie was too popular to
change. His character had taken off and we had won the battle to
keep his streetwise clothing.

Ironically, Fonzie's controversial leather jacket is now on per-
manent display at the Smithsonian Institution in Washington,
D.C. That light-gray windbreaker wound up in a Dumpster on
Paramount's back lot where I threw it.

In television not only do you have to create a concept that sells
but, more important, you have to find one you feel comfortable
with and can repeat week after week. It's more often the speed of
the adequate execution rather than the quality of each individual
episode that matters in prime-time television. Some episodes suffered because we simply ran out of time. Arnold's wedding on
Happy Days and a guest appearance by the Denver Bronco cheerleaders on *Mork & Mindy* immediately come to mind as episodes
that were not up to our usual quality, but you have to find a level
that you won't go below. In a movie you have one two-hour chance
to get your story across to the audience. In television you have just
twenty-two minutes to interest viewers in your story and entice
them to watch again week after week and, you hope, year after
year.

Producing television involves bringing characters into people's living rooms and, contrary to popular myth, the viewers are not sitting still. They're not even sitting down. Most Americans feel they can watch television while doing something else. It's the only medium that's watched this way, except for U.S. Supreme Court Justice Ruth Bader Ginsburg, who apparently reads her mail with a pen flashlight in dark movie theaters. Television viewers are usually making dinner, reading a newspaper, or putting up a curtain rod. To get their attention your show has to be funny enough to make a person put down what he's doing and take a look.

While the actors on my shows often took home awards, as a whole the shows weren't the most critically acclaimed. However, they had longevity. When *Happy Days* ran for eleven years, we were pretty confident that people were putting down their curtain rods.

Many of the shows I produced in the 1970s continue to be seen around the world in the 1990s. People in Uruguay might be skipping dessert to see if Fonzie's motorcycle makes it over the trash cans. Henry Winkler met American hostage Terry Anderson, who told him that they watched *Happy Days* reruns with the guards during their long confinement in Iran. I can only attribute the longevity of *Happy Days* to the time we spent on each show to develop the characters. In situation comedy you have to create characters the audience can love or else they won't laugh.

The best characters are the kind that you can take from your life, like I did when I based Fonzie on Pete Wagner. My childhood in the Bronx has always been a rich place for material. Most of my friends were members of the Bronx Falcons, an athletic club that played baseball, basketball, and other sports. We were a street gang for a while but changed to sports when we realized all the other gangs were beating the hell out of us. The Falcons included Gideon Trokan, the smartest boy in my building, who played piano and taught me how to play chess and went to Hebrew school six days a week; John "Duke" Wellington, a great athlete and handsome boy from my church, who dressed well because his mom worked at Lord & Taylor; Martin Garbus, a cynical and bookish intellectual risk taker who would start an argument over anything (perhaps foreshadowing his career as a lawyer); Larry "Big Bab" Babich, our tallest kid, who never stopped talking;

Robert "Bobby" Schwabe, our neighborhood Joe DiMaggio, who
rarely spoke; and Harvey "Butch" Keenan, the happiest and funniest kid around despite that his mother, Fanny, yelled at him a
lot. Bernard "Bunny" Gwertzman and I packed up sandwiches
and ran away one day to pursue our dream of joining the Yankees.
We got only as far as the subway because we couldn't figure out
how to get to New Jersey where the tryouts were. (Bunny is now
the head of The *New York Times* foreign bureau and knows how to
get anyplace in the world.) There also was a boy named Vincent
Ragusa ("the Big Ragu") whose greatest talent was attaching a
rope to an ice truck and then pulling it with his teeth. Everybody
came with a story in those days.

In the Bronx in the 1950s, we didn't know anything about
girls. But there was a boy on my block named Melvin Yabkow who
did. When we were about twelve he was fourteen and would tell us
these brilliant things like "Blow in their ear." Then he told us to
get a wooden match, stand on a street corner, and light it on the
zippers of our flies to be cool. So I'd stand on the corner and when
a girl walked by, I'd light a match off my zipper. Later when I told
the story on David Letterman's show, I added that we were trying
to attract nymphomaniacs but instead we got pyromaniacs!

I thought about my old friends often as I tried to make the
characters on *Happy Days*, and on all of my sitcoms, likable. The
characters had to be as special as the Falcons so someone would
want to invite them into their living room. That's what television
is all about. Well-written characters will linger in people's minds
instead of fading away when the network inevitably cancels a
show. Ten years later, people still stop me on the street and say, "I
grew up on *Happy Days*." They're usually shaking my hand with
one hand and giving me a script with the other, but it's still a compliment. I think the references to Fonzie in *Pulp Fiction* and
Laverne and Shirley in *Wayne's World* are testaments to the fact
that the characters are still floating around in people's minds and
in reruns.

In the 1970s, I was strictly a sitcom producer, and it wasn't
just by a whim: I looked around at show business and asked

myself, "Which job would be the best one to do while raising a family?" As a sitcom producer I worked five days a week and no weekends. I had a schedule that varied from 10 A.M. to midnight, or sometimes noon to midnight, which allowed me time to have a work life and a family life too.

Writing a few episodes for *I Spy* was about the closest I ever came to an action-adventure format. I just wanted to make charming family shows that dealt with people in living rooms and the sitcom format seemed to be the one for me.

When I was designing my shows I reached back to my years as a writer and tried to figure out what had made Danny Thomas's and Sheldon Leonard's sitcoms so successful. Their philosophy was that you needed three things to make a hit sitcom: First, you needed the right cast and a premise, coupled with writers and producers capable of executing that premise. Second, you needed the right time slot together with a strong relationship with a network geared toward marketing your show. Third, you needed the foresight and luck to be producing the show at the right time in history. Creativity, time slot, time in history—their big three became mine.

I quickly discovered that if you have only one or two of these elements, it's not enough. I missed the mark with shows like *Barefoot in the Park*, *The Little People*, *Who's Watching the Kids*, and *Joanie Loves Chachi*. You can't just have a great batch of actors or writers or the perfect time slot or a topical theme. I think you need all three if your show is going to live out the season.

Happy Days had all three: a strong creative package, a dream time slot at 8 P.M. Tuesday nights, and the right time in history. The show never would have been a hit in the 1960s but in the 1970s, people were ready for nostalgia. *Laverne & Shirley* also had a solid premise and an enviable time slot at 8:30 behind *Happy Days*, and it came on the air when there weren't any other blue-collar women on television—the perfect time in history.

Many producers think their show will catch on if only they had a little more time. Well, there isn't much extra time in television today; it just costs too much money. In the 1970s we might have gotten as many as thirty episodes for a show to find an audience; today you pray for at least three episodes. My TV series version of

Nothing in Common went off the air after seven episodes but I believe that every good product will always find an audience, just not necessarily the year you produce it. This kind of wishful thinking is usually a disappointment to a network executive because he wants a hit now, but it can be rewarding for a writer-producer because he wants to see his work done at any time.

Jerry and I pitched a pilot called *Sheriff Who??* to NBC in the 1960s. It was a sitcom about an outlaw, Evil Roy Slade, who ran around the Old West robbing banks. We proposed a season of episodes in which Evil Roy would chase or kill town sheriffs, played by a different guest star each week. The show was meant to be a satire about all the old westerns we had ever seen. It was our definitive statement against violence. Unfortunately, everybody thought *it* was violent and no one wanted to buy the show. The powers of the industry told us to forget about it; satire sitcoms never work anyway. Lowell Ganz once said the purpose of being a writer is to be misunderstood, and Jerry and I certainly were with *Sheriff Who??*

Flash forward to 1971. Jerry and I now have some clout in television and *Sheriff Who??* is sold as a two-hour movie of the week. We reworked the original pilot and cast the parts with comedians, including John Astin (as Evil Roy Slade), Milton Berle, Dom DeLuise, Mickey Rooney, and Dick Shawn in supporting parts. We were excited. We imagined that if the movie was a big success, we might be able to spin off the TV show we had always wanted.

Unfortunately, even as a movie of the week retitled *Evil Roy Slade*, it didn't work. It was campy and funny in a dark way, but very few people got it. Slade's band of robbers were a mean and cocky bunch, not the kind you'd invite over for dinner unless you liked eating with your hands up. Apparently, not only didn't audiences want to eat with Evil Roy and his gang; they didn't want them in their living rooms, either. It's not bad to aim for the offbeat, off-the-wall humor, but you always have to be ready to fail. Four people laughed at *Evil Roy Slade* and Jerry said that was more than enough. But the network said it wasn't.

In 1974, Mel Brooks found success with *Blazing Saddles* and proved that audiences would respond to dark, satirical humor about the Old West in a movie. Eventually, even *Evil Roy Slade* found an audience of its own on late-night television. The film is a sort of cult hit now and a favorite among insomniacs across the country. Over the years it has attracted a loyal and eclectic fan club that has included Salvador Dalí, Roseanne, and Alice Cooper, who had *Evil Roy Slade* T-shirts made up for his band. More recently, I met *In Living Color*'s Damon Wayans on an airplane and he told me he loved *Evil Roy Slade*. This startled me when I realized that he probably wasn't even born when we wrote the pilot. This just proves that all good shows can find some kind of audience, even if it might be a small but loyal one.

When I was a television producer, the experts said that you needed about twenty-one million viewers to have a hit. They estimated that about seven million watched for laughs, seven million for warmth and sentimentality, and another seven million because of a certain actor or a challenging sophisticated new situation. The last seven million were the hardest group to attract. Some shows would get the first seven million with just plain laughs right from the start, but then go off the air in a year.

Television survives on and lives for ratings. That's just the way it works. After a while I started to feel like we owed the audience something in return. When you're reaching more than twenty-one million people, which *Happy Days*, *Laverne & Shirley*, and *Mork & Mindy* did, you start to think, "Hey, maybe I have an obligation to enlighten as well as entertain." I never wanted to be preachy, but we started exploring more substantial issues on the shows such as diabetes, the handicapped, and mental health. These topics worked well thematically within each show's framework. *Laverne & Shirley* was about survival. *Happy Days* explored the pain of growing up. *Mork & Mindy* looked at the harsh realities of our life and society through the innocent eyes of an alien. Each show was already set up to handle both humorous and more serious topics.

When we'd slip in a message, we'd try to disguise it with humor. If a man stands in a three-piece suit and teaches a lesson on a sitcom the audience isn't going to tolerate it. But if you stick him in a Martian suit and put him in a black box with a voice-over from a guy named Orson, you can talk about solar energy and have people sit up and listen.

No one ever said that producing a television series was easy. The grueling schedule of turning out a show every week is what provides such a great training ground for people who go on to other careers, like directing movies. Requiring a combination of discipline and speed, sitcoms are probably one of the more difficult entertainment forms. In twenty-two minutes you have to introduce all of the characters, tell what the show is about, be hilariously funny, satisfy eight network executives dressed in suits in New York, and make sure those Nielsen families keep their dials tuned for next week. Yet once you have a hit, the reward is that there is truly no other form of entertainment that can reach as many people or has the impact of television.

One year I received a letter from a history professor at Northwestern. In one of his classes, he asked a lecture hall full of students, "When was the first time that you became aware of the potential for nuclear war?" The majority of the students said it was from a *Happy Days* episode in which the Cunningham family considered building a bomb shelter.

Chapter Six

How the TV Producer Supervises Hostile Writers

Polite Story Conferences Lead to Polite Scripts

Producer Lee Rich once said to me, "If you're running into a brick wall, stop. You don't want to hit your head because you'll need it for later." His words would prove to be prophetic for a series called *The New Odd Couple.* If there was ever an award given to a sitcom for worst concept and bad timing, *The New Odd Couple* would have taken home the prize. But the concept and timing were the least of its problems. The show was built upon the twisted philosophy that a sitcom could actually be produced without writers. It was probably the only bad idea that Michael Eisner, one of the best television minds around, ever had. And it was my bad idea that I went along with him. But after all, here was the man who had gotten *Happy Days* and *Laverne & Shirley* on the air.

After seeing a production of *Hello, Dolly!* with Pearl Bailey filling Carol Channing's shoes in the title role, Eisner decided that Paramount should dust off the original *Odd Couple* scripts and reshoot them exactly as written ten years later with an all-black cast starring Demond Wilson and Ron Glass. Everybody agreed. The underlying problem, however, was that the new series was based on greed: If the studio didn't need new scripts, then they wouldn't have to hire new writers. This would save them lots of money and aggravation. It also would undermine the basic process of sitcom, which is a bunch of writers sitting around pitching the best possible jokes.

Paramount owned the rights to all the old scripts and ABC was more than willing to back the concept because *The Odd Couple* was now huge in syndication. Paramount asked if I would supervise the show. My first response was no. It was 1982 and I was already directing feature films and slowly phasing myself out of television. I changed my mind because I knew that if I said yes, more than seventy-five people, many minorities, would get jobs immediately. They got me the way they usually got me, not with money or power but with the promise that I could create work for other people. It was a battle between artistic integrity and people eating, and I sided with the food.

Although I agreed to be associated with the show, I was unable to save it from self-destruction. Words written for two square New York Jewish men in their forties just didn't sound right coming out of the mouths of two hip thirty-year-old African-American men. Even though they hired a skeleton staff to adjust some of the dialogue, it wasn't a quick fix. To make a sitcom work you need writers creating new material for the actors. You can't just squeeze new actors into old scripts. Demond and Ron admirably and doggedly gave it their best shot, but *The New Odd Couple* never made it through its first season. I called up Paramount and said, "Stop. We're headed for a brick wall."

The industry's temptation to try to eliminate writers from television to cut down on cost has increased since *The New Odd Couple*. Today television is filled with home-video programs, magazine shows, and other reality-based programming that use only a few writers or none at all. Danny Thomas and Sheldon Leonard never would have bypassed writers because they believed in writers and they treated each of us as if we were one of the most important players on their team.

Instead of making us work in dark, smoked-filled conference rooms, they planned pitching trips for us each year. We traveled to places like Palm Springs and San Francisco to lay out scripts for the coming season. Those trips demonstrated a real dedication to the writers. Unlike most studio and network executives today, Danny and Sheldon recognized the importance of nurturing and training young writers. The only time Sheldon ever lied to Jerry and me was when he told us that if we wrote for *I Spy* we'd get a trip to the Far East. Instead, he gave us a coffee-table book about Asia—to share.

People always ask me about the driving force in television in the 1970s, and I tell them it was that the most successful producers I knew loved their shows. I loved *Happy Days*. Sherwood Schwartz loved *The Brady Bunch*. Norman Lear loved *All in the Family*. And we all enjoyed working with the writers on our shows. But in the early 1980s, things began to change and many people who once had disdain for the medium were suddenly lured into television writing and producing because of the promise of high salaries. According to the Writers Guild, the minimum payment for a thirty-minute network prime-time story and teleplay in 1970 was around $1,500, compared with $15,000 by 1994. Clearly, the financial incentive was there.

However, I've always thought that the best producer was not the one taking home the biggest salary but the one who understood the process of writing. Each writer works in a slightly different way, and you can't just listen to the loudest or pushiest one on your staff. Sometimes the best material will come from the shy, quiet guy sitting in the corner with his nose in a script. On *The Dick Van Dyke Show*, Carl Reiner, the antithesis of the word "shy," was nevertheless very encouraging to the quiet and less assertive writers and always made it a point to listen to them.

The pitching sessions on *The Dick Van Dyke Show* could get very loud with writers screaming and yelling out ideas like people bidding at an auction. I was usually paralyzed by shyness and my bad accent and didn't say much. Once in a while, Carl would quiet the room, turn to me, and ask for an idea or opinion. His attention and patience gave me the confidence to speak up. Years later Carl told me that he wasn't just being kind; he was being smart. When he used to work with Mel Brooks and Neil Simon on *Your Show of Shows*, Mel would yell and pitch ideas and monopolize everyone's attention. But every so often, Carl would quiet the room so Neil could speak. Needless to say, Neil's quiet thoughts proved to be big loud laughs.

The only one on *The Dick Van Dyke Show* who was shyer than me when it came to verbally pitching a story was Dale McRaven. Dale's partner, Carl Kleinschmitt, always did the pitching for the two of them; Dale never said a word. One day Kleinschmitt called in sick and Dale was faced with the prospect of pitching their story all by himself. Right before the meeting, Jerry and I found Dale throwing up in the men's room. He told us he just couldn't stand up alone in front of the rest of the writing staff and describe his story. As he leaned over the toilet, he was able to tell us his plot line and we went back and pitched it for him (actually Jerry pitched and I nodded a lot). Dale later conquered his fear and went on to become one of the creators and producers of *Mork & Mindy* where he listened to other scared writers pitch their stories.

A writer pitches scripts to head writers and producers, and producers must pitch ideas for sitcoms to studio executives, network representatives, and stars. It's always easier to get them to listen to your pitch when you already have another hit show on the air. During the second season of *Happy Days*, I went with my wife to a resort in Marco, Florida, to attend an ABC television convention where we spent time with Fred Silverman, the network's top television executive. A few months earlier, Fred had been the head of NBC and spent his days trying to figure out a way to beat *Happy Days* in the ratings. Now he was the head of ABC and preoccupied with keeping *Happy Days* at the top of the Nielsen charts. Such is show business. One day at the convention Fred and I were eating lunch and he said, "I like *Happy Days*. What else do you have?"

Doing business while eating has never been my strength. I had shrimp Louie salad dripping down my chin and the man was asking me to pitch to him with a mouthful.

"I don't have anything else," I mumbled.

"Yes, I'm sure you do. You need something else to make a match with *Happy Days*. The key to television is getting a full hour. You need to package two shows. *Happy Days* is at eight o'clock, so now you need an eight-thirty show that goes well with *Happy Days*. So, what else do you have?"

Quickly trying to spear a baby tomato from my plate without squirting it on my shirt, I suddenly remembered two characters named Laverne and Shirley. They had been very popular when they appeared on *Happy Days*, and I thought this might be the perfect opportunity to get my divorced single-mom-with-a-child sister Penny a steady acting job.

"Well, Fred," I said, pushing back my salad plate, "there were these two single blue-collar girls on *Happy Days* . . . They work in a beer factory."

"What are their names?" Fred asked, getting right to the core of the series.

"Laverne and Shirley."

"Two blue-collar girls . . . working at a beer factory . . . running around single in the 1950s . . . Perfect! I love it. Let's make it a show. But make it fast," said Fred.

And that's how *Laverne & Shirley* was created. We made a ten-minute pilot that we shot one night after *Happy Days*, using Fonzie's apartment as the set. While that was probably the world's easiest television pilot pitch, a much harder one was pitching *The Odd Couple* to Tony Randall. Paramount told Jerry Belson and me to take our pilot script for *The Odd Couple* to Tony and talk him into doing a television series. Just a few years earlier, Jerry and I had been practicing our pitches in a bathroom mirror, and the prospect of pitching a whole show to a famous, talented, and intimidating actor seemed a little beyond us. How could Tony Randall ever be charmed by two guys like us? We couldn't imagine, so we devised a plan.

Tony was appearing at the Pheasant Run Playhouse outside Chicago in a production of *The Odd Couple*. We did some quick research and discovered that Tony's greatest love was opera. I knew about jazz and Jerry was familiar with rock and roll, but we both came up blank on opera. Then I recalled that an attractive and very bright college girlfriend of mine, Cynthia Peterson, who lived in Chicago was an expert on opera. So when we went to meet Tony, we brought her along. For two hours she and Tony talked about opera and then for ten minutes he talked to us about *The Odd Couple* series. The next day Tony signed the deal to star in the series and proved that ten minutes of pitching and 120 minutes of opera were more than enough to convince him. Jerry and I had learned the key to pitching a new series: Do it in a conducive atmosphere, not necessarily conducive to you but to the people you're pitching to.

When producers aren't trying to sell ideas to famous actors, they spend their time trying to discover the next big star. Shortly after my sister Penny moved to California, she started taking acting classes with Harvey Lembeck's improv theater group. One night I went to see Penny perform and I noticed a funny guy with a big nose in her class. His name was Al Molinaro and in one of the improvs he played a very funny priest taking confessions. Penny had told me his story earlier: He was about forty and had just embarked on a career as an actor following a long stint as a loan collector. He was raw but very funny and after the performance I followed him to his car.

"Mr. Molinaro, you're terrific! I hope we can work together some day," I said.

Al briskly thanked me for my compliment and ducked into his car.

He didn't know I was a producer and mistook me for another actor praising his work. It wasn't like I wore this big sign that said I'M A TELEVISION PRODUCER. Dressed in jeans and a windbreaker, I looked more like a stagehand than a producer. (Actors beware: Many television producers don't wear Armani.) I wasn't offended. I thought maybe he had another job lined up or didn't want to work in television. Later, when he found out that I was a producer, he was mortified and thought he had blown his entire career in a windy parking lot.

We started casting for *The Odd Couple* a few weeks later. Al sent me his picture and résumé to audition for the role of Murray the Cop, a character described in the script breakdown as "a pug-nosed Irishman." But Jerry and I decided to take a chance on Al because of all the men who auditioned, he was the funniest. Actors should remember that even if the breakdown says "Irish" and you're "Italian," go for it anyway; you have nothing to lose. The part of Fonzie originally called for a "six-foot tall blond guy" and look who I ended up with and how brilliant he was. Most comedy producers, when in doubt, will always cast the funniest actor no matter what the part calls for.

I hold up Al's story as an example when I tell people that it's never too late to follow your dream. At forty, he had a business collecting delinquent loans and making people's lives sad and by forty-five he was Murray the Cop on television making people laugh.

Being a writer-producer has its advantages: For example, you can change the rules of the game to fit your show. On *Happy Days*, William Bickley and Michael Warren invented the concept of the "six o'clock writers," which meant they gave up some money but got to leave at six each night to go home and be with their families. Later in their careers they went on to become "midnight writers," guys who usually run the show because of pure stamina: They can stay up later than anyone else.

I found that we had to invent new ways to motivate the writers each season. Writing on a sitcom is not like laying bricks; yelling and screaming might make somebody lay bricks faster, but it won't get a staff of creative writers to pick up the pace. On *The Odd Couple* we developed the concept of the "two-rowed writing table."

The staff writers sat in chairs around a long table and the apprentice writers sat in chairs behind them. If an apprentice had an idea, he wrote it on a scrap of paper and handed it to one of the staff writers. The staff writer would then read the joke or line out loud to the group, which sometimes included the actors, producers, and director. If the joke turned out to be a dud, or if Tony put his finger in his mouth and gagged, or Jack spat pieces of his cigar butt on the floor with disdain, the staff writer would cover and say *he* wrote it. If, however, the others liked the material and Tony and Jack laughed, *then* the staff writer would give the apprentice credit. That was the rule: Protect the rookies until they were strong enough to try it on their own.

That's how we made *The Odd Couple* a very safe place for new writers. An apprentice could learn and grow without the other guys beating the hell out of him. The key was never to yell at the young writers in front of the actors because some stars just don't understand how the writing process works. Marion Ross, who played Mrs. Cunningham on *Happy Days* for eleven years, once said, "Which of these young men is my writer?" as if every actor on the show had his own personal writer. To protect themselves, writers needed to put up a united front.

However, if a young writer gave a staff writer a particularly bad joke, there was still plenty of room for teasing later.

"What was that piece of crap you gave me?" a staff writer might say to an apprentice when they were away from the writing table. "Edit your stuff before you hand it to me next time. Did you see the way Jack and Tony looked at me? Like all my ideas sucked."

Yelling was acceptable, but the apprentices were rarely humiliated in front of the entire staff. (That honor was reserved for the staff writers.) I thought my great design of our writing table was all about nurturing writers. How proud I was to watch the young apprentices move up so quickly and become staff writers. I was shocked the day I found out it had little to do with my motivation, but truthfully more to do with dinner.

Often we would order in food and work with the writers while we all ate. The staff writers could set their food on the table but the apprentices had to balance their meals on their laps while sitting in the chairs behind the staff writers. Recently, writer Marty Nadler told me that the biggest incentive to become a staff writer was being able to put your food on the table.

On my shows I approved of and encouraged arguing around the writing tables, even if I had to play the referee. We ran our script meetings by Samuel Goldwyn's philosophy: "Polite story conferences lead to polite scripts." Fighting is good. Henry Winkler once said to Lowell Ganz, "I can't possibly say this line."

Lowell came back with, "You could if you were taller." There were rumors that several writers on *Laverne & Shirley* daydreamed about running down cast members with their cars.

In the 1970s, polite scripts led to polite sitcoms, which got canceled. To avoid being canceled, we reserved yelling for the writer's meetings, particularly on *The Odd Couple*. We argued. We screamed. We bickered. We did anything it took to get a good script out each week. This seemed to work until one week when the yelling got so out of control on *The Odd Couple* that I had to put a stop to it.

"Okay, this week I'm going to write the script by myself, so everybody take a break," I said.

Sometimes simplicity can help bring order back to a situation. I sat down and wrote "The Odd Monks," an episode in which Oscar and Felix visit a monastery and are forced to take a twenty-four-hour vow of silence. It was the perfect way to show the writers how disputes about dialogue can be solved: Simply eliminate the dialogue altogether and build a whole show around physical comedy.

In one scene that took place during their vow of silence, they were washing dishes when Felix discovered an enormous pot that Oscar had done only a cursory job of washing. To show his disgust at the sloppy job, Felix stuck his head way down inside the pot to rescrub it. While he was inside, Oscar took a steel ladle and smacked it hard against the side of the pot. Felix popped up like he had just been deafened.

Since the actors couldn't be monks in every episode, I had to figure out a permanent way to keep the writers inspired throughout the season. I discovered a long-term solution by hiring a mixture of old and young writers. I had many young writers on staff who were full of enthusiasm and energy. However, because many were on their first job, they lacked the discipline that comes with experience. On my shows I decided to hire older writers, in their late fifties and sixties, to help the younger writers. The arrangement not only worked, but also gave me the opportunity to hire many of the writers who had first given me my start: Harry Crane, Milt Josefsberg, Walter Kempley, and Bob Howard.

Of course it wasn't perfect. One day Harry Crane went for a cancer biopsy and came back in time for the *Happy Days* run-through. Sitting with the other writers in the bleachers, Harry, a cynical comedy veteran who had written for Dean Martin, Jerry Lewis, and Frank Sinatra, looked down with disdain on the young cast below, which at the time included a thinly credited twelve-year-old named Scott Baio. Harry said, "Look at that for fairness. I'm dying and Scott Baio is a star." It turns out Harry Crane did not die and Scott Baio grew up to become a wonderful actor, starring in two series, and a fine comedy director.

When it came to pitching new scripts, having a mixture of old and new writers created new dynamics.

"I've got an idea," a young writer would say. "Fonzie has fallen for a girl, but her parents want to move the family to New York City."

Harry Crane would interrupt, "Judy Garland, *Meet Me in St. Louis*, 1944. Here's how the plot goes."

Harry knew all the old movies and would tell the young writers about story structures that were invented before they were even born. Most of the young guys only knew Judy Garland from *The Wizard of Oz*, but they listened when the veterans talked about plot.

Another young writer would say, "Mrs. C gets obsessed with a handsome tennis teacher."

"Did it with Mary Livingston on *Jack Benny*. It goes like this," Milt Josefsberg would offer.

"Laverne and Shirley have a leak in their overhead plumbing and they use lots of pots and pans to catch the drips," a third young voice would say.

"Once used a visual like that on *Beat the Clock*. Here's where the jokes were," Bob Howard would volunteer.

Unfortunately, today Hollywood is plagued by ageism. Actors, producers, and even writers are getting face-lifts, tummy tucks, and dying their hair just to get jobs from twenty-four-year-old television executives and movie producers. I think Richard Gere and I are the only two people with gray hair still working steadily in show business. It's a shame. On my television series, I saw the positive effects that the combination of experience and youth could have on creativity.

While I tried to share my experience with the young writers, other lessons we had to learn together. More than on any other show, we learned together on *Mork & Mindy* . . . what *not* to do.

After the triumphant first season, things slowly started to fall apart. First, I left to go to New York to do my play *The Roast* and my supervising contributions to *Mork & Mindy* became very limited. Then the big blow came when ABC, in a colossal mistake, took the number-one show, *Mork & Mindy*, and moved it to a new time slot. They moved it from Thursday at 8 P.M. to Sunday at 8 P.M. against CBS's *Archie Bunker's Place*. This move, despite protests from me, producers Bruce Johnson and Dale McRaven, and Paramount, was done in my opinion because of greed, power, and Herculean stupidity.

No longer was I dealing with ABC's wise and sensitive Leonard Goldenson or Martin Starger, an innovative friend of comedy, who kept *The Odd Couple* on the air despite its ratings, or ABC programming chief Fred Pierce, who shepherded *Happy Days* through its early struggle. Now there were new people and they wanted to show they could beat *Archie Bunker's Place* and break CBS's hold on Sunday night. They lost. I lost. The show lost, and in doing so caused a lot of aggravation and inferior creativity.

To compete more effectively in the new time slot, we were forced during the second season to attract more young people by giving Mork and Mindy two companions, sister and brother deli owners played by Gina Hecht and Jay Thomas. But in the shuffle we made a big error by getting rid of Mindy's dad, Conrad Janis, and grandmother, Elizabeth Kerr. We were goaded by the network, which wanted to weed out forty-five-plus actors from the prime-time lineup.

Later realizing that rarely has a sitcom been a success without a father or mother figure, we quickly called Conrad and Elizabeth and got them both back.

During the third season, the network moved the show back to Thursday night, but we had lost our momentum. To try to revive the show, the network requested we "sex up Mork and Mindy" and "incorporate some T & A" into the format. We made several desperate attempts with episodes featuring Raquel Welch, the Denver Bronco cheerleaders, and poor Robin wearing various dresses. We even tried a young up and coming comic named David Letterman but nothing seemed to spark the audience's attention until we introduced a character named Exidor.

Exidor, part benevolent schizophrenic homeless man and part religious zealot, became a friend of Mork's and caused a noticeable

surge in the ratings and viewer mail. The first few shows with
Mork and Exidor were hilarious to the studio audience. Spurred on
by Exidor's popularity, the writers became addicted to him. The
audience, however, quickly grew bored with the repetition. Too
much of a good thing can ruin even a top-rated sitcom. When you
find something hot, you have to learn how to use it in moderation
to cultivate long-term loyalty.

Then there was an attempt to return the show to its original
premise: Mork the innocent exploring the foibles of Earth like a
wide-eyed child. That was the concept that had made the show so
popular to begin with. There was only one problem—Robin and
the writers were bored. They wanted to change the character.
They wanted Mork to be hip rather than naïve. What they didn't
understand was that people watch television for consistency, not
for change.

We made a last-ditch effort during the final season of *Mork* to
save the show by bringing on Jonathan Winters, one of Robin's and
my comic heroes. We thought Jonathan's presence would inspire
Robin and help boost our ratings at the same time. When Jonathan
and Robin improvised during the warm-ups it was brilliant. But as
soon as the cameras started to roll and they had to censor their
dirty material and stick to the script, the scenes weren't as good.
Things got to the point where some people would come for the
warm-up, then leave before the filming started.

Robin is still the funniest, wittiest, and quickest comedian I've
ever seen and one of the better human beings. In 1990, I was given
a Lifetime Achievement Award from the American Comedy
Awards and my sister Penny and Robin, who were filming
Awakenings on location, sent a videotape to the ceremony to congratulate me. When they played the tape in front of the audience,
they explained it had been shot at four in the morning, and it was
clear they were both tired and groggy. At one point when Penny
was explaining the set behind them, she had meant to say that
they were shooting their film at a mental institution. But instead,
because she was so tired, her words came out "We're filming now
at a menstrual institution." Robin, not missing a beat, said, "Yes,
Garry, it's a period piece."

Most of Robin's pranks on the set of *Mork & Mindy* involved

Pam Dawber. He was always slipping in unrehearsed off-color jokes just to shock her. But one day she wanted to shock him, so we gave her the punch line to one of his gags. In front of the studio audience, he stopped in the middle of a scene and asked her, "What do you get when you cross a donkey with an onion?" She wryly came back with, "A piece of ass that will make your eyes water!" It was the only time I ever saw Robin startled.

The only time I ever saw Robin scared was when we filmed an episode in which Mork dressed up as a Denver Bronco cheerleader. At the time, the Broncos had a small but skittish Shetland pony as their mascot and the producers wanted Robin to climb onto the horse in his cheerleader uniform and ride it. When it came time to shoot the scene, Robin was more skittish than the pony. If your stars are not comfortable doing something, try to avoid it despite the pressure for ratings.

Robin, however, was fearless when it came to comedy. He would do all kinds of crazy things, including taking off his clothes. Nothing was too outrageous for him. When we filmed an episode called "Mork Gets Mindy-itis," in which Mork has an allergic reaction to Mindy and ends up thinking that he is she, Robin pulled one of his infamous stunts. Again wearing a dress, he knocked on the door to Mindy's apartment. When Pam opened the door, Robin lifted up his dress and showed Pam and the studio audience that he wasn't wearing any underwear. Pam slammed the door, but not before the cameramen got it all on film. Later, fearing someone might sell the film to the *National Enquirer*, Robin went to the producers and asked that the film be destroyed. It promptly was.

The censors didn't know what hit them when *Mork & Mindy* came along. On *Happy Days*, I'd get notes like "Fonzie can't say the word 'virgin' on the air," so instead we would have him say "pure as the driven snow." On *Mork* they didn't just give us notes but recommendations to cut whole scenes. For Robin it became almost a contest as he tried to slip in things like the Serbo-Croatian or Yiddish words for "shit" just to see if he could get it by the censors.

Despite the fun everyone was having behind the scenes, by the end we had lost our audience for good and there wasn't anything we could do to write *Mork & Mindy* back into the top of the ratings. Its first year the show had been a hit, but after ABC's time-slot tinkering I think *Mork & Mindy* never recovered. In the end, not even the voices of Exidor or Robin's genius could save the show from uttering its final "Nanoo-nanoo."

I never wanted any of the writers to make my shows their life's work because I knew my shows weren't going to last anybody's lifetime. I wanted them to come, learn the craft, and then move on with their own dreams. I think one of my strengths was that I knew how to pick a writer with potential. Some of them decided to stay in television and become producers, like Arthur Silver (*Married . . . with Children*), Jeff Franklin (*Full House*), William Bickley, Michael Warren, and John Collins (*Perfect Strangers*), David Duclon, Gary Menteer, and Fred Fox, Jr. (*Family Matters*), while others went on to film, like Lowell Ganz and Babaloo Mandel (*Splash* and *Parenthood*), Harvey Miller and Chuck Shyer (*Private Benjamin*), Bob Brunner (*Exit to Eden*), and Brian Levant (*The Flintstones*).

Working with new writers was always one of my favorite functions of television. I enjoyed teaching them the lessons others had taught me. Jerry Belson, however, was a self-admitted non-teacher. He used to get so frustrated with the new writers on *The Odd Couple* that he said their hands should be placed in a meat grinder and mangled so that they couldn't type again. Jerry and I viewed the writing staff differently: He thought they were out to ruin the nation's humor; I thought they showed promise.

While I liked working with the writers, there were two things that would provoke me to fire a writer: One, if he wrote the phrase "Oh, no!" he received a warning and if he did it a second time I let him go. And two, if he wrote the stage direction "Looks at wristwatch and says line 'I have to go.'" Those to me were the two worst sins of television writing. A third sin, which meant no raise, was writing the "flip screen visual." A lead character says, "I'm not going to wear this tuxedo, dear." Then the TV screen flips over to show the character at a formal affair wearing the tuxedo.

On *Happy Days*, I was having trouble with some of the writers because they were writing scripts about the "day players" (actors who come in for one or two episodes and sometimes work one or two days) instead of the stars. On *The Dick Van Dyke Show*, Carl Reiner used to say, "Don't write the whole show about the mailman. He can only bring the premise." It's one thing to write scripts that focus on the relationships between the main and supporting characters (as we did on *The Danny Thomas Show* with Danny and the kids), but you can't devote an entire episode to a guy who's getting Screen Actors Guild minimum to play a butcher on one show and probably won't be seen ever again.

That's what I tried to teach my writers on *Happy Days*, but they just weren't getting it. So one day I came into a writers meeting and put up on the wall a chart that gave the names of all the actors on the show beside their weekly salaries.

"Look, here," I said, "Fonzie makes $60,000 an episode and the guy who's playing the cop this week makes $750 a show. If you write a whole script starring the cop, I still have to pay Henry Winkler $60,000." As I looked around the room, I could see both understanding and envy in the writers' eyes: understanding because they finally got what I was talking about and envy because they didn't know Henry was making so damn much money.

Another thing the new writers didn't understand was the occasional need for compromise in order to finish. One time it was after midnight and I was running a *Happy Days* writers table. I turned to a young writer and said, "Go and type up your joke for me." He hesitated and then said, "But Garry, you said this joke wasn't funny." I looked at him through my tired bloodshot eyes and said, "At nine o'clock the joke wasn't funny. At midnight it's hysterical."

I enjoyed watching the writers grow, but I didn't really socialize with them much. I kept hearing about other television shows being one big happy family off the set. I didn't think it *had* to be like that because of something that happened years earlier to Woody Allen.

When Fred Freeman and I were writing for *The Jack Paar Show*, we used to hang out in the Village comedy clubs in New York with other young writers. We all envied Woody because he was a staff writer for *The Garry Moore Show* and was paid $1,500 a week, more than most of us made in a month. One day

Woody told us that he had been fired. We all gathered around him and listened as he shared the details. We learned that Garry Moore hosted a brunch every Sunday at his home and insisted that every member of the cast and writing staff attend the brunch. Woody was painfully shy and refused to go to the brunch. Moore said, "No brunch, no job" and fired Woody. A $1,500 a week job taken away just like that because a guy wouldn't schmooze over eggs Benedict.

I decided that if I ever had a show, I would never force anybody to do anything he didn't want to do, except create. When we organized the *Happy Days* softball team, I encouraged everyone to join in, but I never made it mandatory. I love sports and thought it would be a healthy activity for the show, but I never pushed anyone to play. And I never forced a writer to eat a meal with me. After seeing me eat, many were thankful.

Chapter Seven

How the TV Show Runner Supervises Everyone Else, Including Relatives

Hire Some People with Whom You Wouldn't Have Lunch

When you're putting together a sitcom, a prime element is a strong cast. When Jerry and I signed on to produce *The Odd Couple*, we had no cast at all.

Basically, we had Neil Simon's concept and our pilot script but no Oscar and Felix. Jack Lemmon, Walter Matthau, and Art Carney had been wonderful in the stage and film versions, but they were all unavailable for the series. Paramount's initial wish list included Mickey Rooney as Oscar and Dean Martin as Felix. When it came down to Mickey and Dean, Jerry and I decided to quit. They were not our idea of perfect casting or a way to live a calm, healthy life. Learning when to quit in television is critical; you have to be willing to walk away if the basic package doesn't meet your creative needs. As it turned out, Paramount called us back and said they had another idea.

They wanted to pursue Tony Randall for the part of Felix. Now they were talking some sense. After using our ace in the hole opera friend to get Tony, Jerry and I set our sights on Oscar. I had my own ideas about the role. In addition to writing scripts in the early 1960s, my army friend Fred Roos (who later became a big movie producer) and I had operated, along with Patricia McQueeney and Herbert Malina, a personal management consulting firm called Compass Management. Our client list included Penny Marshall, Cindy Williams, Martin Sheen, Teri Garr, Kay Lenz, Ben Vereen, and Harrison Ford, and writers such as Lowell Ganz, William Bickley, and Michael Warren. We knew a lot of out-of-work actors who needed someone to help them break into the business; we did things like prepare them for auditions. So, I wasn't a stranger to casting and often wrote down the names of actors who I thought had "it."

When casting for Oscar, I remembered an actor I saw play opposite Ethel Merman in a Broadway production of *Gypsy*. He had a nonflashy supporting part as her theatrical manager and never sang a solo. Matter of fact, when Ethel sang, she often required the other actors to face her with their backs to the audience. This actor did that and since Ethel spritzed saliva as she sang, he spent most of the show getting soaking wet. Still, at the end when he took a bow the audience cheered. Why? Because they liked him. To me likability was the critical factor. He also had a great face, which was once described as a sexy dachshund, and he was a master of reaction. And when he reacted, he was brave enough to do nothing. No eye popping, no eyebrow raises, no mouth dropping. Nothing. Sometimes the funniest reaction is deadpan. (Jack Benny made a career of it.) Deadpan reactions to Felix's absurdities were a must for Oscar and that's why I loved Jack Klugman for the part.

After talking it over, Jerry and I told Paramount that we wanted Jack Klugman for Oscar. A studio executive said, "Oh, we don't think Jack Klugman is right for the part. We have some tape on him." I asked to see the tape and quickly discovered that they had the wrong guy. It wasn't Jack Klugman, but a mustachioed actor named Jack Kruschen, who was good but not right for the part. While we were busy looking at footage of the wrong actor, Jack Klugman was busy winning an Emmy for his role in *The*

Defenders. Then ABC put in their two cents: "Jack Klugman can't play Oscar because he won an Emmy for 'The Defenders.' He's a dramatic actor. He's not funny."

This kind of narrow thinking demonstrates why network executives are network executives and not television producers. (David Letterman once referred to network executives as "a higher form of weasel.") They have strange skills, like the ability to read upside down from the notes on a producer's desk, but that's about as impressive as it gets. Basically, I feel most network guys lack vision; they can see only what something *is*, not what it has the potential to become. Jerry and I knew that Klugman could do comedy, but what we didn't know was if he would accept the part.

We insisted that Paramount approach Jack and when our names were mentioned, he said, "I remember those guys. They wrote that great first draft of a movie called *The Grasshopper*." It's encouraging to know that there are still some people in Hollywood with memories longer than a television season. Jack signed a deal to play Oscar and we were ready to roll. In sitcoms, half the battle takes place before you ever get your show on the air. As a producer, you need the patience and strength to fight for your casting choices because you're the one who's going to have to live with them. If an actor is a pain in the ass, it is possible to get through twelve weeks with him on a movie shoot, but not five years on a television series.

Part of what always excited me about a television series was the magic of casting. When I first worked with Scott Baio, Crystal Bernard, and Ted McGinley on *Happy Days*, I felt they would be big in television. But I thought that Donna Pescow and Robert Hays from *Angie* also would make it, and they didn't. There's always an element of risk involved, especially when you put two people on screen together for the first time. With Tony and Jack, you could spot the chemistry before they stepped in front of the camera.

When we shot the exteriors for the opening credits in New York, I hired a limousine where Tony and Jack could sit between takes. They weren't in the limo for more than two seconds when Tony leaped out.

"I can't be in a car with that man. He's smoking a cigarette!"

"I can't afford two limos, Tony. Why don't you take turns?"

"But I can't go back in there after him. It'll be all smoky. Bad for my sinuses."

"Well, I'm not going to stop smoking just for him," Jack said, as he stepped out of the limo amid a cloud of smoke.

They both stood outside arguing and nobody sat in the limo.

They weren't just acting. They were actually living the roles of Oscar and Felix. Sadly, years later it would be Tony who begged Jack to stop smoking to save his throat. With Tony and Jack the magic was always there, but with other actors sometimes it takes you by surprise.

After seeing that there were no blue-collar women on television, we decided to introduce two working-class women as dates for Fonzie and Richie on an episode of *Happy Days*. When it came to casting, we were running behind schedule and we didn't have time to hold auditions. I had to come up with two actresses fast who could play tough girls.

I immediately thought of Penny, whose last steady job had been playing Myrna Turner on *The Odd Couple*. In the meantime, Penny and her friend Cindy Williams had teamed up as writing partners. While Cindy had a promising movie career after appearing in Francis Ford Coppola's film *The Conversation*, and Penny paid the rent by doing commercials, in between acting jobs they wrote spec scripts together.

As a favor, I asked Penny and Cindy to help me out on an episode of *Happy Days*. It was a one-time shot and I figured they could use the extra money. Before we knew it, magic occurred. The moment Laverne and Shirley appeared on *Happy Days*, it became obvious that Penny and Cindy had something very special on screen. During the rehearsal, Sam Rosen, a veteran cameraman, called me over and made me look at a two-shot of Penny and Cindy through his lens. Sam said, "Sell that two-shot. That's a series." You can't anticipate that kind of chemistry. You just have to set it in motion and see if it takes off. That night when we filmed the show in front of a live audience, the real people told us their opinion. Their loud applause said, "We like those girls." Then all it took was Fred Silverman to nudge me along before Penny and Cindy would have a series to call their own.

While a producer has to be part casting director, he also has to be part minister to deal with the tantrums and temperaments of the actors on a sitcom. I once told an actress that eyes were very important in film and she should work on opening her eyes wider. In her quest for success, she had surgery to *make* her eyes open wider. I once asked another actress what her ultimate dream was and she said, "Global adulation."

I suspect that Valium might have been invented to help television producers handle actors. Prozac was created later to help actors deal with producers. Since the 1960s pot has always been a favorite of writers so they don't have to listen to anybody. Long hours and short deadlines cause emotions to run high on even the best run series, and it's the producer's job to pinpoint what's wrong and make it better, much like a parent. Actors, it follows, can sometimes be children: some well behaved, others eternally stuck in the terrible twos. For me, *Happy Days* had a dream cast, but *Laverne & Shirley* was a producer's nightmare. The actors were usually cranky, like a kindergarten class that had missed nap time.

There were dark days on *Laverne & Shirley*. Right from the beginning both Penny and Cindy argued with the writers. If a writer made it through an entire season, he was given a gold star. The *Happy Days* cast pretty much acted like a family both in front of and behind the camera. Their fun was putting glasses up to the sound stage wall to listen to the cast of *Laverne & Shirley* fight next door.

Laverne & Shirley was not a show where the writers and actors ate lunch together, and Penny and Cindy were well aware of their unpopularity: For Christmas one year they handed out dart boards with their faces as the bull's-eyes.

The difference in climate between the two shows wasn't just a fluke. The *Happy Days* cast had strong outside interests that included spouses, children, and hobbies. But as a whole, the cast of *Laverne & Shirley* didn't have a life. During the early years of the show, Cindy had dating troubles and Penny got a divorce (headlines rang out: LAVERNE AND MEATHEAD KAPUT). Their personal lives were not a fairy tale. One night Penny and Cindy came out to a three-minute standing ovation at the end of filming an episode. When I later congratulated them they said, "Yeah . . . but we have no dates tonight."

Even Michael McKean and David Lander, who gave birth to the outrageous Lenny and Squiggy, were cynical and angry about life. The cast hung out together because they were communally depressed. Misery was one subject they could all agree on. The only cast members who never complained were veteran actors Phil Foster and Betty Garrett (a woman who had been supporting her family since her husband, Larry Parks, had been black-listed in the 1950s). Phil and Betty would come up to me and say, "What are these kids complaining about? They have a job."

Why were they unhappy? I think it was because although their show was an undisputed hit, and very often the number-one rated series in America, they had very little critical acclaim or accolades from their peer group of writers and actors. Penny and Cindy were in the center of the movers and shakers of young Hollywood life and every night they were with people who would comment on their work. But the physical comedy that Penny and Cindy were doing didn't fit into any category and most of their friends didn't know what to make of it.

At a party Rob Reiner might say, "On *All in the Family* today we dealt with bigotry." Then James Brooks would say, "On *Rhoda* we focused on honesty in a marriage." Finally Penny would mumble, "Today, Cindy and I hung on meat hooks." Rob might ask, "To show the oppression of blue-collar workers?" All Penny could say back was, "No, we just hung on meat hooks." The only time Penny and Cindy were sought out by friends for their work was to help raise money for charity or to meet out-of-town relatives who wanted tickets to *Laverne & Shirley*.

In the beginning, the tension bonded Penny and Cindy together but, eventually, the anxiety began to take its toll on their relationship. Cindy worried that my relationship as Penny's brother might tip the scale in Penny's favor and Penny became jealous when she thought Cindy got better treatment. An unforgettable image is the day Cindy made her manager come in with a stopwatch to time how long Cindy was on screen compared to Penny. Things finally came to a head shortly after Cindy married Bill Hudson and became pregnant.

It all began quite amicably, and I tried to create the perfect arrangement to accommodate her pregnancy. The plan was that Cindy would shoot several shows at the beginning of her pregnancy and then be out for ten episodes. She wanted to be paid for all the episodes. To explain her character's absence, I married her off to a businessman in London. Even the best laid plans can blow up in your face, and that's what happened.

Cindy as a pregnant woman began to quarrel with Paramount and our staff over her working conditions and schedule until one day, when I wasn't on the set, there was a blowup. The next day Cindy filed a $20 million lawsuit against me and Paramount alleging that we tried to force her off the show. My role suddenly changed from producer to minister as I ran around the set holding hands, hugging people, and patting heads while muttering, "Everything's going to be all right. The show will go on."

The lawsuit was settled out of court, but Cindy never returned to the show. At first, I felt betrayed because Cindy and I were friends. I had known her for years and she had given us our family dog after the birth of my son. We named the dog Cindy. What could I tell my kids: We have to change the name of the dog because she left the series? I had tried to avoid the business side of show business, yet there I was caught in the middle of it.

I couldn't blame her for choosing her family over the show. *Laverne & Shirley* was a great place to be if you didn't have a life, but now Cindy had a life with her husband and a baby. I wished her well, kept the name of our family dog, and continued the show without her. Ironically, on the recent *Laverne & Shirley* reunion show the cast said how much they all missed the series. Many people never realize how good they have it until it's not there anymore.

When I wasn't ministering to the troubles on *Laverne & Shirley*, I was trying to figure out how much fun I could have and still get my job done. Part of my fun was called "Camp

Marshallmount." During the period when I had several shows on the air at once I would assemble the cast and crew from each show on a sound stage at the beginning of the season for an annual back-to-work meeting called "Camp Marshallmount."

It was a time for the various cast members and crew from all the shows to mingle because once production started most people were too busy to socialize. Dressed in khaki pants, a whistle around my neck, and a T-shirt with the camp motto LIFE IS MORE IMPORTANT THAN SHOW BUSINESS, I welcomed the campers back. We passed out camp buttons, threw candy into the bleachers, performed skits, and sang songs. As a child I had always loved the camaraderie of camp and now I was the leader of my own television camp.

You might be asking, is this how you produce a sitcom? Well, yes, that's how I did it. People always said I ran my shows like a camp. For eight years in the 1970s, I had more than four hundred people working for me, most of them under the age of thirty. I worried that if I didn't make it fun and if I didn't somehow create a sense of professional pride, then the young people would get into drinking, divorce, drugs, or worse—not be able to concentrate on their jobs. Each day I would look at Ron Howard's eyes and if any other actor's pupils were bigger than Ron's, then I began to suspect he was on drugs.

Each show had at least one camp counselor, or authority figure, in the cast who could show the younger actors that it was possible to have a life in front of and behind the camera. We had people like Tom Bosley and Marion Ross on *Happy Days*, Phil Foster and Betty Garrett on *Laverne & Shirley*, Conrad Janis and Elizabeth Kerr on *Mork & Mindy*, and Doris Roberts on *Angie*. And, of course, on *The Odd Couple*, Jack and Tony supported each other. Behind the camera, my father, producer Tony Marshall, and executive producers Tom Miller, Eddie Milkis, Bob Boyett, and director Jerry Paris helped complete the roster of camp counselors.

While the activities on *The Odd Couple* included various forms of gambling (one day the guy who took the bets on the set seriously asked for screen credit as "Bookmaker"), on my other shows we had more wholesome camp-style activities like yoga lessons, AA meetings, basketball games, and dance classes. For the ambitious campers, we taught informal technical film workshops. We encouraged the actors to learn about directing, producing, and camera lenses. Ron Howard, Anson Williams, Scott Baio, Henry Winkler, and Penny are all directors today and part of the credit goes to the nurturing atmosphere we created on the sets. It wasn't just something in the water; these people worked very hard to learn another craft. When you walked on the set, it was more common to see an actor behind the camera learning a new shot than sitting in his dressing room complaining to his publicity person about visibility.

Our activity lineup carried over to the weekends when we launched a traveling softball team called the Happy Days All-Stars, spearheaded by Nick Abdo, Brian Levant, and others. The team played pregames at major league stadiums across the United States to raise money for charity and traveled to Japan and Germany to entertain the U.S. Army. The softball team gave the actors a chance to meet their fans face-to-face and to bond on the road. Thirty people traveling on a team bus through Wisconsin at midnight is heavy bonding. After Ron Howard slid head first into home plate during a game in San Diego, the writers spent the bus ride home figuring out how to work a black eye into the following week's episode.

Even though we resembled a camp, there was a serious side to our organization and my dad, the only one at the camp who wore a suit, played the hatchet man when we needed him. He was good at firing people.

Dad produced many of my shows, but didn't get very involved with the comedy. Comedy to him was a guy with a New Jersey accent pronouncing "boid" instead of "bird." He sat in a big office with a cigar never far from his hand and a lunchtime cocktail never far from his mind. He represented ten stern, powerful executives all rolled into one. If anybody asked, "Who's the boss?" and it related to money, we pointed toward my dad.

I also liked to have mother types around. I think one of the best training grounds for working in television is to be a mother. Women who have raised children often have the patience for dealing with actors. On a résumé the word "mother" or phrase "raised children" carried more weight with me than a page full of production experience and personal references from other major shows.

One of the best mothers I ever hired was my younger sister, Ronny. She moved to Hollywood in the early 1970s, divorced and with three little girls. She had a college degree from Northwestern, but her work experience was limited to brief stints as a gas meter reader and a substitute teacher. After she started out as a secretary at the Screen Actors Guild, we hired her as a production assistant on *Happy Days* because she had become an expert on unions and contracts. In four years she worked her way up to producer. At night she raised her own children — Penny Lee, Judy, and Wendy — and by day she helped us raise the kids on *Happy Days*. I think they all turned out pretty good.

With my father and Ronny as producers and Penny starring in *Laverne & Shirley*, it was no secret that I, like Danny Thomas, enjoyed working with my family. Our offices were on the Paramount lot in building G, and on any given day I could walk down the hall and it felt like Thanksgiving. After "king of the spin-off," the most common phrase used by the press to describe me was "master of nepotism." Some people in Hollywood pronounce "nepotism" like a dirty word, but I tried to make it an acceptable art form. I worked with my family for two reasons: They were talented and they made me feel more comfortable. There aren't many people in Hollywood whom you can trust completely and if a family member can do the job, then it can only help you, too. I believe this is true of any business.

On my shows, the philosophy was that everybody had to get his job done, and I was there to help. If someone couldn't work under those conditions, then he was replaced by others who could. The quality of the work superseded the camaraderie of the staff. It was like a sports team: Who cares if the third baseman is a guy you wouldn't have lunch with? He can hit and field the ball. I built a big business by hiring many people whom I didn't necessarily want to have lunch with. Any television series can be a grind for all the players, both cast and crew. If you found the pace too tedious, it showed and you moved on. If you found it exhilarating and had a talent for the craft, you moved up. My motto was I didn't have to love everybody; I just had to love their work.

•   •   •

When it came to my procedures for running my sitcoms, I borrowed many of the elements that had worked so well for Danny Thomas. *The Danny Thomas Show* was filmed before a live studio audience of about three hundred people and before each show Danny would come out and perform some jokes and songs. It was a wonderful forum for Danny to try out new stories and reintroduce some old ones from his nightclub act. And, of course, the studio audience enjoyed the extra laughs.

I also filmed my shows on the Paramount lot before a live audience, mostly because I felt it encouraged the actors. Real people, those who don't make their living in the entertainment industry, are the best judges of what is funny. They can play the part of an objective referee in all comedy disagreements simply by laughing or not during the filming of the show. If nobody in the audience laughed at a joke our whole staff thought was funny, that usually meant there were too many friends, family members, or studio executives in the bleachers. I'd have one of the ushers run out to the street and round up some real people. A tourist from Topeka is going to laugh louder, and certainly more honestly, than the worst audience of all: the star's agent.

A half-hour sitcom can take more than three hours to shoot, so to keep the audience entertained in between setups I dusted off my rusty stand-up personality and trotted out my old army routine. Since I was still rather shy and inhibited, it didn't come easily for me. But after doing thirty-six warm-ups on *Hey Landlord!* and more than one hundred on *The Odd Couple*, I finally started to loosen up and have some fun. By the time *Happy Days* and *Laverne & Shirley* came around, I even looked forward to the warm-ups.

When I became too busy to do them myself, other writers and producers took my place. They would introduce the cast, provide informative chatter between takes ("There are mikes above your head and it would help if you laughed upward"), and throw candy bars into the bleachers during intermission. As the crew tossed the candy bars, they would do jokes like "Next, we're going to throw milk," "In the winter we throw soup," or "We have Snickers, Milky Ways, and something called botulism."

Later, we hired professional stand-up comedians to do the

warm-ups on the shows. Three of the best were Marty Nadler, Ray Combs, who would later host *Family Feud,* and Michael Preminger, who wrote *Nothing in Common* with Rick Podell. The *Mork & Mindy* filmings were legendary because at least once each show, either during the warm-up or between scene setups, Robin Williams would playfully grab the microphone. He would climb up and over the railing into the stands and interview members of the audience, ad-libbing jokes and doing impressions, such as the one he did of Fred Astaire dancing in the streets of Manhattan and stepping in dog poop.

Once the warm-ups helped me overcome my fear of public speaking, I lectured at universities and television writing classes around town and, oddly enough, received invitations from the eulogy circuit. Around this time, Jerry Belson's father died and Jerry asked me to read a letter at the funeral. I got my biggest laugh when Jerry also made me read an introduction for myself that he had written: "Hello, I'm Garry Marshall. Remember me? I'm the one who throws the candy bars. Well, not today." The mourners, many of the same people who had been to the filming of my television shows, were quite amused. There was Jerry once again with the unspeakable at his own father's funeral. I then read the letter that Jerry had written to his father in which he described all of the good things his father had done for him.

Jerry's letter was beautifully written and there was not a dry eye when I finished reading. I always felt it was sad that his dad never got to hear it or read it. After the funeral I went home and wrote each of my parents a similar letter thanking them for all of the good things. Of course, there had been bad things, but I left them out like Jerry had because everybody knows about them. Neither of my parents ever mentioned the letters to me, but I know they both showed them to their friends.

Most of my shows used the three-camera format, except for the first season of *The Odd Couple* when we used one camera and a laugh track, and the first year of *Happy Days* when we tried for an artistic, nostalgic texture and shot with one camera like a movie is made. The three-camera format was invented by Desi Arnaz for

Lucy to capture her physical comedy. Having three cameras allowed Desi and Lucy to take chances with their comedy while making sure the laughs were captured on film the first time (physical comedy is rarely funny during a second take). The three-camera format allowed me to take some chances of my own, particularly with physical comedy, because if one camera didn't get it, another one would.

On *Mork & Mindy*, however, even three cameras weren't enough. When we began the show the word around town was that it wouldn't work. Most television executives believed that the hip, satirical humor of *Saturday Night Live* couldn't be duplicated in the eight o'clock family-time slot, which was known as the flagship time slot of prime-time television. Whenever anyone says that something can't be done, that challenges me and I try even harder to do it. The eight o'clock time slot had become a new challenge for me each year. I introduced sophisticated comedy with *The Odd Couple*, nostalgic comedy with *Happy Days*, and slapstick humor with *Laverne & Shirley*. Now I wanted to make irreverent, hip comedy work, too. Once we found Robin, I knew it would work if we could just figure out a way to capture his spontaneity on film.

The first season the cameramen were exhausted. Robin was jumping and running around the set, making Orkan noises and playing with props, but rarely hitting his marks, so the camera couldn't focus on him. The first few weeks some of his best jokes had to be cut out because they were blurry.

"Well, if Robin doesn't stand on his marks, then he won't get on TV," said some of the irritated cameramen.

But Robin felt that he had to have freedom of movement. Yelling at someone again didn't seem to be the answer since they both were right. So I tried to adjust the situation to get the best results. The solution: I added a fourth camera just to follow Robin. It cost more money, but it allowed Robin the room to improvise and gave us more coverage.

I also started showing Robin some of the dailies. I usually made it a policy not to show actors the dailies, because most actors look only at themselves and their opinion is too biased to be constructive. I changed the rules with Robin because I wanted him to see where the cameras were getting him *and* where they were losing him. When we added the fourth camera and Robin made more of an effort to hit his marks, we began capturing more of Mork's antics in the center of the screen. It's important for a producer to make adjustments to an actor's working style, especially if he's as funny as Robin.

As a producer, you have to have some rules that you allow to be broken and others that you don't. On my shows the one thing I couldn't tolerate was when an actor broke the fourth wall and stepped outside his character in front of the studio audience. It was the one thing that could rattle my calm, soft-spoken attitude and make me scream. When my mother was producing her dance shows in our basement, she taught me that entertainment was an illusion for the audience that should never be broken. She said, "Put your best foot forward. What happens backstage is nobody's business but your own." I told the actors on my shows, don't break the illusion no matter what. Unfortunately, it happened twice.

The first person to break it was Tony on *The Odd Couple.* Jack, Tony, and I always got along so well that when it happened all three of us were shocked. One day we were rehearsing and a few visitors came into the bleachers to watch. The actors lost their way in the scene and Tony started yelling at the director, Jerry Paris.

"Jerry, I can't act while you're running around like a nut," Tony said.

I glared across the stage at Tony and he knew immediately that I was angry. He quickly turned toward the audience and tried to make amends.

"You see folks, that's what an actor does when he makes a mistake. He tries to embarrass the director," said Tony.

The damage had been done: His character had lost credibility in front of the audience. I yelled and Tony apologized. The next day he was standing outside my office door at eight o'clock in the morning apologizing again.

"You're forgiven," I said.

"But I've never seen you so upset. I'm sorry, Garry."

I never yelled at Tony again because it took too long to make up.

The other time I lost control was on *Happy Days* and it was with—believe it or not—Henry Winkler, a man whose dedication on screen and altruistic endeavors off screen give a good name to the acting profession. However, one Friday night after the filming of the show we had a fight. Typically, when the show was over each cast member would come out to take a bow. It happened that on this particular night Henry was rushing off to catch an airplane. Instead of taking his usual gracious bow, he came out and screamed at the director, who needed Henry to stay around to do a few pickups (reshoots of a scene that a camera missed the first time). The audience just sat there, stunned, watching two highly paid grown men act like children.

I was furious and followed Henry as he walked behind the curtain and onto the set of Arnold's malt shop, which was safely out of the audience's view. I grabbed him by his leather jacket and shouted, "Never, ever throw a tantrum in front of the audience!" One of the cameramen, Sam Rosen, hurried over and broke us up and I was able to pull myself back together. Henry and I apologized, and it never happened again because he respected just how strongly I felt about maintaining the illusion and integrity of the characters. We've been best friends ever since.

Regardless of what the newspapers or magazines write, the cast of a television series should get along in front of the audience. It's important because television is based on people's comfort with the characters. They should like them no matter what they see on the covers of the supermarket tabloids. The audience loves Roseanne. They love Delta Burke. They love Oprah. The press can destroy movie stars but only the audience can get tired of television actors.

It takes a secure TV series cast to work with guest stars and *Happy Days* was one of the most secure. The cast not only welcomed guest stars but also gave new actors the room to become stars. They were so stable in their own show that they weren't concerned with butting egos. When Robin Williams first appeared on *Happy Days* as the alien Mork, the cast gave him room to shine. On most other sitcoms, the series regulars would have asked that the guest star not steal the show or would have given him the cold shoulder if he had.

The cast of *Happy Days* is one of the reasons that Robin got

Mork & Mindy, Penny and Cindy got *Laverne & Shirley*, and Erin Moran and Scott Baio got *Joanie Loves Chachi*. The actors on *Happy Days* had the popularity to turn whatever they touched into a spin-off. Ron Howard, Henry Winkler, and the other actors on *Happy Days* gave up and coming actors the confidence and the incentive to launch new series.

We based our spin-offs on the cocktail party theory: If you go to a cocktail party and you don't know anyone, then you feel uncomfortable. But if the host comes up and puts his arms around you and introduces you to a few guests, then you begin to feel more at ease. When we started spinning off shows from *Happy Days*, we shot promotional spots where Fonzie literally put his arms around Laverne and Shirley, and later Mork, and said in effect, "Hey, check my friends out. They have a new show." And people did.

The spirit behind *Happy Days* wasn't invisible. It had a name: Jerry Paris. Jerry was the director of the show for eleven years and during that time he gave it the consistency, warmth, and dedication that kept it on the air. Unfortunately, next door *Laverne & Shirley* never found a director or producer who would stay around for very long. After I directed the *Laverne & Shirley* pilot, the long parade of guest directors and producers began.

One season Penny and Cindy handpicked writer Monica Johnson, Jerry Belson's sister who later cowrote *Lost in America*, to produce the show, but even *she* succumbed to the pressure and began to sleep at the studio. The morning she came to the set wearing her pajamas it was clear that Monica had had enough and it was time to give someone else a try. *Happy Days* had the stability that *Laverne & Shirley* never had, but it didn't make *Laverne & Shirley* less funny. Putting together a show and just getting it on the air is one thing, but launching a show that can sail through many rough years of ratings wars is something much more difficult. Despite the different atmospheres, both shows did this: *Laverne & Shirley* lasted eight years and *Happy Days* ran for eleven.

While the dynamics of the cast and crew are critical to the success of any sitcom, the bottom line is always money and inevitably if you work in television you have to deal with high-priced talent.

At least on *Happy Days* no one let the amount of money they were making go to their heads; there weren't any lawsuits or prima donnas and everyone had the same size dressing room.

From a financial point, the studio loved *Happy Days* right from the start. The costumes, music, and themes could never go out of style in reruns because the show was out of date to begin with. Studio executives smile when you talk about rerun potential.

While the studio and network were making money, so were the actors. Most of the actors on *Happy Days* and *Laverne & Shirley* were young kids who went from having no salary to making five figures a week. I was a little taken aback at the irony the day I walked onto the *Happy Days* set to find three nineteen-year-olds sitting around talking about their escrows. It was also no wonder that those recently successful kids sometimes walked around the set looking like they had just won the lottery. During the first season of *Laverne & Shirley*, I got word from Paramount's accounting office that Cindy Williams wasn't cashing her paychecks. I called Cindy into my office to find out what was going on.

"Cindy, are you cashing your paychecks?" I asked.

"No."

"Why not? Where are they?"

"In my sock drawer," she said.

"What are they doing in your sock drawer?"

"That's where I hide them for a rainy day," she said.

She probably had thirty thousand dollars' worth of checks wedged in between her knee-highs and tennis socks. After a brief discussion on the safety of the U.S. banking system, I convinced Cindy to take her checks to a bank and deposit them so Paramount could balance its books.

Several years later, Penny came to me one day and asked where her paycheck was. Everyone in the cast of *Laverne & Shirley* had gotten her check for that week except Penny. I told her not to worry, that I would track it down. At the time, Penny was making about $25,000 an episode. That was a pretty big check to misplace, so I set off to find out what happened.

I walked to the Paramount administration building and learned that the paychecks had been given to my father, who at the time was the executive producer on *Laverne & Shirley*. I went back to our building and to my father's office, which sat directly across from mine.

"Pop, do you have Penny's paycheck?"

"Yes, I do," he replied.

"Where is it?"

"In my pocket," he said, lighting a cigar.

"What's her paycheck doing in your pocket?"

"I'm withholding my daughter's check because she was fresh with me earlier today," he said, as he took a long drag from his cigar. "And I'm not giving it back until she apologizes."

"Pop, you can't take it away like it's her allowance! She's a big star."

Eventually, I got Penny, the star, to apologize to her father, the producer, and she got her check.

Did I forget to mention the drawback of working with your family? No matter how big a star you become, your parents never let you forget you're their child.

My favorite story about Penny and money happened on *The Odd Couple.* One year Paramount gave the entire supporting cast except Penny a small raise. An executive confided to me off the record that the studio felt "Penny is Garry's sister. She won't quit no matter what we do to her." Penny felt terrible, so I asked them to give her the raise; they said there was no money in the budget. I went back to Penny and told her that this time it wasn't worth the fight and she should forget about it. Besides, she had only a small supporting part, which gave her very little bargaining power.

"Penny, someday when you are a star you can ask Paramount for an even bigger raise," I said, "but not now."

Flash forward to 1979 when *Laverne & Shirley* was number one in the ratings. When it came time for Penny to renegotiate her new deal with Paramount, she called me on the phone and uttered only one word.

"Now?" she asked.

"Now!" I replied.

Penny asked for triple her salary, and she got it. (Cindy benefited too because they were paid the same.) It's always important to negotiate from a position of strength. Penny had something Paramount wanted and would have paid almost anything to keep her. So if you get passed over for a raise the first time, don't worry. If you're worth it, your time will come. The most important thing to remember about show business money is that it's okay to believe in *revenge;* I do. Not revenge to hurt somebody, but to get what you deserve after being passed over. Everyone will get his turn. If you have talent, you will get the money you deserve—and then they will pay you *too much* money.

I had learned this lesson years earlier when I wrote for *Love, American Style* under the name Samuro Mitsubi. In addition to writing scripts for the series, I wrote blackout sequences, which appeared in between the main stories each week. Some of them had dialogue while others were sight gags, like a hotel bellman carrying a bride over the threshold while the groom watched. I got paid a couple hundred dollars a year for turning in 150 blackouts. I thought I was being underpaid, but when I asked for a raise the producers always turned me down. *I* was big but I guess Samuro wasn't.

A few years later, *Love, American Style* was sold into syndication. Most of the shows carried my blackouts, and when they realized this they called me and said, "Garry, we need those blackouts for syndication. We'd like to offer you $500 for all of them." I sent back a note: "Your offer was very nice. However, I want $10,000 because you screwed me before." And they paid me. A hard concept for some young people to understand is that when you start out you can allow them to take advantage because, truthfully, you may not be very good yet. But when you are good, you turn around and get even, and they let you, willingly, without any animosity, because you are now, in the most used phrase in show business, "worth it!"

When I came into television I thought I was just a writer. But by pursuing a career as a head writer, and learning how to choose the best ideas from other writers, I was able to leave television a producer. What television had taught me most of all was how to be emphatic. Sheldon Leonard's words still hold true today: "Make a decision, right or wrong, because most of the people in show business are afraid to make a decision." One of the hardest decisions I ever had to make was to decide that it was time for me to move on.

Chapter Eight

Directing Movies—The Most Expensive Form of Self-expression

I Get Paid to Watch Julia Roberts Smile and Tom Hanks Cry

In the early 1980s, I went to a dinner party at a friend's house and spent most of the evening sitting in a corner talking to Albert Brooks, Harvey Miller, James Brooks, and Chuck Shyer, all directors. While the other guests mingled over coffee and dessert, my wife came over to chide us for being so aloof. "Everybody is afraid to come over and talk to you guys," she said. "You're so intimidating sitting here talking artistic film director stuff. Come join the group." The fact was that we weren't discussing the social implications of violence in film or debating the breakdown of the studio system. We were saying, "Does your cinematographer shout at you?" "Are you always waiting for makeup?" "Do you know the names of the different camera lenses yet?" "Are you too afraid to film in the rain or make an explosion shot?" "What kind of hat do you wear?" We were five first-time film directors hiding in the corner, scared to death.

That's why I went into film: to be scared again. After twenty years, television was no longer challenging for me. I would go to some rehearsals of *Joanie Loves Chachi* and count the number of lights in the ceiling grids. I pressed too hard to come up with future spin-offs: Lenny and Squiggy join the army, Ralph Malph becomes a holistic dentist, Joanie and Chachi open a bed and breakfast, Potsie becomes a sex therapist. I was losing my concentration and starting to do bad work.

Just as I was losing my passion, so was television. Television producers, spurred on more by money than pride in their shows, were beginning to concentrate on merely winning their time slots. Reality shows were replacing comedy shows and television was becoming crueler and adopting a Machiavellian approach: "Let's get a hit fast no matter what."

Under this climate my series *Hey Landlord!* wouldn't have lasted thirty-six minutes, let alone thirty-six weeks, and *60 Minutes* never would have been given the five years that it took to find its loyal audience. Prime time was beginning to resemble a battlefield: The networks had started to use their shows like a fleet of kamikaze planes, manipulating and moving my shows around the weekly lineup to kill shows on competing networks. Don Hewitt, the producer of *60 Minutes*, said, "Television isn't about seeing it or hearing it. It's about feeling it." I believed that too, but I didn't seem to be in the majority anymore.

I finally became tired of the pressure from Paramount and ABC to create a new show every season. Many executives were pushing writers to spread themselves thin so that they could keep their own jobs. If an executive backed a Garry Marshall pilot that failed, he could keep his job because it would be my fault. If he backed a new producer's pilot that failed, it would be the executive's fault and quite possibly he would lose his job too.

Anyway, the day I told the lighting man on *Happy Days* that two of his lights were burned out, I decided to leave TV to become a film director. I also couldn't stay up until midnight anymore and I had heard film directors got to go to bed earlier. This turned out to be a lie, but what did I know?

●　　●　　●

Directing was not a completely blurry concept to me, but my experience was limited to the small screen. I'd directed episodes of *Love, American Style*, *The Odd Couple*, *Happy Days*, and *Laverne & Shirley* and had learned a tremendous amount from watching other television directors such as Jerry Paris, Hal Cooper, John Rich, Jay Sandrich, and Alan Rafkin. The best I could hope for was that there would be some similarities between television and film directing.

I had always admired Billy Wilder's *The Apartment* and Michelangelo Antonioni's *Blowup* because they both showed such a respect for detail and romance. I loved the films of Frank Capra and Preston Sturges because they had happy endings. Despite the fact that happy endings weren't the most politically correct way to end a movie in the 1980s, that's the way I hoped to end mine.

I was pretty sure from the beginning that comedy was the right road for me as a director. I once had a conversation with a young aspiring director and he told me that from the moment he saw the scene in which Vanessa Redgrave's head got cut off in the 1971 movie *Mary, Queen of Scots*, he had been drawn to the macabre and wanted to make macabre films. Well, I had seen that movie too, but it had had a different effect on me: I thought about how I could have made the same scene funny. What if the man assigned to cut her head off had a sinus cold that day, or he had to call in sick so another guy had to cover for him? What would happen if it was the executioner's first day? I was always looking at a story from a comedy viewpoint, and I actually wrote that skit, called "The Executioner's First Job," for an ill-fated 1970s review.

I also was inspired by French director Jacques Tati and his wonderful eye for visual comedy in such films as *Mon Oncle* and *Mr. Hulot's Holiday*. Tati's work showed me the freedom film allowed a director. Unlike television, where you had to keep all the characters smack in the center of the screen, in film you could place them anywhere you wanted—the side, top, back, bottom. In film the eyes of the audience could pick up the characters wherever you put them.

My first artistic step in becoming a director was to question my name. All the great film directors seemed to have such rich, one-of-a-kind names like Elia Kazan, King Vidor, Cecil B. DeMille,

Francis Ford Coppola, and Martin Scorsese. Maybe my name was too common and too closely associated with television. Perhaps I should use my father's original last name and call myself Garibaldi Masciarelli. After some thought, and a persuasive argument from my wife, a blond, blue-eyed girl from Ohio who didn't want to be referred to as Mrs. Masciarelli, I decided it was better to switch clothing than my name.

Instead of the baseball caps I had worn on my television shows, I started wearing baseball jackets with sports team logos on them. I thought the jackets might keep me warm, help me stand out, and perhaps appeal to the crew's various team loyalties.

When I made the decision to direct movies, I instantly went from being the confident wise old sage of television to the new kid on the block of film. One minute I was at the top of the totem pole and the next minute I wasn't even on it. I was forty-seven years old and regardless of what anybody tells you, to start a new career at forty-seven is daunting. Moving into film was like the first day at a new school where everybody knows the rules but you. They also seemed to know each other.

When you don't know the rules, you have to do your homework. I asked all of my friends for advice on directing. The designer and producer Polly Platt reminded me of William Wyler's words: "The key to directing is to resist the temptation to be a swell fellow." Everyone wants to be liked, but the key to directing is that you don't want everyone to *like* you all the time. If you want to be adored on a movie set, don't be the director, be the caterer. Everyone loves lunch.

James Brooks told me about a phenomenon called "eye-rolling time," when you tell the cast and crew an idea and they nod yes but their eyes roll in disbelief the minute you turn away. I had to learn to stand behind my own opinion. Jerry Paris told me that when things got too overwhelming, I should take a walk around the block. Mel Brooks encouraged me to fire someone from the movie the first day to gain the respect of the cast and crew.

Many directors and industry veterans, from Steven Spielberg to Sam Rosen, told me to shoot as much film as I could because once I got in the editing room, ultimately I wouldn't have enough. And finally, the man who would direct three *Godfather* epics and

had survived a jungle shoot on *Apocalypse Now,* Francis Ford
Coppola, put his arm around me and gave me perhaps the most
practical advice of all: "Be prepared to change your shoes a lot
because your feet are going to get tired." Armed with all of this
advice I was ready to direct a movie, but I had one small problem:
Nobody would hire me.

     A director usually becomes attached to a script in one of three
ways: He develops a project himself with other writers; he writes a
script himself; or he is hired by a studio or production company to
direct a script that has already been written. When you're a new
director, as I was, and you take the studio or production company
route, you basically have to take the script they give you. After
being turned down by some of the big-name studios and production companies around town, I pursued a new group called ABC
Motion Pictures, which had a distribution arrangement with
Twentieth Century Fox. My television shows had made a lot of
money for ABC, so they were willing to take a chance and let me
direct a feature film.
     The head of ABC Motion Pictures, Brandon Stoddard, hired
me to direct because he knew I could at least fix a script. He gave
me a script called *Young Doctors in Love,* written by former television writers Michael Elias and Rich Eustis. It was a zany satire
about hospital life and the studio needed someone to guide the
writers in a rewrite. I wasn't in the position to say, "Oh, gee, I
really had something else in mind." I was just thrilled that he was
going to let me direct any script.
     So I got my wish. On *Young Doctors in Love,* I went to work
every day scared to death. Most of the time I worried about money
in the budget. In movies if you lose a day of shooting it costs the
studio about $100,000. I used to drive to work each morning with
this sinking feeling in my stomach that somebody had given me
$100,000 to hold and I had just misplaced it. But I quickly learned
that it was okay to feel that way, and I had the support of a wonderful new producer named Jerry Bruckheimer.
     You have to know as a director that it's acceptable to make a
mistake. All directors make mistakes, even on films that cost mil-

lions of dollars; perhaps *especially* on films that cost millions because you have so much more to worry about. On a big-budget studio picture, a director usually shoots an average of two to two and a half pages a day on a shoot of about forty to sixty days. Inevitably on every shoot you are going to make mistakes, but you try not to make them cost you an entire day. If an actor gets sick, the wrong set is built, or God makes it rain, you try to work around it if you can. In 1994 when we were shooting *Exit to Eden*, I had to lead a group of seventy-five cast and crew members out of Malibu as the orange and yellow fires swept furiously toward our location. You can't anticipate disaster, but you have to remember you're in charge when it happens.

When you make a mistake as a director, however, you don't necessarily have to tell everybody that it's because you were scared. Shoulder the blame and move on. Then later you can reveal your fear to your spouse, therapist, or favorite bartender, but don't let the actors see you panic. It's your job to be strong and lead the cast and crew. There can be only one captain and you're wearing the hat, so lead them—even if you're still really trying to figure out what the hell you're doing and what you want to say with the movie. As Frank Capra said, "Only the morally courageous are worthy of speaking to their fellowman for two hours in the dark."

After I didn't completely fall on my face with *Young Doctors in Love*—it made a respectable showing at the box office and was a surprising hit in Sweden, where they have socialized medicine and enjoy making fun of doctors—ABC Motion Pictures let me direct another film. This time it was a nostalgic coming-of-age comedy called *The Flamingo Kid*, which took place in the early 1960s.

Producer Michael Phillips said he first heard about the script in 1974 when he was playing canasta with Mama Cass and she mentioned that her friend Neal (no relation) Marshall had written a script, then titled *Sweet Ginger Brown*. Michael optioned the script and later received it as part of his divorce settlement from ex-wife Julia *You'll Never Eat Lunch in This Town Again* Phillips. Michael and I first met to talk about the script in 1982. I don't even play cards, but *The Flamingo Kid* was the turning point of my film career as a director. The movie not only made money, but also earned a batch of fine reviews. Suddenly studio executives from places like Tri-Star, MGM, and Twentieth Century Fox started calling me.

I had earned the clout to choose my own projects and now it was time for me to make some decisions. In general, directing a film can take about a year of your life: four months for preproduction, ten to eighteen weeks for shooting, and about five months for postproduction. I decided that I would try to choose films that I felt passionate about. I can do anything for a month, but a year is too long to spend on a project that's just *nice*.

I put the word out to agents and friends that I wanted scripts with poignancy and one of the first scripts I got was about a talking horse. I learned that I had to be more specific: poignant scripts without animals. I never got over my television failure, *Me and the Chimp*. Eventually, I got the kind of human comedies and comedy-dramas I was looking for. Along the way, though, I made some mistakes: I regret turning down the movies *Flashdance* and *Reuben, Reuben*.

I chose *Nothing in Common* because of its serious themes and the father and son angle appealed to me. I went with *Overboard* because I wanted to direct a romantic comedy and Goldie Hawn, an actress I've always found hilarious, sexy, and lovable, was attached to the project. I selected *Beaches* because I wanted to work with Bette Midler and Barbara Hershey and thought the script's friendship between two women would be new and a challenge for me. When *Pretty Woman* came across my desk, the characters' sexuality appealed to me. During my years in television the closest I had ever come to sex was when Joanie gave Chachi a hickey.

In the late 1980s, Scott Rudin, a very smart producer then at Twentieth Century Fox, called me and said, "How would you like to go to New York and see an Off-Broadway play called *Frankie and Johnny in the Clair de Lune?*" Scott said that if I liked the play, I could have breakfast with playwright Terrence McNally the next morning and discuss directing *Frankie and Johnny* as a movie.

I flew to New York, saw the play, and liked it. As I was preparing to have bacon and eggs with Terrence McNally the next morning, Scott called me to say the deal was off.

"You're out, Garry. Paramount just bought the play for Mike Nichols to direct."

"Does this mean I don't get breakfast with Terrence McNally?" I asked.

"No, you don't. He's eating with Mike," Scott said.

"Scott, what are you doing for breakfast?" I asked.

"I've already eaten."

So I hung up the phone and ordered room service. I was disappointed because I'd felt an immediate connection with the play about a coffeeshop waitress and short-order cook looking for love. But what could I do? I had no choice but to look for another film to direct.

Several years later, after the success of *Pretty Woman*, Mike Nichols dropped out as the director of *Frankie and Johnny* and Paramount asked if I was still interested. I quickly said yes, even though it meant I had to temporarily break away from Disney, for which I had done my last two films, *Beaches* and *Pretty Woman*. That's the kind of director I had decided to be: a director who wasn't attached to any studio. I didn't want to direct just any film. I wanted to direct a film I cared about and felt connected to even if some people didn't like it. I wanted to direct *Frankie and Johnny* and Paramount had it, so I went with them. Maybe it wasn't the best business move, but I'm not a businessman.

You have to decide what drives you as a director: the size of the deal, the power of the studio, or the script's potential to bring you prizes and awards. I care about the quality of the script, the people involved, and especially whether it will be fun to do for a year. Who are the stars? Is it an actor I've been dying to work with? Who runs the studio? (This can change daily. During *Frankie and Johnny*, Paramount went through three studio heads.) I also care about the location. I'm not the kind of guy who wants to pick up and move to South America for a five-month shoot (my food allergies rule out most foreign locations immediately). Will the studio hire the producers I want? Hollywood is all about packaging and if I don't like the box, then I won't even bother to unwrap it.

I always wanted to direct positive, uplifting films that reached for the heart rather than the mind, the emotions rather than the intellect. I liked romances and sentimental films and movies that could be classified under the heading "Gentle Hilarity." I knew I wasn't cut out to be a great stunt director who made films filled with never-before-seen special effects or an avant-garde director who shot Freudian moments or used snow as an existential metaphor. I wanted to make films that celebrated the human spirit and highlighted the good in human beings through both comedy and drama.

And, like my television work, I wanted to make movies that appealed to mainstream audiences. When my children were small I used to take them to the movies and nearly die of boredom. I would get so restless that I would have to leave my kids in the theater while I went into the lobby to read. I'd check on the kids every once in a while, but in between I'd feel guilty imagining that some terrible person in the theater was clobbering my kids over the head with a popcorn box. I wanted to make films that anyone could go to, and maybe some that kids and parents could watch together and *both* enjoy.

The only real film directing mentor I ever had was Polly Platt, who was my set designer on *Young Doctors in Love.* Most people were too polite when I asked for their opinion, but Polly would often put her fingers in her mouth and pretend that she was gagging when I showed her a scene that wasn't working. I was lucky to have Polly around, because traditionally there are very few mentors for directors. There are film schools with professors and guest lecturers, but they usually don't have the equipment to adequately prepare a director for real-life situations that come up on the set. Instead, most directors have to simply learn from watching other films or from their own mistakes, which is what I was forced to do when Polly wasn't around.

There are various kinds of directors: There's a director who works through fear, yelling at the actors. There's a director who stresses the intellectual and organic subtext of the plot. There's a director who works through silence, never speaking to the actors. And there is a director who works through begging. Penny and I are the begging kind. If a shot isn't working or an actor is having trouble, Penny will hold her stomach and say, "I'm getting so nauseous. Please get this shot right so we can all go home." It usually works. Understand clearly that you can be sick or in pain in front of actors, but never scared.

The cast and crew look to the director to maintain the vision of the film and to protect the integrity of the characters. If it's a comedy, you have to make sure it's funny. If it's a drama, you have to keep it on course and sustain the honesty and tension. But the director must see to it that everyone is making the *same* film. More specifically, the director and the studio must be making the same picture. A studio doesn't give a director a multimillion-dollar budget and just say "Wing it." Certain results are expected and this must be communicated.

The director and the studio have to agree on the premise of a film right from the beginning. If they don't, the project could become a disaster, which is the reason I became associated with *Beaches*. Mark Rydell (who did one of my favorite films, *The Rose*) started as the director on the project but had a disagreement with Disney over what the film was about. David Hoberman and Jeffrey Katzenberg brought me in; I had the same vision as the studio and they gave me the job.

Oddly enough, directors rarely get fired by a studio for being afraid. Most often they get taken off a movie for tooting their own horn too loudly. A first-time director might say to a studio executive, "I'm going to make this scene perfect. Just the way you want it." But inevitably when the studio executive sees the dailies and the scene is not perfect, he'll feel let down, which translates into "mad executive." You might get a few more chances but after a while, the studio stops believing you and starts to worry.

I take the opposite approach: "Hey, we'll see what happens. I'm going to give it my best shot." Then when you do a good job, let the studio executive congratulate you. If you promise too much, the executives will only end up being disappointed. Studio executives are the men and women in expensive clothes who put fear into your crew. I always understood that it was *their* money, so they had a right to say something. You don't necessarily have to listen, but you should let them speak. Also, if you're asking for an extra million dollars, it helps to say "please."

The most critical time to maintain control of a movie is during the first two weeks. The key is don't go over budget those first two weeks. If you do, the studio will think you are off to a shaky start and the executives will visit you without smiles on their faces. If you hire a smart production manager, he will schedule some of your easier scenes in this first period. During the first two weeks a new director must be on his best behavior and is basically on probation.

I know what it takes to fire a director because when I was a film producer I fired one. Why? For the first month and a half, he refused to start shooting. When he finally did, it wasn't worth the six-week wait, so we let him go. If you make a mistake during the third or fourth week, the studio will sometimes be more compassionate. If you make a mistake during the last few weeks, you're usually off the hook because the studio is too busy planning the publicity and marketing campaigns. Hollywood's motto is screw up later rather than earlier.

I always thought that when I became a film director I would have plenty of time to make and perfect my pictures. We were always rushed in television. One day we were doing a big musical production number on *Laverne & Shirley* and we had a visit from Steven Spielberg, who was in the middle of directing *1941*. Steven was amazed to discover that we were shooting our eleven-minute musical sequence in *one day*. He said that on a movie he'd have at least ten days to shoot it. I thought, How wonderful; if I ever become a film director I'll have so much time. Wrong. There's never enough time in film, either. That's why many people from television can make the transition to film. We're used to short deadlines. On the set, when the sun is going down and I'm three shots behind, I feel like I'm back in television again. The trick is learning to be quick and cinematic at the same time.

There are many ways for an artist to express himself and surely all of them are cheaper than making a movie with a price tag of $100,000 a day, and an average budget of $20 million to

$40 million. But when you're a director, you have to deal with the money. In the beginning I tried to ignore it and let the producers worry about it. You just can't do that because the studio will still hold you accountable.

On *Pretty Woman*, it cost ten thousand dollars a day to rent The Rex restaurant in downtown Los Angeles for the scene where Edward (Richard Gere) takes Vivian (Julia Roberts) along on a business dinner. Because of the cost we had only two days, and I had to use my time wisely. Finances are what creep onto the set when you're shooting your movie. You're trying to create the most beautiful shot ever seen on film, and there's a guy in a suit yelling at you, saying, "One hundred extras will cost too much. Can we hire ten chubby ones and have them spread out?" When you're really in trouble, the answer is to use cardboard people, as I did in several musical numbers in *Beaches* and Penny did in the stadium shots of *A League of Their Own*. The basic rule to remember is: Put the money on the screen, not into actors, limos, dinners, or gifts.

One of the best characteristics a director can have is the ability to compromise wisely. If you don't want to compromise you can go off and make your own movie, but unfortunately you may have to use your own money, too. And you're gonna need a lot of it. (My budget on *Exit to Eden* was $25 million and that's considered low budget these days.) Learning how to compromise is essential on big-budget studio films so you can fight for scenes you consider absolutely crucial. (Independent films give you much more creative control when shooting, but then later marketing and distribution of your picture has its own kind of hell. The 1990s, however, seem to be a decade where the awards are going to the independent films and that will help them get a wider distribution and in many cases rerelease.) Before I start shooting, I go through my script and block out the scenes I'm willing to compromise on and those I won't.

It usually breaks down like this: Twenty-five percent of the arguments don't matter, so I let the studio win. Fifty percent of the arguments can go either way; some I win, some they win. However, the last 25 percent I have to win at all cost or I won't be able to make my movie. My advice is win that 25 percent or quit. It may seem like a small amount, but if you let the studio win lots of little battles, then you can still win·the war. The trick is not to compromise when you're exhausted or running behind schedule. Compromise when you are clear-headed and full of ideas.

Michael Eisner once said, "Garry Marshall doesn't direct a movie. He hosts a movie." That's pretty accurate. Just as on my television shows, I run a loose ship. I want everyone to get along while *they're* working because I hate tension while *I'm* working. I don't care if two people kill each other at the wrap party as long as they can get along during the shoot. Movie sets are extremely intense and it's critical that petty squabbles are kept to a minimum. One way to do this is to make each person feel as if he's one of the most important players on the team. I let anyone make a suggestion on a film, from the smallest star to the biggest Teamster, because everyone is part of the process. I have no use for people who play it safe and refuse to give suggestions. On my set everybody can speak if he waits his turn.

But just because I listen to everyone doesn't mean I always take that advice. Ultimately, a director must of course make his own decisions. On *Pretty Woman* there were four very bright opinionated producers and they were always giving me their ideas. One was constantly worried about the cost. Another was concerned that Richard Gere's portrayal of the businessman be realistic. Another was interested in how the film would play with European audiences. The fourth cared about protecting the screenwriter's original words (a rather predictable position because this producer also happened to be the screenwriter's manager).

With all of these producers tugging at me, I ran the risk of steering the film in four different directions. I stepped back, took a deep breath, and tried to maintain an overview. When you're shooting you try to keep the whole story in your mind, but you never know if you've succeeded until you reach the editing room. The producers also try to concentrate on the whole story, but usually their story is a lot cheaper than yours.

The producers and I had big arguments over the ending to

Pretty Woman. One suggestion was that Vivian should literally return to walking the streets as a prostitute. Then Edward would drive by again, as in the movie's opening. He'd see her, she'd see him, and we'd end on a closeup of Julia's sensational smile. Another idea was to have her waiting inside his limousine when he got in to go to the airport. Yet another proposal was for Vivian to be driving on a street one way, Edward driving the other way, and for them to meet in an intersection where they'd smile at each other. While I loved Julia's smile throughout the picture, it seemed too easy to end on a closeup of it.

All of these ideas were cheaper than my idea: for them to meet outside her apartment building as he climbed up her fire escape like Prince Charming. I asked David Hoberman, then president of Touchstone/Walt Disney Pictures, to go with my idea. He agreed, despite the expense, because it fit better with the spirit of the film. *Pretty Woman* deserved a fairy-tale ending. However, I was stuck on a last line for Vivian and I turned to executive producer Laura Ziskin for advice.

"What would a woman say?"

"She rescued him right back."

EXTERIOR VIVIAN'S APARTMENT — DAY
(Edward and Vivian climb toward each other on the fire escape.)

EDWARD

So what happened after he climbed the tower and rescued her?
ANGLE ON VIVIAN'S FACE
(An expression of the purest joy. She takes Edward in her arms and speaks to him softly.)

VIVIAN

She rescued him right back.
(They kiss. The sun breaks through the clouds. The Happy Man street talker comes by babbling.)

HAPPY MAN

Welcome to Hollywood. What's your dream? Everybody
comes here. This is Hollywood, land of dreams. Some
dreams come true, some don't. But keep on dreamin'.
This is Hollywood. Always time to dream. So, keep on
dreamin'. . .
(Follow the Happy Man to a BLACK SCREEN.)

I once worked with a cinematographer who told me that I
didn't command enough authority to be a film director. One day
he brought me a ladder and asked me to stand on top of it. He
wanted me to yell at the actors and scream at the crew. Stand tall
on this perch, he said. This is the way you should control the set.
I climbed up the ladder, yelled, and almost fell off. It just wasn't
my style. I wanted to control the whole set while sitting in the corner, with my eyes closed, sucking on a toothpick (a habit I
adopted after I quit smoking). You have to find a way to work
that suits you.

I'm from the John Huston and Fred Zinnemann school of
soft-spoken directors who talk quietly so people will be forced to
hang on their every word and listen to them. I also get results
from mumbling and half the time no one knows what I'm really
saying. Sometimes I talk so fast that the crew doesn't understand
what I want, but they're too afraid to ask me to repeat it. Over
the years, I have taught the people who work with me to speak up
when they are confused. The code phrase is "Garry, say it in
English." Lately, I've even been anticipating their response and I
say to myself "English," and then I repeat myself in a clearer and
more concise way.

Sometimes, however, I forget to articulate my thoughts altogether. One day on *Pretty Woman*, Richard and Julia were delayed
in makeup, so I shot several inserts of a waiter, played by comedian Allan Kent, catching a snail. The crew rolled their eyes but I
ignored them. When Julia finally arrived, I shot several scenes of
her flipping the snail into the air. I was working so hard that I forgot to tell Julia that I was going to intercut her scene with a shot
of the waiter. She just trusted me and did her part. When Julia and

Richard finally saw the edited version of the scene, they were completely surprised and amused to see what I had done with it. They never knew the waiter was going to catch the snail, and it turned out to be one of the funnier moments in the movie. A director always has to think of the big picture, even when the cast and crew are focused on only one scene.

There was a scene near the end of *Nothing in Common* when Tom Hanks and his cold, stoic father, played by Jackie Gleason, meet in a hospital just after the father has pulled through a serious operation.

There were many, many suggestions on how to shoot this moment.

"Tom should cry."

"Tom should not cry at all."

"He should cry earlier when the father first gets sick."

"Tom would never cry in front of his father."

"Tom is a comedian and he did a TV series (*Bosom Buddies*) where he wore a dress for heaven's sake! Nobody wants to see him cry."

And on and on.

Tom and I felt he should cry because in looking at the overall story, the scene fell at a critical point where he finally releases all his feelings after years of hostility toward his father. We shot the scene like this: Gleason is wheeled back to the room from surgery and is still asleep on the gurney when Tom comes in. Tom leans over the gurney, touches his father, and tears come. Just before we cut away from this moment, we see Gleason's eyes open.

It was a perfect scene to complete the dramatic arc of the story. I remember watching Tom's depth and emotion in the scene and thinking, "More than a funny guy."

A director has to be part psychiatrist, part teacher, and part parent to everyone on the set. Part lover is not such a good idea because it represents a loss of control on the set. Many people entering show business find the responsibilities of being a director too overwhelming and they go on to other jobs. There are many talented people who have directed one picture—some very good pictures—and have never been heard from again.

On the good side, I once read an article that said film directors and orchestra conductors lead long lives because their hearts are always pumping fast. Probably because they are always waving their hands at someone. Sometimes directing can feel more like a race than an art form. The bottom line is that no matter what, a director has to learn how to be creative while exhausted. If you can manage to stay on budget, make the movie you want to make, keep the actors and crew happy, and still stand up for your vision all while overtired, then you've won a great prize: a chance to direct another film.

Chapter Nine

Handling Movie Stars Without Having a Psychology Degree

Charting Moods and Menstrual Cycles

Several years ago when I lectured at the American Film Institute in Los Angeles, I was startled to see how much the students knew about directing. They were up to date on the latest technology, knew which lenses to use to achieve different shots, and were comfortable behind state-of-the-art sound and editing systems. Many of them honestly knew more about the mechanics of film directing than I did. This was ironic considering that I had directed seven feature films and most of them hadn't directed even one.

What was obvious, however, was that they didn't understand this: Directing is about more than just the nuts and bolts and technical process. That can be learned. It's also about the people, which is much more difficult to master. More important than selecting the right camera lens is learning how to get the star out of his trailer. More important than knowing the cranes and alternating lengths of the dissolves is knowing the mood of an actor and using his mood to stretch the actor to a better performance. I do this through gentleness, which often confuses my co-workers. Most people in Hollywood don't understand the power of gentleness.

An experienced director will always do some kind of research on the actors before starting a film. I go to their agent. I call up their publicist. I take their closest friend to lunch. I do anything I can to find out what they're really like. After meeting with Kate Nelligan, I wanted to cast her as Cora, the key role of a sharp-tongued waitress, in *Frankie and Johnny*. But the rumor at the time was that Kate was trouble.

I try to steer clear of troublemakers, even if they can act. So to find out for myself, I went to Terrence McNally, who had worked with Kate in New York and asked him, "Is Kate trouble? If not, why the bad rap?" And he said, "No. Absolutely not. In the past she's been unhappy on certain projects because of dumb people, but I think she's fabulous." Then I spoke to Barbra Streisand, who directed Kate in *The Prince of Tides*. Streisand said, "She's wonderful. I got along with her. You'll get along with her." So I went ahead and hired Kate. Terrence and Barbra were right: Kate was fabulous and ended up winning a British Academy Award for her performance in *Frankie and Johnny*.

I always take the time to find out about my actors' past as well as their present. When I spoke to Richard Gere about taking on the role of Edward in *Pretty Woman*, I mentioned that Hector Elizondo would be playing the hotel manager and that they would have several scenes together. I said this because I'd found out earlier that both Hector and Richard had been in *American Gigolo* and had gotten along very well on that set. Richard didn't decide to take the part just because of Hector, but it's always important to appeal to an actor's comfort level. If he's going to be acting with someone he likes, he'll have a better time and probably give a better performance.

I also discovered that one of Richard's passions is Buddhism, which led to a wonderful moment in my own life. Most actors introduce you to their agents, but Richard introduced me to the Dalai Lama of Tibet. We met during one of the Dalai Lama's visits to Los Angeles. Richard gave me the worst possible introduction. He said,

"His Holiness, I'd like you to meet Garry Marshall, one of the funniest men you'll ever meet." I was tongue-tied. I wanted to say something profound, but all I could think of was that we were both fifty-four. So I blurted it out: "We're the same age." The Dalai Lama said, "And I think we've both done pretty well."

While movie deals are made every day, sometimes you've got to be crafty to get an actor to commit to your project. When it came time to cast the father in *Nothing in Common*, we batted about the names of comedians like Sid Caesar and Dick Van Dyke. My first choice was Jackie Gleason. But as much as I wanted him, I had my doubts that we could get him because Gleason hadn't worked in years.

However, Ray Stark, one of the producers on the film, was a friend of Gleason's and was determined to give it a shot. Ray took *Nothing in Common* to Gleason and the two men discussed the script. While Gleason liked the story, he was reticent to take on a new project. But Ray knew what buttons to push.

"Jackie, if you retire now your last movie will have been *Smokey and the Bandit Part II*. Is that how you want to be remembered?"

Gleason signed with us that day.

Nothing in Common was Gleason's final film and he seemed happy with the result. If you find out what your actors care about and what kind of baggage they're carrying, it's easier to make your casting wish list come true.

On the first day of a shoot, I always let my lead actors know that they're the only ones on the set who are allowed to whine. Their performance can make or break a film, so if they want to whine every once in a while they can. Stars can be babies and learning to pacify them is part of the job and I don't have a problem with that. However, I believe that every star also has the ability to behave like an adult for at least an hour a day. So on the first day I take my stars aside and say, "I'm going to treat you like a temperamental artist. But there will come a time, say when we're behind schedule or the sun is going down, when I will ask you to be an adult." This reasoning has worked with every actor I've directed from big stars to

up-and-coming stars to never-going-to-be stars. When it really
counted, they were adults and helped me solve the problems.

On *Overboard,* Kurt Russell proved to be an asset in front of
and behind the camera. He looked like a movie star, he acted like
a movie star, but unlike most movie stars one day he helped the
crew move heavy camera equipment up a hill so we could rush to
beat the setting sun. Another day he helped remind Goldie Hawn,
his costar and life partner, that it was adult time. We were filming a scene in the middle of Long Beach Harbor and the water
was safe because the Coast Guard was with us, but the tempera-
ture was like ice. Goldie was wearing a sleeveless gold evening
gown and the scene called for her to jump into the ocean with a
life preserver on.

She did the scene twice, but unfortunately I didn't get the shot.
When you're shooting from a row boat, between the director
yelling "Action!" and the actors actually responding, you can drift
ten yards or more in the water and lose your camera angle. So we
had to do the scene again. When I broke the news to Goldie, she
didn't take it well.

"No, no, no," she yelled. "It's *freezing* out there. I don't want
to go back in the water. I'm done."

As the Coast Guard stood by and my crew waited for me to set
up the next shot, I thought of several persuasive reasons for her to
jump in again. The artistic reason was that she was a fearless
actress and this was a wonderful scene with which to end the
movie. The organic and emotional reason was that her character
was in love and she wanted to leap off the ship to be with her
boyfriend. Just as I was about to speak, Kurt came to the rescue.

"Goldie, for the money you're getting to do this picture, you've
got to jump in the water right now."

"Oh . . . you're right," she said, and got up and prepared to
jump into the water again . . . and once more.

In dealing with actors you've never worked with before or
never met, the best bet is to open up a line of communication
with them right way. I always begin by asking questions like
"What's the worst thing a director ever did to you?" or "What do

At the age of forty-seven, I decided to start a new
career as a movie director. *People* magazine used to
refer to me as Garry *Happy Days* Marshall and later
switched to Garry *Pretty Woman* Marshall.

From the streets of the Bronx to a sidewalk in Hollywood. Surrounded by
family and friends on November 23, 1983, I got a star on Hollywood
Boulevard's Walk of Fame.

Portland, Oregon, 1983: a group photo of the Happy Days All-Stars softball team, which included Tom Hanks (*center, standing*), Crystal Bernard (*center, kneeling*), and Ron Howard (*standing, second from right*).

Closet athlete, Mrs. C., a.k.a. Marion Ross, steps up to the plate and swings for the fences.

Hanging out with Laura San Giacomo, who costarred in *Pretty Woman* and appeared in a production of *Wrong Turn at Lungfish* in Los Angeles.

With my sisters Penny and Ronny visiting my dad, who at eighty-seven still likes to wear a suit.

May 1980: watching the sign of my play *The Roast* come down from Broadway's Winter Garden Theatre. The sign ran longer than the play.

HENDERSON PRODUCTIONS

PHOTO BY JOAN MARCUS

The various casts of *Wrong Turn at Lungfish:*

Fritz Weaver, Calista Flockhart, Michael E. Knight, and my daughter Kathleen.

HENDERSON PRODUCTIONS

Stephanie Niznik, Tony Danza, me, and Jami Gertz.

HENDERSON PRODUCTIONS

Tony Danza, Kelli Williams, Laurie Metcalf, and George C. Scott.

At the Carl Reiner Celebrity Tennis Tournament in La Costa with Norman
Lear, Carl Reiner, Mel Brooks, and Anne Bancroft. Good comedy minds.
Fair backhands.

How sweet it was:
with writing partner
Jerry Belson and
Debbie Reynolds as we
filmed *How Sweet It Is*,
our first produced
screenplay and our
first screen credit as
producers.

Hiding from the Las Vegas sun with Jacqueline Bisset on the set of *The Grasshopper*. The movie was later a cult hit, which is show business talk for it didn't make any money. But I liked it.

The cast from my movie *Young Doctors in Love*, which included Sean Young; Michael McKean, who played Lenny on *Laverne & Shirley*; and Ted McGinley, from *Happy Days* and later *Married . . . with Children*.

Taking time out in between scenes on *Young Doctors in Love* to play basketball with Hector Elizondo (in his costume from the movie) and several crew members.

With my lucky charm, actor Hector Elizondo, star of TV's *Chicago Hope*. I hope he's in every movie I ever direct.

My daughter, Kathleen, helping me out during *The Flamingo Kid* by running around the track like a horse.

Matt Dillon and Hector Elizondo in a sensitive father-son scene from *The Flamingo Kid.*

Preparing a shot with the gang from *The Flamingo Kid*, which included Fisher Stevens, Marisa Tomei, Brian McNamara, Bronson Pinchot, and Matt Dillon (*sitting down*).

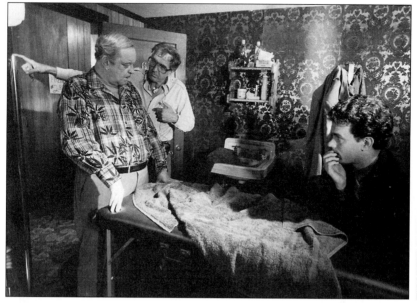

Directing two major stars from different decades:
working with Jackie Gleason and Tom Hanks on a scene that was
eventually cut from *Nothing in Common.*

Taking a break with Jackie Gleason and Tom Hanks on the set of *Nothing in Common.* Tom hadn't won an Oscar yet so he didn't get a chair.

Seeing double on the set of *Overboard* with Goldie Hawn and her stunt double.

Directing Goldie Hawn and Kurt Russell in a romantic moment from *Overboard*. Love scenes are my favorite, especially when you have the advantage of built-in chemistry.

you hate most about a director?" Actors are usually very honest
with me. They've said things like "I hate it when a director yells
at me in front of the crew" or "This one director wouldn't let me
call him by his first name and it really made me mad." The most
common complaint has been that directors lie about everything
from scheduling to nude scenes. It's important in a director's
working relationship to take the time to find out what makes an
actor happy and what frightens him. (This philosophy includes
asking the actresses what kind of aftershave they prefer. If an
actress hates Aramis, I'm certainly not going to wear it on the set
every day.)

To avoid big problems with actors I try to confront small ones
early by having personal talks often. In 1984, when producer
Alexandra Rose brought me the script of *Nothing in Common* with
Tom Hanks attached to it, I was very excited and immediately
committed to direct. However, just before we started shooting,
Tom seemed to be out of sorts, which was strange because he was
usually so amiable. Being the secure person that I am, I assumed
the problem was my fault.

Tom and I weren't strangers. He had done an episode of
Happy Days, shot his series *Bosom Buddies* on the Paramount lot,
and had even played on the *Happy Days* softball team. So when I
saw that something was bothering him, I asked for a personal talk.
That's when I found out that he was getting a divorce the week we
were starting to shoot *Nothing in Common*. We discussed it pri-
vately for a while, and then I said that I was sorry and would try
to make the job as easy as possible for him. Sometimes you have
to be a supportive director and a supportive friend. No matter how
amicable a splitup is, it's never easy. But Tom got through it all
like a gentleman and is now married to Rita Wilson, a very funny
and talented actress.

Thanks to Tom and Jackie Gleason, the film turned out to be
one of my best. Tom personally helped Sela Ward and Bess
Armstrong turn in top performances and he was wonderful on
screen and off. I'm glad we talked at the beginning of *Nothing in
Common*.

Tom has no entourage, but most big stars do. If you have a
problem with a star and he doesn't want to discuss it, talk with

someone who works for him. A secretary, an assistant, or an associate can give you insight into an actor or actress. A director should make it a point to be friends with these people and show them that you respect them. Most people are rude to a star's entourage because they feel they are sycophants. I don't judge people on their job, but on their behavior. Remember, the saying is true, in Hollywood a secretary or personal assistant today could be the head of a studio tomorrow.

After an exhausting night on a long shoot, it was four o'clock in the morning on the set of *Pretty Woman* and Julia Roberts fainted. The crew buzzed with the news that she might be sick or have appendicitis. But I had gotten to know Julia, and I suspected that something else was up.

"Sweetheart, when was the last time you had anything to eat?" I asked her.

"Yesterday I ate an avocado," Julia said.

She was a young actress just too busy to waste time on food.

"You probably should have eaten two avocados and maybe you could have made it through tonight."

She laughed, I hugged her, and then fed her some tuna fish.

Julia was not the first nor the last star to have a problem that affected one of my movies. Barbara Hershey showed up with silicone-filled lips a few days before shooting *Beaches* and Jim Brown was arrested over a fight while we were filming *The Grasshopper*. No matter what came up, no matter what the problem, we found a solution each time: We fed Julia. We carefully shot Barbara's lips. We bailed Jim out.

My philosophy about movies is similar to Debbie Reynolds's. She had written into her deal on *How Sweet It Is* that she could have time off each week to attend her daughter Carrie's Brownie troop meeting. I had written into my *Pretty Woman* contract that I could have two days off to attend my daughter Lori's wedding. I always find a way to lead a real life while making a movie at the same time.

•   •   •

Those who thought I pushed the limits of nepotism in television were in for another surprise when I went into film. I made it a point to surround myself with family, friends, and trusted colleagues on every film, even if I had to have my preferences written into my contract with the studio. I wasn't just being self-indulgent; I was protecting myself. I had come across a lot of hostile people in the movie business and I felt that friendly faces would help insulate me from the enemy.

I usually rely on my family the most when I'm in trouble, like the day it rained on *Beaches*. We were shooting a scene with Bette and I was petrified that her wig would get wet and put us back three hours. Wigs take a long time to prepare on any film but a wet wig can turn into a nightmare. What about a second wig, you ask? Ha! Wigs don't grow on trees and we didn't have enough money left in the budget for that.

So, I cast my son as the car rental agent who holds an umbrella over Bette's head and walks her to her car. This way I could say, "Scott, no matter what you do, protect her red hair or you won't get your allowance this week. If you get any water on that wig, I'll kill you." You can say that type of thing to a son but not to a nervous young actor. A son won't call his agent or manager to complain. It took seven takes, but I ended up with a great shot despite the rain and Scott was able to add the phrase "wig protector" to his résumé.

Nepotism also came in handy during *The Flamingo Kid* when we were filming a scene at the Yonkers Raceway in New York at four o'clock in the morning. I was trying to get a shot of the crowd in the bleachers as they watched the horses, only we didn't have any horses. The deal on the horses was that they went home at midnight. We were planning to use an insert of some stock footage later, but I needed a finishing line shot of the crowd to make it work. The actors' eyes had to follow one spot as if a horse were making its way around the track. I scanned the set for someone who could run fast like a horse but who didn't have an agent.

My daughter Kathleen, a high school actress fresh from her role in the play *Antigone*, was visiting the set that night, so I asked her to run around the racetrack. "Forget your motivation as an actress. Just run like a horse," I told her. The arrangement worked out perfectly: My daughter ran, the actors as the crowd watched her, and I was able to get my shot. Of course, the next day Kathleen phoned her mother in Los Angeles and complained that "Daddy made me run like a horse!" She was happier later playing the role of a waitress in another scene. (You might be asking why didn't we have a car or truck drive around the track? We tried that first but the noise ruined the sound track. My daughter's running was quieter; we even told her to huff, puff, and breathe quietly.)

When I'm not busy directing my family, I try to find a part for Hector Elizondo. He has appeared in each of my eight films. While he's a close friend and a great actor, that's only part of why I use him. More important is his professionalism; it helps keep the other actors in line. My friend, actor, and now A-list movie director Ron Howard did the same thing on *Happy Days* and served as a role model for my other TV shows too. When Hector and I first teamed up on *Young Doctors in Love*, I found it invaluable to have him on the set because we were using so many fledgling actors. Nobody dared act up because Hector's composure and professionalism would have made them look bad. Similarly, Richard Crenna played the role of comedy mentor on the set of *The Flamingo Kid* and could often be seen tapping out the comedy rhythm of a joke with a pencil so the other young actors could hear the importance of the beat.

Authority figures can help bring a sense of calm to a potentially raucous set. And when you find one you work well with stick with him, especially if he can play basketball like Hector. On the set of *Young Doctors* we would shoot baskets during lunchtime and then I would help Hector put on his dress and we'd go shoot a scene. Once he played a game in full costume: flowered dress, face makeup, and pantyhose. He scored a lot of points. Nobody would guard him.

I also work with Hector because he can make the other actors look so good on screen. When we were casting *Pretty Woman*, Disney didn't want to pay Hector's salary. I got so mad that I paid half his salary myself. After Disney saw how good he was in the dailies, they paid me back, but it demonstrated how serious I am about working with the actors I want and need. Hector's consistency as an actor is something that I've grown to depend on.

In *Pretty Woman*, because Julia was so young and relatively inexperienced, I wanted to surround her with a strong supporting cast, which included Hector. Just before the two of them were about to rehearse their scene in the hotel manager's office, I asked Hector to deliver his lines in a leading manner, as if he knew the answers and were too polite to say them out loud. Then I told Julia that no matter what Hector said, she should keep nodding her head.

MR. THOMPSON

Miss Vivian . . . things that go on in other hotels don't happen at the Regent Beverly Wilshire.
(Vivian says nothing.)

MR. THOMPSON

Mr. Lewis, however, is a very *special* customer. And we like to think of our *special customers* as *friends*. As a customer, we would expect Mr. Lewis to sign in any additional guests. But as a friend, we're willing to overlook it. I'm assuming you're a . . . relative?
(Vivian finds herself nodding.)

MR. THOMPSON

I thought so. You must be his . . . ?

VIVIAN

(NODS)
Niece?

MR. THOMPSON

Of course. Naturally when Mr. Lewis leaves, I won't see you in this hotel again. I assume you have no other *uncles* in this hotel.
(Vivian bites her lower lip and nods.)

Then I told Julia to blow her nose very hard into the handkerchief that Hector gave her. She didn't understand exactly why, but I told her we'd cut to Hector's reaction later and it would be funny because it was his beautiful, monogrammed handkerchief. The scene worked very well thanks to Hector's stability and Julia's trust. After eight films together, Hector sometimes knows where I'm headed before I do. That's one of the benefits of working with an actor more than once.

Fortunately, many of my friends and family have talent or I wouldn't have gotten away with using them. Show business won't tolerate bad acting for very long, even from the actor with the most well-connected family tree. In Hollywood, it's difficult to find real faces, those that haven't undergone a trendy face peel or a nip and tuck here and there. In certain parts I like to use actors who have real faces: the owner of my favorite Italian restaurant, the juggler who sits behind me at the Raider football games, and many of my childhood friends show up on the call sheets of my movies. Tom Hanks calls it my Crony Count, and after working with Penny on *Big* and *A League of Their Own*, he told me that my sister has a Crony Count almost as long as mine. I guess it runs in the family.

While friends and family make me comfortable, I also like to put my actors at ease, especially the younger ones. The best way I know how is to keep them busy. As on my television shows, I never wanted my movie actors to get bored because boredom can lead to trouble. *The Flamingo Kid* was probably the movie in which I worked with the greatest number of actors in their twenties, including Matt Dillon, Janet Jones, Fisher Stevens, Brian McNamara, Leon Robinson, Bronson Pinchot, and at the time an unknown Marisa Tomei. Before we headed to New York for location shooting, I figured out an activity that we could all do together. A film shoot is not quite long enough to launch a softball team, so I had a basketball net set up instead. The cast and crew, both men and women, shot hoops before work, after work, and between takes. Instead of coffee breaks, we took basketball breaks. The minute I saw a group of kids heading off to a trailer to hang out, I'd grab the nearest megaphone and yell, "Game time!" It worked for me. When we weren't playing basketball, we played tennis and Janet Jones was a great player.

When you direct kids you have to play by a different set of

rules than you do with adults. If an adult gets tired, you can usually get a few more good takes out of him. But when an eight-year-old says he's tired, you probably got your best take twenty minutes ago. Besides staying awake, the hardest thing to get a child actor to do is cry. On *Overboard*, I worked with four little boys, ages six to twelve, and in one scene six-year-old Jeffrey Wiseman had to cry. It's common in a case like this to just squirt some special drops into the kid's eyes and wait for them to tear up. Because Jeffrey was so young, I didn't want to fool around with any drops.

So early in the shoot, I asked Jeffrey what was the saddest thing he could think of. He said it was the day his dog Fluffy died. I told him there would come a time during the film when I would ask him to remember Fluffy. Not now, but soon. Several days later when the cameras were rolling, I asked Jeffrey about Fluffy. He started to tear up when he shared his story with the cast and crew. Then we rolled right into the scene with the dialogue as written. We didn't have to mess around and put anything in his eyes, and we got a take we could use. The next day Jeffrey whispered in my ear, "You aren't going to talk about Fluffy again, are you?" I said, "No. No. That's it for Fluffy."

I know there were probably a hundred other well-trained child actors to choose from, but the problem is that many of them look like well-trained child actors on screen, too. Hollywood kids come to auditions with blow-dried hair and look like rich Munchkins. A four-year-old who just used hair spray doesn't look like a real kid to me. However, when you hire real kids, you've got to be prepared for anything. In another scene from *Overboard*, Jeffrey was supposed to take out a handmade macaroni necklace from his pocket and give it to Goldie. He whipped it out with such gusto that he smacked Goldie right in the forehead with the necklace. She nearly passed out and said, "Garry, I feel stars circling around my head like a cartoon character." With kids, sometimes learning to cry is easier than mastering the props.

When they're not hurting the other actors, you have to watch out for the kids hurting themselves and be ready to improvise. Fortunately, movies are about illusion, so you can usually find a solution without hurting your story. We filmed a scene in

Overboard where the four boys were chasing Goldie through the woods. The next day, before we could finish shooting the scene, one of the little boys twisted his ankle. He was too hurt to run, big budget, big stars, major motion picture or not. We had already shot part of the scene so we couldn't just cut him out.

This is where my television background came in handy. We always had a way. We had to have a way—and fast. I solved our problem with a mask. We showed the beginning of the chase scene and then cut to a new scene where the boys put on scary monster masks and said, "Hey, let's scare Mom!" Once the boys started running with the masks on, I used another little boy of the same height to replace my wounded actor.

The last thing to remember about kids is that you can never forget that they are kids. We cast Mayim Bialik (the star of *Blossom*) to play a young Bette Midler in *Beaches*. Mayim was great as Bette except for one thing: Mayim has blue eyes and Bette has brown. We had the prop department order Mayim some brown contact lenses. Everything would have been fine except, of course, they ordered only one pair of contact lenses and one day little Mayim lost a lens. There we were, shooting a $30 million movie and our production schedule was threatened because a kid lost a contact lens.

When you work with kids you have to anticipate things like this and order half a dozen backup lenses to protect yourself. We had a backup pair, but they were at the doctor's office ten minutes away. We sent a couple of crew members to the optometrist's office to get the other pair, but it was Saturday and his office was closed. The doctor was in Palm Springs. Over the phone I gave my crew permission to break the doctor's door down. Unfortunately, we were too far behind schedule to wait for the lenses, so we had to shoot part of a restaurant scene in which Mayim had one blue eye and one brown one. Remember: Kids are kids and they lose things, so have a backup with you on the set and not in China. (The budget memo on *Beaches* that read "cost of optometrist's door repair" raised a few eyebrows at the studio, but they still paid it.)

As usual, before we started shooting *Pretty Woman,* I talked a lot with Julia Roberts and Richard Gere about their lives. I discovered that Richard is an accomplished musician and can play several instruments, including the piano, guitar, and trumpet. So we had him write and play some of his own music on the piano in *Pretty Woman*. The scene added another dimension to the film and to the audience's view of Richard as an actor. We also thought that having the two characters make love on top of a piano would be a novelty. Little did we know that down the street Michelle Pfeiffer was perched on top of a piano with Jeff Bridges on the set of *The Fabulous Baker Boys*. I guess it was a big year for sex on baby grands.

Another thing I look for in actors is what they do when they're nervous. When she's uncomfortable, Julia Roberts reaches around and snaps the back of her bra. It's just a little unconscious nervous tic that we used in the film to help the behavior of her fish-out-of-water character. It's finding that kind of material that reminds a director to keep his eyes on the actors at all times, even when they're not performing. One day the cast took a break while the crew fixed a broken light. While Julia and Richard were waiting, they compared the size of their hands. It was a tender, very natural moment and I later had them re-create it on film in the scene where they take a bath together. I could probably stay at home making up things for the actors to do, but natural behavior always comes across better on screen.

I saw Michelle Pfeiffer at the catering truck ordering a bagel one day on *Frankie and Johnny*. When she discovered they were all out of bagels, she started to cry. I was ready to run to the nearest deli to buy her a dozen bagels, but she said it wasn't that important. It turned out she was having her period and everything made her cry. I didn't try to cheer her up but made it a positive thing because she had several crying scenes in the movie. After lunch, we sat down with the production schedule and, with Michelle's approval, plotted the crying scenes around her menstrual cycle. This made these scenes easier for everyone, especially Michelle. Yes, I'm a filmmaker and I chart menstrual cycles. Later I saw Michelle walking around the set with a sign she had pinned on the back of her bathrobe that read BEWARE PMS.

I originally learned the importance of women's cycles from Debbie Reynolds on *How Sweet It Is*. We were sitting in our first big production meeting with Debbie and ten others talking about a swimming sequence. Suddenly, Debbie secretly passed me a note that said, "Garry, ask me when my period is." Now, I was a first-time producer who knew nothing and I wanted to impress the others, but I didn't know what to make of this note. Was she coming on to me during the height of the meeting? I looked at Debbie and she gave me an encouraging nod. "Errrr . . . Debbie," I said, "when is your period?" She smiled and said, "Oh, what a bright producer Garry is. That's such a smart question for him to ask. You all should know my menstrual cycle so you can schedule the swimming sequences around my period."

When I'm not getting to know the actors, I think actors should get to know each other. Before *Frankie and Johnny*, Michelle Pfeiffer and Al Pacino had worked together on *Scarface*, but on that film, Al had been the big star and Michelle was just the newcomer. Their working relationship on that film could not have been described as close; he didn't say more than two words to her off screen. I wanted them to get reacquainted on *Frankie and Johnny*. I had them come to my house for an informal rehearsal.

In the beginning, the conversation moved rather slowly, but after a while Michelle picked up the pace. She became very animated and asked Al all sorts of personal questions: "What's your favorite color? Your favorite food? Your favorite time of year?" Al, being the shy, reclusive kind of actor that he is, got very defensive and said, "What are you trying to be Michelle, a talk show host?" Eventually, even Al settled down and stopped looking at Michelle as if she were Sally Jessy Raphael.

I asked them what they liked best about their bodies. Michelle said she liked her neckline but thought her hands were too big. I believe she referred to them as "meat hooks." So we had her character constantly opening jars for other people to call attention to her strong hands. Al said he liked his eyes but thought his posture was terrible. Later when we shot the scene in the flower mart, Al was wearing a trench coat and Michelle turned to him and said, "Can you stand up straighter? I feel like I'm working with Columbo."

As much as a director tries to get along with the actors, disagreements are inevitable and I've found that when you do fight with the stars it's best to do it one on one. To fight with the actors in front of the crew is disruptive to the set and to the publicity department because your spat could end up on the cover of a magazine. When a fight breaks out, I usually clear the set or take the actor aside to discuss his problem in private.

Some actors need to let off steam now and then. That's okay. Bette Midler was an actress from the "school of steam." During the *Beaches* shoot, whenever Bette would come screaming toward me with something that irritated her, I would clear the set and give her my complete attention. But one day when she did it, I didn't clear the set.

"What's wrong?" she asked. "Why aren't you clearing the set?"

"Because you're absolutely right and I want everyone to hear you," I said.

And that's the way we worked. When I felt she was making too big a deal out of something, I cleared the set and told her so, but I wouldn't embarrass her. But when she was right, I told her she was. Total honesty proved to be the best way to work with Bette.

Many actor-director fights involve the script and that's unfortunate because the script is usually an actor's least competent area. Actors can contribute a great line or a gesture that will enhance a scene, but most don't understand screenplay structure. To avoid script arguments, I encourage the actors to become involved in other areas of production. Dana Delany helped make the selections for her wardrobe on *Exit to Eden*. On *Flamingo Kid*, Matt Dillon participated in some of the crew's favorite pranks, including the ritual that required each actor to get a whipped-cream pie thrown in his face on his last day. On *Frankie and Johnny*, Michelle helped the prop department by dressing the set with some personal items from her house. I've found that these kinds of extracurricular activities can help relax the stars and keep them from messing around with the script. Bette volunteered to police the extras' wardrobe and all flower arrangements on *Beaches*. If an extra was wearing clothing from the wrong decade or if the flower beds and greenery looked too dead, we heard about it from Bette.

Sometimes actors fight among themselves and a director should learn how to keep the peace. You must motivate the actors and keep their relationship from deteriorating any more than it has to. During *Beaches*, Bette and Barbara Hershey got along

famously until one day when the script called for a scene in which
Bette paints Barbara's toenails as a gesture of friendship because
Barbara's character was pregnant. As we walked onto the set to
rehearse the scene, Bette took one look at Barbara's toenails and
said, "Oh, Barb, you've got such gnarly toenails. You gotta start
gardening with your shoes on." Bette was only joking but Barbara,
an actress of great class and concentration, was clearly disrupted.
I couldn't run the risk of her staying that way. In the story, C.C.
and Hillary were supposed to be best friends but that wouldn't
come across if I had one unhappy actress off screen. So I tried to
make Barbara feel better and diffuse the issue by showing Bette
my not so attractive toenails.

Once in a while you might find that it's impossible to keep personal feelings out of a scene. In that case, you have to try to incorporate them into the movie. In another scene in *Beaches*, Bette
slaps John Heard across the face after they exchange wedding
vows. It was her character's way of making sure her new husband
didn't forget the moment. I wanted John to do a comedy take after
the slap; maybe something amusing with his eyes. As it turned out,
the week we shot the scene John was going through a divorce that
involved child custody. He had so much internal turmoil that when
Bette slapped him, it was impossible for him to do anything other
than wince like it really hurt. Real wincing and real hurting just
aren't funny. (Watch the Three Stooges. They understood it perfectly.) I had to figure out something else. After Bette slapped
John, I had the camera cut to the justice of the peace, played by
Hector Elizondo. Hector did a funny take and we were able to
move on. By the end of the film, with Bette's help John had gotten
himself back together and we shot a beautiful, poignant scene in
which he and Bette break up on the stoop outside his theater.

Sometimes you can keep an actor happy just by handing him
a better line. The writers were giving Julia Roberts many funny
things to do in *Pretty Woman*, and one day Richard Gere said,
"You don't really need me. You just need an image of a suit and
tie. Why don't I just go home and you can film my suit." He was
doing a brilliant job, but he was clearly feeling left out. I told him
we'd work on something funny for him to say in the opera scene.

INTERIOR SAN FRANCISCO OPERA HOUSE BOX — NIGHT
(As the lights come up, Vivian wipes off her tear-ruined
mascara. She sighs, happy.)
(The OLDER WOMAN in the next box smiles at her.)

OLDER WOMAN

Did you enjoy the opera, dear?

VIVIAN

(TEARFULLY)
Oh, it was so good I almost peed in my pants.

Richard thought it would be funny for his character to say, "I
don't know her," referring to Vivian. But at this point in the movie,
Edward was falling in love with Vivian, so it would be only natural for him to try to cover for her.

OLDER WOMAN

Did you enjoy the opera, dear?

VIVIAN

(TEARFULLY)
Oh, it was so good I almost peed in my pants.

OLDER WOMAN

(STARTLED BY VIVIAN'S REMARK)
What?

EDWARD

She said she liked it better than *Pirates of Penzance*.

The new line was in character for Edward, made Richard
happy, and made the audience laugh.

•   •   •

Casting is a fragile business in Hollywood and the industry is filled with stories of what might have been. Originally, Jeffrey Katzenberg and I discussed Madonna for the lead in *Pretty Woman.* I even met with Madonna at a French restaurant and she suggested some other actresses because she felt Vivian should be played by someone under twenty-one. Producer Steve Reuther later brought me that twenty-one-year-old named Julia Roberts. Matthew Broderick was supposed to do Matt Dillon's role in *The Flamingo Kid* but the deal fell apart. We considered Al Pacino for Richard Gere's part in *Pretty Woman*, but Al couldn't commit to it at the time.

My sister Penny and Jack Nicholson talked about starring together in *Frankie and Johnny*, as did Barbra Streisand and her ex-husband Elliott Gould. Emma Thompson read for the role of Cora in *Frankie and Johnny* with a letter-perfect Brooklyn accent. In *Beaches*, Anne Archer almost played Barbara Hershey's role and director David Lynch and producer Don Simpson were in the running for Spalding Gray's part. I met with Bridget Fonda and Nicole Kidman for Dana Delany's role and Sharon Stone for Rosie O'Donnell's part in *Exit to Eden.*

Sometimes you guess right. Sometimes you guess wrong. Or sometimes the information you're given can be misleading. When we were casting *Exit to Eden*, I was interested in Dana Delany and watched a clip of her riding a horse sidesaddle in the movie *Tombstone.* I thought how wonderful. She's an accomplished horseback rider. I'll write a horseback riding scene into my movie, too. After I hired Dana, I learned that in *Tombstone* the costume department had added a third leg to her dress to make it look like she was riding sidesaddle because she wasn't really that great a horsewoman. Instead of hiring an actress who had experience with horses, I had one who had experience with a fake leg. However, Dana did prove to have the elegance and bravery required to tackle the part of Lisa, the erotic dominatrix, in *Exit to Eden.*

When casting works, you'll know it right from the start. The first day on the set of *The Flamingo Kid* when I saw the light hit Matt Dillon's cheekbones, I knew for the first time what the phrase "star quality" really meant.

•   •   •

Each actor works a bit differently. Some love to rehearse. Others like to tackle a scene cold. Some stay in character even off camera while others are the characters only when you yell "Action!" and still others come in and out. On the set of *Pretty Woman*, Richard prepared for the big fight scene in the hotel room by not speaking to Julia the entire day preceding the scene. Julia came to me upset that day and asked why Richard was mad at her. I said, "It's just for today, dear. He'll talk to you again tomorrow." He did.

Jackie Gleason would leave the set of *Nothing in Common* every day at five sharp and head right for the nearest bar. On *Beaches*, Barbara liked to rehearse a scene over and over until we got it down and she also enjoyed talking with the crew between scenes. Bette, on the other hand, loved to tackle a scene for the first time with the cameras rolling and preferred hanging out in her trailer with her little girl between scenes. Al Pacino had his own private writers to enhance his role in *Frankie and Johnny*. Richard Gere liked to spend time raising money for Buddhists. Goldie Hawn liked to have her kids with her on the set. One of my best memories from *Overboard* is holding her little boy in my arms while yelling "Action!" to Goldie on the set.

It's okay to let everybody do what he wants to be happy, but there must be a commitment to the film schedule too. No matter how big your stars, you have to know somewhere in the back of your mind that you can do the movie without them. Even stars can let you down and you have to be prepared when they do. Actually, I believe that anyone on a movie set can be replaced, even me.

When I directed *Wrong Turn at Lungfish* in Los Angeles, George C. Scott missed the performance the day after our opening night, which had garnered several mediocre reviews. Pressed for time, producer Jim Freydberg and I struggled to prepare his understudy, an able but nervous actor named Richard McKenzie who requested that we position a plastic bucket off stage so he could throw up between scenes. That night, Richard did an excellent job, but the audience was disappointed. They wanted George C. Scott, not an understudy, regardless of how good the understudy was.

George returned to work the next day, but I continued to feel uneasy because I knew he could do it again. But what was I going to do, fire General Patton? The man is one of our country's greatest living actors and one of my idols. I had to figure out something else. I decided to cover myself. I not so secretly started rehearsing Jack Klugman to replace George in case he didn't show up again. Sure enough, as soon as George heard that I was rehearsing Jack, he was on his best behavior. Sometimes it takes someone waiting in the wings to make an actor give his best performance. There were forty-eight performances of *Lungfish* in Los Angeles, and General Patton did forty-seven of them brilliantly.

You can't be afraid of actors who are considered stars and you certainly can't be afraid to give them direction. That's what a director is there for. Bette Midler said that many of the directors she had worked with in the past were too intimidated by her and too afraid to suggest anything new, and it ended up hurting her performance. You have to take charge and risk the wrath. From an Oscar winner to a young kid making his screen debut, every actor needs direction.

Tom Hanks is a minimalist when it comes to taking direction. He likes it when a director says basic things like "louder," "softer," "slower," "faster," "lighter," "darker," "smarter," "confused," "aware," or "not aware." You can do a whole movie with Tom just by using those words. After we worked together, Tom told me that a director on another film said to him, "I see this scene as char-treuse." And Tom said, "So do I." But he didn't know what the hell the director was talking about. He likes it simple. Other actors require more elaborate direction. Whether your job is to suggest a look, a line, or a whole shift in attitude, it has to complement your vision of the movie.

I think the greatest moment as a director in working with actors is to watch them go someplace they've never gone before, to make them stretch their acting muscles. Directing an actor and making him look the same way he has looked in his last ten films is boring for the actor, director, and often the audience. In TV they like a star to be the same every week. It's not necessarily so in the movies. If someone is too "on the nose" for a part, I keep looking. When we were casting *Frankie and Johnny*, Michelle Pfeiffer and Al Pacino both came to us with some heavy acting baggage.

Michelle was famous for being beautiful and intensely aloof in dramas, and Al was well known for being volatile and angry in thrillers and epic sagas. But they were both eager to try a warm comedy-drama and that's what made the casting work.

Kate Nelligan also played against type in *Frankie and Johnny*. Kate was a Shakespearean actress with several Tony nominations. When she read for the part of Cora in *Frankie and Johnny*, however, she was wearing a tight miniskirt and had her hair teased. She looked more like a coffeeshop waitress than Lady Macbeth. Kate was not the first actress whom we thought of for the role but she was interested in it because she said to me, "You're the only director in town who thinks I do sexy parts!"

I decided to go with her because it was such a different kind of role for her and one the movie audience had never seen her do before. Audiences like to be surprised and one of the ways to do that is through off-beat casting. Kate was a classical actress who could speak with my Bronx accent when she wanted to. Whenever she went awry with her accent in a scene, she would turn to me and say, "Garry, come talk to me for a minute."

Many of the actors I work with are uneasy with comedy and half the fun is teaching them how to be comfortable. I'm always fascinated when I find a pretty actress who also has the potential to be funny because it's a rare combination. There are plenty of funny women and many beautiful women in Hollywood but only a handful of actresses, like Goldie Hawn, Julia Roberts, and Meg Ryan, are considered to be both. Years ago there was an English actress named Kay Kendall and she was one of the first truly funny and beautiful women I had ever seen. She could make people laugh and swoon, and I thought that was something very special. Unfortunately, she died in her early thirties from cancer, but she proved without a doubt how well comedy and glamour could be combined.

When it came time for me to direct women, I looked for that same combination. I took the lessons that Lucy had taught me about physical comedy and shared them with Sean Young in *Young Doctors in Love*, Barbara Hershey in *Beaches*, Michelle Pfeiffer in *Frankie and Johnny*, and Dana Delany in *Exit to Eden*. These women were strong dramatic actresses who had not done a lot of comedy. We explored how physical comedy could enhance their characters' range. Michelle getting peanut butter stuck to the roof of her mouth while home alone was a wonderful moment and got solid laughs.

When I'm not trying to make pretty women funny, I have been known to make a brooding actor smile. Before they did movies with me, Matt Dillon, Richard Gere, Al Pacino, and the Australian actor Paul Mercurio were known for their sexy, sulking poses. I didn't want any of that. Comedy doesn't work when an actor is looking down at his shoes, talking into his tie, hunched over smoking a cigarette, or staring straight ahead as if looking down the barrel of a gun. In comedy, an actor's head has to be high up in the air. The moment I saw Matt dropping his head I would say, "No brooding. Do that in your next film. This is a comedy."

On *Nothing in Common*, I had a different kind of challenge: I started with two actors known for their comedy and tried to steer them toward drama. The transition with Jackie and Tom seemed to be going smoothly until we got to the first scene in the hospital room where Jackie and Tom have a sensitive father-son talk. It had to be a very poignant scene. Any comic knows, however, that a hospital room is like a bee's nest full of humor. Gleason suggested that before we did any hospital scenes we needed to have an exorcism to purge the room of all its jokes.

Tom, Jackie, and I went into the hospital room and took turns saying every joke we could think of. We did bedpan shtick, jokes about doctors and nurses, gags about the bed's going up and down, and pranks with the television clicker. Finally, when Jackie was satisfied that there were no more jokes floating around the room, we proceeded with the scene and were able to give it the serious intensity it deserved.

Becoming an actor is one of my best ways to improve my directing and learn how to cope with other actors' foibles. It's one thing to say to an actor, "I understand what you're going through," and another thing to do it. My first acting job was as a gangster named Big Leonard in an episode of *Hey Landlord!* My character, named as a tribute to Sheldon Leonard, was a forerunner to the casino owner I later played in Albert Brooks's movie *Lost in America*. In the 1960s, I appeared as a boxing referee on *The Dick Van Dyke Show* and occasionally during the 1970s in my own television shows, mostly in off-beat cameos. Whenever I found the opportunity I would write a small musical combo into one of the shows. It made my mother feel like all those years of playing the drums weren't wasted.

My old army friend Fred Roos got me my first feature role in the 1968 movie *Psych-Out*, starring Jack Nicholson and Bruce Dern. I played a straitlaced narcotics agent, a role that Fred often cast me in because he knew I owned a nice blue suit, which I used for musical gigs as a drummer. After that I appeared in various films directed by my sister Penny, Ron Howard, Albert Brooks, and Michael Hoffman. It also helps for every director to see how other directors work.

For me the best part of acting is that I get a chance to relax. When a light breaks or a costume doesn't fit, I don't have to worry about it. I head to the catering truck for another donut. When Albert Brooks asked me to appear as a casino owner in *Lost in America*, I had just finished directing *The Flamingo Kid* and was exhausted. The thought of acting in someone else's movie sounded like going to a health spa to me.

Working with Albert, however, would prove to be no vacation. When I direct a movie, I usually do four or five takes for each shot. Albert is the kind of director who shoots at least fifteen takes for each shot. In the movie, my character was supposed to get increasingly irritated with Albert's character. In real life I didn't have to act: I *was* becoming annoyed because Albert did so many takes. I was getting so tired that I finally said, "Albert, what's wrong with the scene? Can I help you out? We seem to have the beginning down. Why don't we just start in the middle of the scene and move on with it?"

He agreed and we started from the middle. I followed his lead and we improvised but suddenly, he gave me the opening line from the first part of the scene. Out of frustration, I roared with laughter, but still kept acting. Albert kept my laughter in the film. It was so natural, it worked. Albert also made me say "Santi Claus" so many takes in a row that I wanted to strangle him. I'm now embarrassed I ever questioned Albert's judgment: Ten years later, people still come up to me and say, "Santi Claus."

Appearing in *Lost in America* increased my visibility in Hollywood so much so that my wife began to raffle me off at charity functions: "Come to the free clinic auction and win a dinner with director and actor Garry Marshall." "Come to the music center bazaar and bid on lunch with Garry Marshall." I would go to eat with the winners and they would say things like, "Mr. Marshall, my daughter could be a wonderful heart surgeon like her dad, but what she really wants to be is an actress. Can you talk to her?" Or I might go into a restaurant and several women would wink at me. I would say to my wife, "Look, honey, those girls think I'm cute." She'd say, "No they don't. They just think you'll make them into Julia Roberts." For better or worse, acting moved me into a whole new arena where I was no longer just a name, but now a face, too.

My most recent acting job has been a recurring role as the head of the network on *Murphy Brown*. There are many reasons why I like working on this TV series: It's a busy, entertaining set with intelligent, talented actors; the set is near my house and I don't have to take the freeway; and being on a top-rated network show keeps me eligible to play in celebrity softball games.

I think an asset to my acting career is that my dental bridge slips every evening and to compensate for it, I start overenunciating. Although I remember a time on the set of *A League of Their Own* when I was all dressed up and mingling among thirty beautiful girls when suddenly Penny yelled in front of cast and crew, "Wait! Wait! Let's shoot my brother now. I don't want to shoot him after five o'clock because his bridge slips!" After that a lot of the girls weren't that interested in talking to me.

Most people's bridges slip at five or six o'clock at night. Not a helpful hint for directing Johnny Depp or Brad Pitt, but maybe for other actors. My appearance in *Soapdish* as a network executive also demonstrates that you never know what is going to work in a movie. Hollywood people still come up to me and say, "You know the words I like? I like the word 'peppy' and the word 'cheap,' Peppy and cheap," which was just one of the many lines from *Soapdish* that caught on. Why? It's the truth about Hollywood. They love anything that is "peppy and cheap."

In *Lost in America*, I used my love of the nightclub performers who had given me my start in show business. When we were shooting, Albert abandoned his own script and took several ad-libbed jabs at Wayne Newton. I countered his lines with my own: "You can't say that about Wayne. I like Wayne Newton." It was natural and honest and it worked. I do like Wayne Newton. Albert encourages actors to ad-lib from life. Honesty is one of the toughest emotions to re-create on film, so if you can take it from life, it's going to look better up there on the big screen. Orson Welles said, "There are two activities that you never believe in movies: prayer and copulation." Honesty works on the screen and off, too. Lying only seems to work when making a deal or reporting your picture's grosses.

Dipping into your own past to create a moment on screen can be very painful. Once on *Pretty Woman*, Julia was having a difficult time in a scene in which Richard's character talks about his father. In real life, Julia's father had passed away several years earlier and she was having trouble dealing with this. When Richard said, "I hadn't spoken to [my dad] in fourteen and a half years; I wasn't there when he died," it was clearly very painful for Julia. I didn't pry but held her tight in between takes and had makeup standing close by to touch up her mascara. Sometimes a hug can be the best way to deal with a problem.

I needed more than a few hugs, however, when I took over George C. Scott's part in *Wrong Turn at Lungfish*. George's contract was up and we had *two* weeks before actor Fritz Weaver was slated to take over the lead. In the meantime, we had a choice: temporarily close down the play or get another actor to fill in. No other actor wanted to rehearse *four* weeks to work only *two* weeks. I had the part almost memorized from directing, so *I* jumped in. Playing a blind man onstage in front of hundreds of people was scary, replacing George C. Scott playing a blind man was absurd, but when it really went over the top was the night I walked out to play a blind man and there in the third row was Al Pacino, who had just won an Academy Award for playing a blind man in *Scent of a Woman*. When Al came backstage afterward to see me he was very kind.

During *Lungfish*'s six-month New York run things went from

very absurd—like Jami Gertz toughing out the last third of the play with a fractured arm after getting hurt in the fight sequence and an exhausted Michael Knight acting all day in his soap opera, then racing over to our theater to do the show at night—to the extremely emotional and poignant—the night Tony Danza's terminally ill mother came to see him in the play. Tony got a standing ovation and his mother asked to be helped from her seat so she could join the applause, too. That was the last time she saw him perform.

Part of working with actors is learning to understand their processes and the reality is that acting can be very terrifying because it's all about rejection. Hollywood is filled with young people who dream of becoming movie stars. The problem is that while the rewards are great, so are the odds. Barbara Hershey once cautioned my aspiring actress daughter Kathleen that you haven't earned the right to call yourself an actress until you've collected at least fifty rejections. Yes, fifty.

The actors who make it in show business are not those who have the most impressive theater reviews, the most names of well-connected producers in their address books, or the most powerful agents. The actors who succeed are those strong enough to handle the constant rejection day after day. Lee Strasberg said that if you take three actors of equal talent, at the end of a certain amount of time one will make it and the other two will quit. Not fail, but quit.

Different Ways the Director Protects Himself from the Crew and Vice Versa

The Bird That Almost Ate Al Pacino

Some directors lock into a script before they start shooting and vow not to change a word. They plan elaborate and detailed story-boards that map out each page of the script, from 1 through 120, and have illustrators and storyboard artists break down their every shot. They have all the bases covered, from the first "cute meet" to the final farewell. On my set, however, anything can happen from last-minute improvisations to total scene rewrites to outright pranks. I believe that making a movie can be fun.

My approach is to maintain an atmosphere free of restraints because I think that's when magic can happen. Each director has his own method. Woody Allen likes to use a hand-held camera to achieve a natural documentary look. Costa-Gavras and Oliver Stone rely on fast-cutting shots to tell their stories while the team of Merchant-Ivory prefers gentle, slow-moving shots. Francis Ford

Coppola often uses panning dolly shots. Like Martin Scorsese, I love to use the steadycam because it allows me to follow the actors from room to room and pick up dialogue on the move.

Each director has his own technical preferences as well as different ideas about how to run a set. There's an accepted way to type a screenplay, a proper way to load the film into the camera, and some unwritten law that says the actors get to eat lunch before the extras, but there's no right or wrong way to run a set.

Some directors discuss the entire script at length with their stars, but Woody Allen sometimes gives actors only the pages for the scenes in which they will appear. Some directors like to maintain a distance from their actors while my sister Penny invites them over to her house for parties on the weekend, and Francis Ford Coppola likes to make them pasta. With comedy, I've found the most productive way to run a set is to go with the flow because it's often the spontaneous and unexpected moments in front of and behind the camera that later become the highlights of your movie.

One day on the set of *Pretty Woman*, Julia showed up for work exhausted—the result of a late-night quarrel with her boyfriend. Usually Julia was the consummate professional, but this was one of the few days when her personal life was out of whack with our production schedule. I told her to do the best she could and we'd try to help her out. A little makeup, a little coffee from the truck, and she would be as good as new.

But she was dragging and seemed quite willing to trade in her entire acting career for a one-hour nap. In one corner, we had an alert Richard dressed in a tuxedo looking very dashing and in the other corner we had Julia, dressed in the soon to become famous red dress, falling asleep. Not exactly the right ingredients for a memorable, romantic scene.

Budget problems dictated that I had no choice but to stick to my schedule. It was the day we shot the scene in which Edward gives Vivian a beautiful, expensive necklace and matching earrings to wear for their evening at the opera. It also was an unusual day because a security guard from Fred's jewelers had accompanied the necklace and earrings, valued at $25,000, to the set and was standing next to me during the scene. I normally don't allow visitors on my set but in this case the deal was no guard no jewelry.

When we started to film the scene, I noticed that the guard began to yawn. Suddenly, I started directing the whole scene just to please the guard.

I took Richard aside and quietly told him that when Julia looked at the necklace again and reached out to touch it in the box, he should snap the soft velvet box closed on her hand as a joke. I thought that at the very least this would wake up Julia and possibly result in an amusing addition to our gag reel. I yelled "Action!" and waited to see what would happen.

When Richard snapped the box, Julia was so surprised that she threw her head back and burst out laughing. It was a lovely, big honest laugh without any inhibition. The stunt not only woke up Julia, but also made the security guard laugh, and gave us a charming moment I ended up leaving in the movie. You can't rehearse comedy too much or it gets flat and the actors get bored. Flat comedy and bored actors do not make a hit.

After eight movies, word has gotten around that crew members who work on my pictures should expect pranks, and if possible to bring some along.

In *Pretty Woman*, as we began to shoot the first bathtub sequence, Julia was feeling pretty uneasy and it was completely understandable. She was a beautiful twenty-one-year-old girl sitting naked in a bathtub surrounded by a dozen big sweaty crew members. Sure there were bubbles in the tub, but bubbles aren't much comfort when there's a big guy with a tattoo on his arm holding a light above your head and saying, "Honey, lean forward a little and push the bubbles up. We can see your boobs." Short of putting Julia in a wet suit, I knew I had to think of something to calm her down.

First, I started a rumor that we were going to put goldfish in the tub. However, this tactic only seemed to make Julia more nervous as she looked for bits of orange beneath the bubbles. It was clear I had to move on to plan B. In the scene, she was supposed to go under the water, then pop up, excited by Richard's offer to pay her three thousand dollars for sex. During a break, I secretly told the crew that the next time Julia went under the water, everyone, from the camera crew to Richard, was to leave the set. A few minutes later, Julia went under and we split. We all scurried out of her sight line and hid wherever we could. She popped up and was startled to see that she was alone. For the rest of the day, Julia was completely at ease with the nudity because she was too busy trying to anticipate our next prank.

When we began shooting *Frankie and Johnny*, Al Pacino was very intense. He often would request up to fifteen takes to get a scene right, and usually just as we were getting tired, he would hypnotize us with a brilliant piece of acting. I think Al is one of the great talents in our industry, but he's very serious and at the start of our movie he was particularly somber. He had been shooting several heavy dramatic movies back to back, but my crew wasn't going to let him remain serious for long. One day we were shooting a scene on the set of a ladies room at a bowling alley, and Al became distracted by his own reflection in a medium-size mirror on the wall. He came bursting through the closed door, started to perform, and suddenly went "Oooooh . . . ahhh!"

I yelled "Cut."

"What's with the 'Oooooh, ahhh'?" I asked.

"Garry, I saw myself in the mirror."

Not sure what to say, I said, "So, how'd you look?"

"No. No. You don't understand. It throws me off. I can't have that mirror."

He asked me to replace the mirror with a smaller version so his attention wouldn't be diverted. I told the cast to take a break while we fixed the problem.

Since Al had asked for a smaller mirror, I asked the crew to bring me the most gigantic mirror they could find. It's unbelievable how fast a prank can improve the speed of a crew. When I called for the big mirror, men who hadn't moved in three days leaped to their feet and initiated the search. The winner was a ten-foot mirror that covered the entire wall of the set. When we had it securely in place, we called the cast back in. Michelle Pfeiffer came on the set first and was easily persuaded to go along with the gag. Al took his place behind the closed bathroom door for his entrance.

"Action!"

Al burst through the door and launched into his speech.

"Of course I don't know you. You don't know me either. We got off to a great start. Why do you want to stop? Woooo!" Al screamed, taken aback.

He's such a disciplined actor that he was able to recite several lines of his speech flawlessly before he looked up and saw the gigantic mirror. And then he laughed.

This wouldn't be the end for Al. His no-nonsense attitude made him an easy target for more practical jokes.

We were shooting a scene—eventually cut from the movie—in which Al's character returns to his apartment and is surprised to find some old friends from prison in his room. We were shooting very late on the Paramount lot and everyone was getting a little groggy. I sensed that both cast and crew needed a little pick-me-up other than the usual supply of bagels and granola. During a break I went to the sound stage next door where they were shooting one of the *Star Trek* movies. I talked to the actors about coming over to our set for a visit and they were game.

Around midnight we were still shooting the same scene, and Al burst through the apartment door for the umpteenth time. But instead of finding our two actors, he found William Shatner, Leonard Nimoy, and DeForest Kelley fully dressed in their *Star Trek* garb. Al broke up and everybody met his *Star Trek* favorites. For the rest of the film, every time Al came through a door he had a suspicious look on his face, never knowing what was on the other side.

Not everyone likes the way I work, and not everyone wants to join the party. On *Nothing in Common*, John Alonzo was the director of photography and for most of the shoot he thought I was crazy. He not only rolled his eyes; he even slapped his head in disbelief on occasion. John, a civilized, cultured man who liked to play opera music while we were setting up a shot, had worked on such legendary films as *Chinatown* and *Norma Rae*. He was a brilliant cinematographer, with far more experience than me, and one of the best hand-held camera operators I've ever seen anywhere.

However, he thought my directing methods were completely

inappropriate, and he found my pranks a waste of time. He thought stars should be treated like Hollywood royalty as in the old days. But many stars today truly aren't as composed and professional and under studio contracts like in the old days. It's the nineties and we're dealing with stars who have shrinks, gurus, psychics, and relatives and some who take drugs to balance themselves but often end up throwing everyone else off balance. The truth is that there are a few stars who are just one taco short of a combo platter. The director's job is to deal with it all.

Whenever something would go wrong on the set of *Nothing in Common*, John immediately wanted to assign blame to the appropriate party. I would take the blame, the same as I had done in TV, just to end the discussion. Gleason, however, called me on it one day.

"Garry, it can't *always* be your fault," Gleason said.

The next day Gleason brought a big chalkboard onto the set and became the arbiter of all on-set disputes. If a problem was my fault Gleason would put a check under my name, or if he determined that someone else—like the propman, the scriptwoman, or John—was to blame, then he would put a check under their name. The arrangement looked like Ralph Kramden as the host of a new quiz show titled *Who's to Blame?* but it got us through the movie.

The less than perfect experience on *Nothing in Common* made me realize an important lesson about directing: Choose your cinematographer wisely. Don't hire the one with the longest list of movie credits. Don't take the one with the most impressive education. Work with the one you get along with best. A director's alliance with a cinematographer is one of the most crucial on a film. You can dream all you want about clever shots and tricky angles, but unless you can communicate your vision to the cinematographer, it's not going to get on film. If you hire a cinematographer who differs somehow from you philosophically, then the crew will sometimes split: Half the crew will listen to you and the other half, particularly the camera operator, will listen to the cinematographer.

I found a cinematographer on *Beaches* who I could really communicate well with, but there was one slight catch: He didn't speak English. Well, let's just say he didn't speak it great, but that didn't matter. Italian-born Dante Spinotti finally understood the way I worked. Our relationship was based on images — *and* guttural sounds and mutual mumbling.

When I wanted a shot, I would say, "Over here . . . hmmmm . . ." "I want her by the thing here . . . ahhhhh . . ." "With the sun coming up over that there . . . mmmmmm."

Dante would nod and mumble something back, usually in Italian, but we understood each other perfectly. We didn't need words.

While Dante and I worked well together on *Beaches* for Disney, things didn't go as smoothly on *Frankie and Johnny,* which I did for Paramount. Throughout the shoot studio executives hounded me because they thought Dante was too slow. Almost every day I'd get a note or a phone call from Paramount requesting that I fire him.

On *Beaches* nobody complained about his pace because Bette and Barbara took so long in hair and makeup that they made Dante look fast. But on *Frankie and Johnny,* we had Michelle using understated makeup and straight hair, and Al, whose cosmetic preparation consisted of running his fingers through his hair. Al and Michelle were always ready and Dante would still be setting up a shot. This gave the illusion that we were behind schedule, so every day I had to protect Dante from the studio. Dealing with the studio was easier since the influential ICM was now my agent and I had more clout. I defended Dante because we worked so well together; communication and talent are more important than speed to me. Of course, the irony is that when the movie was finished, those same Paramount executives who had tried to fire Dante said of *Frankie and Johnny,* "It's our prettiest film of the year!"

After I found Dante, I looked for an art director who I could click with. This is an important job to fill because my sense of color is about as bad as my sense of wardrobe; the only time I felt truly comfortable was in the army, when they told me what to wear and all the khaki matched. I hired Albert Brenner to be art director on *Beaches.* There are some art directors known for their elaborate high-priced sets, but Albert is not one of them. Albert is a great trickster and that's why we got along so well. Whenever it seemed like something couldn't be done, Albert would make it happen, and make it happen cheaply. During *Beaches*, we were scheduled to shoot a scene inside Bergdorf Goodman's perfume department, but at the last minute our deal with the store fell through. Albert said, "Don't worry. I'll build it for you." Pressed for time and money, he built a set that was so beautiful even the most loyal Bergdorf Goodman shoppers were convinced.

For *Pretty Woman*, I wanted to fly to San Francisco to shoot Edward and Vivian's big night at the opera at the famous War Memorial Opera House. I thought the scene deserved the extra money it would cost to go on location. However, my crew wasn't exactly rushing to travel north: We were nearing the end of the shoot, many people were getting weary, and some of the producers thought it would cost too much. Then San Francisco had a huge earthquake, and our shoot there was postponed indefinitely. Various people came up to me with alternatives: "Can we shoot it in L.A. and make it look like San Francisco?" Brilliant ideas like "Can the characters go to a movie instead?" or "Can Edward and Vivian stay home and watch an opera videotape?"

The image of Edward and Vivian watching Verdi's *La Traviata* on a VCR didn't exactly appeal to me. Originally the script called for them to be watching Verdi's *Aïda*, but that opera had elephants. Animals scare me and, thank God, elephants turned out to be too large and too expensive for the scene anyway. So we changed it to Puccini's *La Bohème*. While it was cheap (three people, two old chairs, and a battered table), it was too depressing for our scene, so we switched the opera to *La Traviata* minus the ballroom scene with hundreds of extras.

Once we had our opera nailed down, we had to worry about the set. It cost too much to get three hundred or four hundred extras to re-create an audience, so Albert hung a row of box seats from the side of a sound stage wall. Then all we needed were about eight extras to fill them. In all of my movies I always have my heroes arrive late to an event, or leave early. This way the rest of the audience is already sitting down and you don't need to hire extras, and no one is ever in the lobby except the stars and one lovely usher. In addition, during the opera scene we kept the camera moving around so you couldn't see how small our set really was. Albert the magician had come through.

When I first worked with Albert, I was too afraid to speak up in our production meetings. I was worried that I didn't know enough about design to contribute anything intelligent. Some directors are able to sit down with an art director and say things like "Put the Audubon prints here and the faux Louis XV chair there." I say things like "Put the fancy bird pictures here and the pricey chair over there."

But slowly, the more I learned, the more Albert encouraged me to speak up. We chose the "pointing" method of communication. He gave me pictures and I would point at the ones I liked. On *Beaches* he taught me how we could use different color schemes to express the various phases of the movie: pastels for youth, grays for tough times, reds and golds for success, and muted sunset colors for illness. Albert showed me how art could be used to carry a story.

Sometimes, however, I get a little lazy in the communication department. When I'm working I'm usually in such a hurry that I don't always take the time to speak in well-thought-out sentences with precise vocabulary. Instead I rely on a crude form of shorthand to get my point across. During *Exit to Eden*, we flew to London to score the movie with the composer Patrick Doyle. When we were in the recording studio, Patrick explained to me how the harp adagios would be used in the film. As we started recording, I began blurting out suggestions like "I love that. Give me some more of that harp shit." A less experienced composer might have looked at me with disdain, but Patrick understood. He wrote down on his pad, "More harp shit." Next time I remembered the word "adagio."

I now become cranky when I can't get my special people on a movie. Whether it is Dante, Albert, my favorite first assistant director Ellen Schwartz, or my favorite second assistant director Bettiann Fishman, working with friendly faces makes me feel more comfortable and cuts down on the time it takes to get to know someone new. It's exciting to work with new people, but usually it takes so much longer to find your way.

Like television, film also attracts a variety of producers but in the movies there's a different producer lineup: a creative one, like Alexandra Rose, who might have brought the script to the studio and can sit and nurture the writer; a technical expert, who knows how to mount a production and oversee finances, like Robert Greenhut and Marty Katz; the star's producer, who often heads the star's independent production company, like Bonnie Bruckheimer; and maybe one other producer, who handles foreign distribution and mostly shows up for the cast party and premiere. Sometimes you might also have a packaging producer, like Ray Stark or Scott Rudin, who puts the entire package together. I always hope for at least one producer who will protect me from the studio. Now you know why there are so many people running around Hollywood with the title of producer.

On *The Flamingo Kid*, I worked with Michael Phillips, a producer who did protect me. He knew it was only my second film and that I was still a little green. One day I shot a scene inside a tennis shack. When I thought we were done, I told the crew that it was time to move on. They packed up the equipment (boxes full of heavy cables, lenses, and monitors) and were halfway over to the next set before I realized I had missed an angle at the tennis shack. I took Michael aside.

"Michael," I whispered, "I missed a shot."

"Do you really need it?"

"Yes."

Then Michael announced to the crew, "Okay, everybody, let's go back to the tennis shack. It's my mistake. I need another shot."

He didn't let me humiliate myself in front of the crew. We went back to the shack, I got my shot, and then we were ready to move on. Unfortunately, because Michael can't be there to protect me on every film, I now train my crew to count to ten very slowly before moving on to the next set. This gives me time to change my mind.

My shortest movie shoot lasted fifty days on *Young Doctors in Love* and my longest was seventy-four days on *Frankie and Johnny*. The length of your shoot is determined by the intricacy of your story and how fast you can get it on film. A crew, sometimes made up of more than one hundred people, can lend you support and help speed the process along. But when you're in a crunch, the only one you can really depend on is yourself.

I was directing my first film, *Young Doctors in Love*, and I got to a point a few weeks into the shoot when I knew I was losing everyone. The crew thought I was some incompetent director from the moon and couldn't quite figure out why anyone had put me in charge of a big-budget movie. The consensus seemed to be that I was a television hot shot who had no business directing a film: "He might know how to turn an alien and a hoodlum into stars, but he doesn't know anything about movies." I finished staging a shot one day and turned to my cinematographer, Don Peterman.

"What do you think?" I asked. "How does it look?"

"It looks like the living room of *Happy Days*," Don said with a smile.

I knew I needed to somehow gain the crew's respect and I needed to do it fast. We were scheduled to shoot several scenes outside, but suddenly, despite the weather forecast for another beautiful southern California day, it rained. We had to move to our cover set (an indoor backup set used in case of rain). Unfortunately, only half of that set was built; we would have to shoot in only one direction. We rehearsed the scene and it was very dull. The prospect of shooting a dull scene on half a set did little to excite the cast or crew. Everything was falling apart and the crew was looking at me to lead them.

I took a break and went for a walk. I wanted desperately to show my crew that I was a filmmaker, but what could I do? Shoot something magical through a glass window? Something shocking? Something profound? What kind of shot could I do to make them see that I was a filmmaker? A high shot with a crane through the ceiling? I thought about rewriting the whole scene, but I didn't have time. Suddenly it hit me. The truth was I *wasn't* a filmmaker. At least not yet. I realized that instead of stretching to try to do something I was uncertain about, I had to stick with what I knew best—comedy.

The scene involved several doctors talking in the hospital locker room about a broken romance. I asked for the cinematographer to get me the widest camera lens available. "Seventeen?"

he said. "Sure, whatever." I didn't even know the numbers or names of the lenses yet. I just said, "Get me something wide." I told him to point the lens straight ahead, and "Don't move it during the entire scene."

I let a group of doctors sit in the foreground (because there was no room on the set to stand) and told them to recite their lines as written, no matter what else happened. In the background I had a phone attached to the wall. Then I worked out a routine with actor Gary Friedkin, a person about three feet tall, who was playing the role of Dr. Milton Chamberlain. In the scene the phone rings, a doctor answers it, and then calls Milton away from the group. Milton takes the receiver, has a brief conversation, then goes to hang up the phone. But he discovers that he can't reach the hook to hang up the receiver because it's too high.

He jumps as high as he can and fails to hang up the phone. He runs off stage left and takes a running leap and fails. He runs off stage right and takes another flying leap and fails again. He disappears and comes back pulling himself along the wall while perched on top of a hospital gurney. When Milton finally reaches the phone, he triumphantly slam dunks the receiver. The doctors in the foreground are oblivious to all of this; only the audience is in on it. All it took was one take.

I then heard whispers from the crew, "Oh, *that's* what Garry does. He makes up little bits for the actors to do . . . The man knows nothing about filmmaking, but look what he just did. He took a phone and he made an entire dull scene funny." With that one scene I showed the crew that I might not be well versed in the mechanics of directing, but I knew about comedy. For the rest of the shoot whenever I tripped over a technical question, I could always find a member of the crew who was willing to point me toward the answer. I still think the phone scene in *Young Doctors in Love* is one of the funniest I've ever shot.

Many people who aren't in show business have no idea what a director does, and many people in show business view directing as this incredibly creative process like painting or sculpting. But trust me, it's not all creative. A lot of a director's job involves dealing with contracts, permits, injuries, mood swings, and banal problem solving. We were filming *Nothing in Common* on location in Chicago one day when the weather reached 103 degrees in the shade. It was one of those hot and humid days when all you want to do is put your head in a bowl of ice cubes. When you shoot a movie in the Midwest during the summer, the weather is almost a supporting character. While I was busy questioning why I had ever agreed to shoot a film outside Los Angeles, my cast and crew were struggling to get the work done and stay cool. Jackie Gleason was melting as fast as a Fudgcicle. In between scenes he would go back to his air-conditioned trailer for some relief. Then disaster struck.

Around midday, I got word that the air-conditioning in Gleason's trailer had broken down. This is one of the hazards of directing: Just when you're in the middle of a thought about a particularly artistic shot, someone in the crew confronts you with a problem about air-conditioning. (Did Kazan and Fellini have to worry about things like this? Yes.) The air conditioner was broken and my star was sweating. To hell with art. I had to take charge of air-conditioning. Part of getting a performance out of an actor is learning how to guide them as far away from the word "irritated" as possible. Gleason said he wanted a new trailer right away. A quick check found that it would take several hours to track down a new one. The Great One was not a happy camper. I had to find another solution.

"Hey, give him my trailer," Tom Hanks said.

Besides being a nice guy, Tom was not one of those actors who used his trailer like a bear uses a cave in winter. Tom didn't really care much about his trailer. He preferred to spend time in between scenes throwing a ball around with the crew. So I said, "Why not?"

I went to talk with Gleason, who sat stoically in the dead air of his Winnebago.

"Jackie, can we give you Tom's trailer just for today?" I asked. "He said he doesn't need it."

"No, I don't want to take the kid's trailer. He'll be a star someday. That's not the way things work," he said, offended by the mere suggestion.

This was going to be more difficult than I'd thought. The only way out was to try to make Gleason believe that Tom's trailer was a new one. Normally I don't lie to actors, but in this case the heat drove me to it, and Tom said to give it a shot so we could continue filming. I enlisted some of the prop guys to paint over Tom's name and number on the door of his trailer. The two trailers were parked on different streets, so I asked one of the Teamsters to drive Tom's trailer around the block. A few minutes later he came barreling around the corner and announced, "I have a new air-conditioned trailer for Mr. Gleason!" Jackie was happy. Tom was happy. And we could all go back to work.

When I'm not waging battles against appliances, I'm fighting with the studio over rehearsal time. Most studio executives lie to you. They promise you weeks of rehearsal time but it never happens. This period is limited in television but you have an advantage because the actors know their characters so well. If we were running behind on *Happy Days* and ran short on rehearsal time, Ron Howard didn't say, "Oh, I just need a little more time to get the character of Richie Cunningham down." After the first season, he just did it. I thought when I moved over to film I would have plenty of rehearsal time, but I was wrong.

You think you have rehearsal time but then the wardrobe staff takes your stars for fittings. Then the makeup people borrow them to check out their coloring. Then the hairdressers steal them to see what looks better, a bob or a crew cut. Then the publicity mavens lure them away for photographs. When it comes down to it, if you want to get any quality rehearsal time at all, you've got to make the time yourself.

On *Frankie and Johnny*, a film with more dialogue than most, I rehearsed with Michelle and Al on the weekends. It was the only time when the three of us could escape. We'd meet at one of our homes; we went to Al's place the most because he had the best food and a personal chef. We shot for twelve weeks and ten of those weeks we rehearsed on Saturdays, occasionally on Sundays. At first, we just read the script aloud. Then, eventually, when they felt more comfortable with the words, I got them on their feet to rehearse.

With Michelle and Al, I used a "circle" rehearsal technique

that the Steppenwolf Theatre company had taught me while I was directing *Wrong Turn at Lungfish* in Chicago. Film directors should jump at any chance to direct a play because it can improve their relationship with actors. What's wonderful about the theater is that you get to move the actors around and stage scenes. You don't have to worry about things like flattering closeups or intricate lighting. Theater features an actor from the top of his head to his toes while television is just from the waist up and movies concentrate on the face and eyes. Directing a play gives you a chance to move the whole body around.

In my mind I would draw an imaginary circle around Michelle's and Al's feet. Then I moved the actors around by shifting their circles. I never got inside either circle to interrupt them with an acting note yet, but simply pushed the circles around. If Michelle said a line too quickly, I didn't say, "You're saying that line too harsh or too wimpy." That's too intrusive for a rehearsal. I stayed back and just moved the circles around the set, letting them become familiar with the material.

You hear a lot about actors fighting with directors, and most of the fights occur when a director or a producer enters the circle before the actor is ready. He gets in the actor's face too early. When an actor rehearses a scene, any idiot can tell him ten million things to do. Don't do it. He's not ready. Just move the circles. Eventually, when the actor becomes more comfortable with the material, then you can say, "Too fast." "Too slow." "Louder." "Softer." "This is not very honest." "This line doesn't seem to fit in your mouth. How can we make it more comfortable?" This is the time when the director can step inside the actor's circle.

If you try to talk with an actor before he's ready, he won't hear your words. He'll only hear your tone (usually as rejection) and get defensive. Psychologists say that when a parent is talking with a teenager, the child only hears the first ninety seconds of a conversation and then turns off. This also is a good approach to consider when working with an actor. So try not to get in an actor's face too early, and when you do, your best bet is to say your important information within the first ninety seconds!

•   •   •

A director always has to be on the lookout for things that can hurt his production. Pay attention to some of the warning signs such as: Beware of the props. There's a lovely moment in Terrence McNally's play *Frankie and Johnny in the Clair de Lune* when Johnny looks out Frankie's apartment window and sees a robin. A few beats later Frankie sees the robin, too. In the play, this scene signifies the couple's new life together. To capture the moment on film, we built the interior of an apartment with windows looking onto an adjacent fire escape, and I asked the propmen to order a robin. However, as it turns out, if you bring a robin onto a set or into captivity, it dies. I imagined a tabloid headline: DIRECTOR OF PRETTY WOMAN KILLS BIRD ON SET OF NEW FILM! PACINO AND PFEIFFER STAND BY HORRIFIED!

My crew said, "Garry, don't worry. We're going to *make* you a robin instead." And they did. There was only one catch: The bird cost close to fifteen thousand dollars, which was well beyond what we had initially budgeted for birds. Still, nobody wants to see lovers look out a window and see a dead bird or even a motionless stuffed bird. So I said, "Go ahead. Build me a bird."

They took a stuffed robin and built an elaborate mechanical device inside it so the bird could move. However, with all of the moving parts and wires, the robin turned into a gigantic killer bird rather than the small, feathered friend it was supposed to be. Instead of a prop, it looked more like one of the stars from a horror film called *The Robin Who Ate Frankie and Johnny*. I don't direct scary movies, so I sent the prop department back to the drawing board. For fifteen thousand dollars, I wanted a bird that wasn't going to make the audience cover their eyes in fear.

The propmen came back with a smaller mechanical robin whose head swiveled from side to side. It could even bend down and pick up a magnetic worm. Not exactly something that could pass for one of David Letterman's stupid pet tricks, but I thought it was acceptable. We placed the bird in a tree outside the window and tried the scene with the actors. Al was supposed to walk over to the window and say, "Look, a robin."

I yelled, "Action!"

Al walked over and said, "Look . . . a robot!"

While we applauded the fact that Al had finally gotten the hang of pranks, it was clear to everyone that the mechanical bird was over the top. So it turned out that one of the differences between the play and the movie version of *Frankie and Johnny* is that there's no robin in the film. It took fifteen thousand dollars and several bizarre dead mechanical birds for us to figure this out, but in the end we learned that sometimes the imagination can be more effective than a prop. Al and Michelle "acted" a bird out their window.

Sometimes no matter what the script says, a set can dictate the approach to a scene. The script of *Overboard* called for Dean, a carpenter played by Kurt Russell, to build a closet for Joanna, an heiress played by Goldie Hawn. We wanted the closet to include some custom-made features like shoe boxes and drawers and other accessories that a wealthy woman might have in her home, only in this case it was on her yacht. The set designers got a little excited and ended up making the closet so elaborate that the bill came in at close to ten thousand dollars. And the costume designer felt compelled to fill the closet with lots of fancy dresses, shoes, and hats, which only increased the closet's price tag. But from a directing standpoint the closet worked for the story, so I didn't make a big deal out of it.

When MGM got the bill for the closet, however, they made a big deal about it.

"Ten thousand dollars for a closet? It better be in a sensational scene."

"No, not really," I said. "It's actually just a small scene in the beginning."

"Well, then *make* it a big scene. For ten grand we want to get a nice long look at that damn closet."

We had to go back and rewrite the script so the closet was the center of the scene. We added a long sequence of Dean proudly showing Joanna her new shoe racks. In keeping with her character, Joanna found fault with his work and the scene led to a pivotal moment in the movie when she throws his tools overboard. In the end, the closet and the scene were an asset to the movie. And wealthy women across America dialed up carpenters and said they wanted a closet like the one in *Overboard*. Not bad for one over-the-top closet.

When you work with the art department sometimes you win, as with this closet, and sometimes you lose, as I did with a foot in *Nothing in Common.* In the movie, Jackie Gleason's character is sick and we needed to show the audience just how sick he was and do it quickly. We created a moment in which Tom Hanks reaches down to put a slipper on his father's foot and sees for the first time how severe his father's condition is: A loss of circulation has already turned his toes and foot green. We filmed the scene and then planned to insert a shot of an artificial gangrene foot later.

The art department made a foot, which I thought was quite effective. We shot it and placed the insert in the scene. I didn't hold the camera on it for very long, but according to our producer, Ray Stark, he thought the shot cost us about $10 million at the box office. Before our final cut, Ray had tried to convince me to cut the foot out of the movie, but I was adamant about keeping it in because I thought it showed the drama of the situation. I didn't anticipate that some people in the audience would be turned off by seeing a gangrenous foot ten feet tall on the big screen. I thought they would just accept it as part of the story. Apparently, some of them told their friends, "Don't see that movie. It's got a big, ugly foot."

I never forgot that and later it influenced a decision I made on the *Frankie and Johnny* set. In a tender moment, Frankie tells Johnny about a scar on her scalp that she got from an old, abusive boyfriend. There was some debate on the set about whether I should shoot an insert of the scar. "No way," I said. "I lost ten million dollars over a foot. I'm not going to risk that on a scalp, too." You can mix comedy and drama, but blending in some gross reality is going too far. Sometimes it's better to let the actors "act" the foot or the scar instead of showing the inserts.

My overall approach to hiring crew members is to select people who aren't afraid to make fun of me. I figure if I'm kidding around with the cast and crew, there should at least be a few people on the set who can keep me in line. The crew of *Frankie and Johnny* became quite adept at it. In the film neither of the main characters, Frankie nor Johnny, has a last name. That was the way Terrence wrote the play, and that was the way he wrote the screenplay. It was his preference and I was determined to keep it that way. One day the propman and a sign painter came to me with a question.

"What's Frankie's last name?" asked the propman.

"She doesn't have one," I said.

"Come on . . . " props said impatiently.

"It's the truth," I said. "She doesn't have a last name."

"She has to have a last name," said the sign painter. "It says right here in the script, 'Johnny goes to Frankie's apartment and rings the doorbell.' Garry, on that doorbell *there has to be a last name.*"

They were worried about their jobs, but I wasn't budging.

"No last name," I said.

"But Garry, Johnny comes to the door. He rings the bell and there's got to be a last name on the buzzer," said the propman.

It was beginning to sound like an Abbott and Costello routine.

"No. You guys just don't get it," I said. "It's supposed to be *poetic*. People don't have last names in poetry."

Later that day, we shot the scene. Al walked up to a row of mailboxes, went to press a buzzer, and started laughing. I walked onto the set to see what was going on. It wasn't like Al to lose his concentration. I took a look for myself. In big bold letters, the name above the doorbell read FRANKIE POETIC. Further along in the shoot when we introduced a customer in the diner named Mr. DeLeon, the propman said, "Thank God, finally somebody with a last name."

Chapter Eleven

Riding out the Day-to-Day Storms of Making a Movie Without Drowning

Filmmaking Is Not a Democracy

In most cases people don't go to the movies just to see beautiful costumes, elaborate sets, or well-applied makeup. While all those things are important, moviegoers pay money to hear and see someone tell them a story. The story is critical, and a director has to keep that in mind every day on a film shoot. It's not surprising that many writers make good directors because they've had experience as storytellers. Directors like Nora Ephron, David Mamet, James Brooks, and Blake Edwards were all writers before they became directors and they're still telling stories. In television, I told my stories in a half-hour format. When I started directing movies, I had to adjust my timing to fit the new length; but whether it was a half hour or a two-hour feature movie, it was still a story. If you can't tell a good story, even an oblique one, then don't even sit in the director's chair.

There are many kinds of stories. There are hardware pictures (which rely on props and special effects), external action adventures (with lots of running, jumping, and "You wait here," "You go over there" dialogue), internal dramas (involving cerebral, emotional, or psychological relationships), zany comedies (with kids or pets), fantasies (sometimes with animation), and love stories, one hopes with actors who you want to see kiss. There are very few family movies anymore because our society has ruled that once children reach the age of twelve they wouldn't be caught dead in a theater with their parents.

Being a good storyteller requires telling the story the way you want it told. There will always be someone who disagrees with the way you're telling the story. In *The Flamingo Kid*, there's a scene in which Jeffrey (Matt Dillon) says good-bye to his girlfriend, Carla (Janet Jones). The scene comes at the end of the summer when she has to go back to California. I wanted to make sure the audience understood that the girl left and that she wasn't coming back. She didn't change her mind. She didn't decide to stay. She's not going to surprise him and show up. Girl gone.

To make my point, I followed the good-bye scene between Jeffrey and Carla with a shot of an airplane taking off. When I called for the shot, my editors rolled their eyes and expressed their disappointment. "Garry, a plane taking off? Come on. That's so cliché." It was cliché, but I knew the audience would need it. During preview screenings we had shown the movie without the airplane shot, and many people wrote on their comment cards, "Where did the girl go?"

Unless the audience saw Carla's plane take off, there was still the remote chance that she could come back. Why? Because man is an emotional animal who always believes the girl or the boy will come back. A male zebra leaves a female zebra and all the other zebras know he's gone, including her. But humans always think that maybe they'll get back together. The phrase "out of sight, out of mind" was probably written for zebras because human audiences want to know what happened to the love interest. By inserting the shot of the plane in *The Flamingo Kid*, we were symbolically saying that the summer was over, and so was their relationship. The end of *Casablanca* wasn't played at a bus stop but at an airport so Ingrid Bergman couldn't just turn around and come back. The director was saying, "That's it. She's gone."

For the sake of the story, you never want to mislead the audience, unless it's intentional, a method Jackie Gleason used to call the Wild Turkey theory. If a guy walks into a bar and says, "I'd like a scotch and water, please," that's a straight line and if you follow it with a joke or some crucial plot information, the audience will be able to *hear it*. However, if a guy walks into a bar and says, "I'd like a Wild Turkey, please," the audience won't be able to hear the next few lines because they'll be thinking, "A Wild Turkey? What a strange drink. I wonder why he ordered that?" I feel a director should lead rather than manipulate the audience in the right direction. If a Wild Turkey is key to the character or plot, then leave it in. But if the line is only a setup, then change it to something more pedestrian so it won't stir the audience's interest unnecessarily.

You make choices every day as to how you want to tell your story, and very often it all comes down to my favorite—the banana theory. If a man is walking down the street and there's a banana peel up ahead, as a director you have two choices: You can either show the banana peel and then show him slip on it or you can show him slip, and then see that he fell on the banana peel. There's no right answer. You either let the audience in on the gag or reveal it to them later as a surprise. The point is to choose the shot that will help you tell your story best.

It also depends on who's walking. If it's Tom Hanks or Robin Williams, the walk will be funny, so you can show the banana later or maybe not cut to it at all. However, with other actors, you might cut to the banana first and then show the slip. With bad actors, I suggest you cut to the banana *fast*!

I almost lost sight of my story with *Pretty Woman*. We had already shot the scene in The Rex restaurant where Edward takes Vivian to a business dinner. Several executives at Disney and producers on the film told me that the scene's business discussion about a hostile takeover plan wasn't close to being clear or making sense. We agreed that I should reshoot the scene, and a writer was brought in to rewrite and clarify the business deal. To do that it would cost ten thousand dollars to rent the restaurant for one day and another hundred thousand dollars to cover the day's cost for the actors, crew, and writer. We were all set to go but a few days before the reshoot, I had second thoughts.

I realized that my story wasn't about the business deal. It was about the girl, Vivian. I felt I was right, but I needed to bounce my idea off someone else just to make sure. Here I was, a director about to turn down one hundred thousand dollars to shoot more film. I went right to the top, to Jeffrey Katzenberg. I showed him the scene and asked for his opinion. I told him I was more than willing to reshoot the scene, but I had a feeling that the audience wasn't even going to hear the business discussion.

Jeffrey agreed with me. He said the audience wouldn't be on the edge of their seats trying to follow the financial discussion, but would be waiting to see if Vivian used the right fork in the fancy restaurant. So I edited the scene to make Vivian the center of attention and let the business discussion carry on in the background. After I recut the scene, Vivian popped off the screen. It turned out to be one of the funniest and most pivotal scenes in the film because that's when the audience really falls in love with Vivian for the first time. She freezes her mouth on sorbet, flips a snail into the air, and you love her and Edward loves her.

The point of the scene was that rich people can get away with anything. When she accidentally threw the snail into the air, the waiter didn't just throw her out of the restaurant. Instead he said, "It happens all the time." If you're ever in trouble with a scene and you can't figure out what's wrong, ask yourself, "Is this scene helping me tell my story or enhance my character?"

The best way to protect your story is to go through the script before you start directing a movie and circle the scenes in which you need to maintain total control. I call these my gold scenes.

In *Beaches*, one of my gold scenes was the movie's opening shot, which is also the first shot of Bette's character, C. C. Bloom. The first shot of any character is an indelible image the audience will carry with them for the rest of the movie. With the opening, I wanted to show two things: First, what a big star C.C. was, and second, what an important event she was willing to give up just to be with her sick friend Hillary.

I knew I wanted Bette to be singing in an important arena, but I didn't know where. We tried to book Carnegie Hall, but it was too expensive. Someone suggested shooting the scene at a nightclub, but somehow that didn't carry enough weight. It had to be some place impressive. We needed a familiar site that would make the audience think, "Oh, if she's singing there she must be famous."

We started scouting sites closer to home and found the Hollywood Bowl. The only problem was that we didn't have enough money in the budget to fill the bowl's amphitheater, which holds eighteen thousand people. (That's too many to fill with cardboard cutouts.) I called Disney and told them my dilemma.

"No bowl," they said. "With thousands of extras, it's too expensive."

"What if I fly over it and film the real crowd at night?" I asked.

"No bowl."

A few days later I called Disney back.

"Can I buy an old shot of the bowl filled up?"

I had gone this route before. During *The Flamingo Kid* when I was short on money and desperate for a big Fourth of July fireworks finale, I bought some footage from the old *Love, American Style* TV series. To make the audience forget what a terrible shot it was, we covered it with a voice-over from the owner of the fancy beach club who had been set up to be a cheapskate: "It's time for fireworks. Everybody to the beach. The fireworks are for El Flamingo members only. Non-members, please don't look up." However, I wasn't going to get my way so easily in *Beaches*.

"No bowl," the powers at Disney said again.

Then I came up with an idea and called Jeffrey Katzenberg to run it by him.

"How about if I shoot at the bowl with nobody in it?"

"How?"

"It'll be a rehearsal. Bette rehearsing in the daytime with no audience."

Katzenberg thought for a moment, then said, "You can have the bowl."

So we got the bowl minus the horde of extras. With Bette, a small band, and a couple of stagehands, I was ready. In the film, I showed her rehearsing the opening song "Under the Boardwalk" and immediately the audience could tell that she was a successful performer. It was clear that if C. C. Bloom was willing to give up a night appearing at the Hollywood Bowl for her friend, then it must be a special friendship. I protected one of my gold scenes and kept us within the budget at the same time.

Sometimes I'm so determined to protect a scene that I go overboard to get it. In *The Flamingo Kid* one of my gold scenes was the moment when Jeffrey discovers that his mentor, Phil Brody (played by Richard Crenna), is not without his flaws. One afternoon at the beach club, Jeffrey sees that Phil is cheating at cards. This scene changes the entire direction of the film and it was critical that I got it right. I couldn't just have a club member say, "Oh look, Phil is cheating." Jeffrey had to see it with his own eyes. I created a trick: I had the shadow of a child's hula hoop form a clock on the stomach of a heavyset man, who then used his hands as the hands of the clock to show Phil the number on the cards the other players were holding. "What a good idea," I thought. "It's going to take forever to shoot it," the crew yelled. But we shot it.

Unfortunately, I devised such a clever plan that no one in our first preview audience even remotely understood how Phil was cheating. All the audience got was that Phil *was* cheating and that Jeffrey saw him cheating, but they didn't know exactly how. The whole clock bit on the guy's stomach totally missed. But to be honest, most people didn't care how. It was enough to know that Jeffrey's mentor was a phony. Sometimes you can get so wrapped up in an important scene that you forget your story. A gold scene doesn't always have to be complicated. It just has to be clear.

In most love stories, the actual lovemaking scenes are gold and to shoot them properly you need to have control of your set. The love scenes in *Pretty Woman* took place in the penthouse of the

Regent Beverly Wilshire Hotel. I had a choice: I could either shoot
the scenes in the hotel or have my crew re-create the suite on a
sound stage. I chose the sound stage because it offered me more
control. If I wanted to move a wall or pull up a carpet, a hotel
would make it difficult. It would take too long to get permission
from the hotel manager or hire a wrecking crew.

Shooting on a set offers a director more freedom to move
around with the camera and you don't have to worry about knocking over a hotel vase. The negative side is that sometimes a set
doesn't look real. To create the illusion, I relied on my cinematographer, Chuck Minsky, who lit the shot well, and the production
designer and sound crew, who hid the fact that it was just an
indoor set on a sound stage.

After shooting my share of bedroom scenes, I've discovered
that the best time to schedule a love scene is at the end of your
shoot. It's too difficult to throw two actors into bed on the first day
when they've just met. They're still saying things to each other like
"I loved your last movie" or "Do you take cream in your coffee?"
If you wait until the end of the shoot, they've had a better chance
to get to know each other and are more relaxed. Well, most of the
time. On the set of *Pretty Woman,* even at the end of the shoot,
Julia was still nervous because she had never appeared in the nude
before. Richard, on the other hand, was experienced at taking off
his clothes in movies (a reputation he didn't like).

After surviving the bubble bath scene, Julia went into the bedroom sequence feeling pretty confident. The pranks had loosened
her up and taken some of the edge off her fear. Unfortunately, her
composure didn't last for long: She broke out in a rash all over her
body. If that wasn't bad enough, when I looked through the camera
lens to check the very close two-shot of Richard and Julia in bed, I
saw that a big vein had suddenly popped out on her forehead.

"What the hell is that thing on your forehead, Julia?"

"It happens when I get nervous," she said.

"And that rash?"

"Same thing. Nerves."

"Why are you nervous?" I asked.

"Why do you think? I'm going to do a love scene with Richard
Gere in front of everybody."

We had to stop the scene. I got on the bed with Richard and Julia. Together, he and I massaged her forehead and eventually the vein disappeared. When the propman came back with some calamine lotion for the rash, we were finally able to shoot the scene. Love scenes might look glamorous on the screen, but on the set they usually end up high comedy.

Love scenes can also take a long time to shoot, even when your actors aren't nervous. In a scene from *Frankie and Johnny*, Frankie opens up her bathrobe and stands nude in front of Johnny. It was a difficult scene to shoot, with heavy dialogue and tricky lighting, but very essential because, storywise, it represented Frankie's growing trust in Johnny. We had to capture his lust, her tension, his love, and her apprehension all in scene 105 on the schedule.

The scene was seventeen pages long and we were given two weeks to shoot it. First we shot it as a silhouette, but with her robe open and arms extended Michelle looked like Batman. Then we shot it with shadows, but it made Michelle look like a black figure with a floating head. Finally we got it right when we shot it as a side two-shot with Johnny looking at her. The scene took so long to shoot that the actors started to get tired. Michelle even yawned a few times, which is not the kind of romantic response you want on film.

When we finally finished shooting, I had the sound crew play "Glory, Glory Hallelujah!" over loud speakers. Then I opened a boxful of bright red T-shirts that said I SURVIVED SCENE 105 and gave them to the cast and crew. It was easier to shoot a week on location in New York City than it was to film that one scene.

I can do many things to make actors feel more comfortable during a love scene: surround them with supportive actors, hug them if they're scared, rewrite the scene to make them feel more at ease, or plan a prank to keep their minds off the nudity. One thing I can't fix is chemistry. If two stars do not have chemistry from the beginning, it's impossible for me to generate it on screen. Chemistry isn't a magical concept that some directors see and others don't. It's the way two actors talk together. The way they kiss. The way they simply stand side by side. Richard and Julia certainly had it from the first time I saw them sitting together talking in the living room of Richard's New York apartment. I knew I didn't have to look any further because I had found my Edward and Vivian.

As much as people try, you can't force chemistry to make it work. In *Frankie and Johnny*, the press gave us a lot of flak for not casting Kathy Bates as Frankie. She had been wonderful in the stage version, but the truth was that once we hired Al Pacino, we didn't feel that the two of them had the right chemistry.

Al read with several other actresses, but it wasn't until Michelle Pfeiffer showed up unsolicited that we knew we had found Frankie. She not only had the desire to play Frankie, but also she had already demonstrated in *Scarface* that she had chemistry with Al. That's the key to making a love story work: If the two stars have chemistry, you can usually fix everything else. Some people say you can "act" chemistry, but I don't buy it. Two people can pretend to like each other, but I don't think you can fake the sexual tension you need to make a love scene pop off the screen. There's just something that happens when two people with chemistry touch each other on the screen that can make a love scene believable.

Of course, some say the best chemistry of all is the real thing. Think Hepburn and Tracy. Taylor and Burton. Thompson and Branagh. It's a director's dream to have stars with built-in chemistry. It will save you time. You can even be daring and shoot the love scenes the first day if you want to. On *Overboard* we were able to cut through the initial awkwardness that plagues many screen relationships, put Kurt and Goldie right into bed, and transfer their rapport to the screen. Unfortunately, you're not going to find many real life couples who can actually act, so when you do, film quickly or they could break up tomorrow.

Many producers feel the opposite about this theory. They feel that if the couple is married, then there's no real heat. Two strangers kissing is what an audience often likes better because they live vicariously by saying, "Look at those two make love and they never met before." Love with a stranger is still a turn-on. Which theory is true? No answer. Again, we're not dealing with an exact science.

•   •   •

When I went into directing movies, Phil Foster said, "Put a lot of things in your movies and have lots of people talking at once."

"Really?" I said.

"Yeah."

"But what if people can't follow them all?"

"So they'll come back to see the movie a second time."

Film the extras, animals, signs, cars, and anything in the background to make your movie so interesting and full of such intriguing off-beat unforgettable images that a person won't be able to catch it all the first time. Phil's advice turned out to be a good directing tip as well as sound financial advice. The big blockbusters aren't the movies that everyone sees once but the ones that everyone sees twice.

Young Doctors in Love was a movie that I hoped could do for hospitals what the satire *Airplane!* had done for flying. I planned to spoof everything from operating rooms to bed pans. What I quickly learned, however, was that this approach to directing can put you in the hospital because it's so exhausting. It was no wonder it took three men to direct *Airplane!* I could have used two more on *Young Doctors*.

While *Young Doctors* was by no means a big success, it was somewhat of a hit for my career because it showed that I could direct comedy. I gathered Michael Elias and Rich Eustis in my trailer whenever I could on *Young Doctors*, and we pitched ideas, trying to capitalize on all types of humor, including topical references. We used the hospital's public address system to make voice-over announcements during scenes:

"Your attention, please. E.T., phone home" and "Dr Pepper, please report to the diabetes ward" were a couple of the jokes that made it into the movie. We didn't call attention to them, but just let the audience overhear them.

I didn't want *Young Doctors* to be just funny or amusing. I wanted it to be wacky and zany, and this strategy paid off in Europe, where the film *was* a big success. Some European audiences might not have understood the dialogue, but they reveled in the sight gags. We put goldfish in the intravenous bags. We had candy stripers who wore tap dancing shoes and delivered medication on skateboards. We had a vital sign monitor in the operating room that displayed video games during surgery. We wanted to be irreverent, as in one of our announcements, "Attention, due to a mixup in urology, there will be no apple juice served today."

Moviegoers, particularly the twenty-something generation, are more visually sophisticated than they used to be thanks to the array of cable channels and video games. People are capable of seeing hundreds of images dance across the screen, as on MTV, and they expect their movies to be as entertaining, if not more so. A movie audience can get bored easily and anything you can do to keep them amused will help. I always tried to remember: Beware of the obvious and cultivate the obscure, except where clarity is essential. People don't want you to tell them exactly what's going on. They would rather put the pieces together for themselves.

In *Pretty Woman* we cut out a lot of dialogue that told the audience that Edward's love was changing Vivian's personality. You could see the transformation taking place by the way Julia behaved. My approach was to film her like Bambi. I wanted to show her as a little deer darting in and out of the trees so quickly that you couldn't get a clear look at her until the end of the movie. One of the ways I did this was have her be fidgety. I told Julia that she shouldn't sit down on any of the chairs during her first night in the penthouse.

"Vivian would be too uncomfortable sitting in a chair," I said. "Five minutes ago she was waiting to pick up a trick on the street and now she's in a fancy penthouse. She's out of her element. So she would sit anyplace else *but* in a chair. Show with your body language that she doesn't belong there."

Julia sat on the floor, on a table, on a desk, and anyplace she could possibly climb onto, except a chair. Later, if she had to sit in a chair, she sat in it like a six-year-old with ants in her pants. Finally, at the end of the film when she wears the elegant red dress to the opera, the audience sees her sitting correctly, in a chair, for the first time. When you can show a transformation instead of telling it, the audience feels a greater connection to the characters and has more energy invested in the outcome.

In movies, if you tell the audience too much, they say, "This is too stupid. I'm going home." However, if you tell them too little, they say, "This is too oblique. I'm going home." That's why there aren't more hits out each year: Movies slant too heavily in either direction. To make a hit, a director has to walk that fine line between "too stupid" and "too oblique."

Some directors worry about the critics and strive to make their movies innovative and artistic. Other directors focus on the marketing of the picture and try to cash in on merchandising and other tie-ins. And still other directors try to beat the competition by making a bigger and better picture with more special effects, more famous stars, and exotic locations.

I try to direct my movies as if I were sitting in a dark theater eating a box of popcorn *with* the audience. I try to think like them. If a scene gets too confusing for me or a question pops into my mind, I make sure that I answer it on screen. I don't like people in movie theaters leaning over to each other, asking, "Esther, what's that she's got in her hand?" "How did she get to Pittsburgh?" "Is that her father or her uncle?"

A director is constantly trying to second-guess the audience. In *Pretty Woman*, Vivian was a prostitute and the average viewer assumes that prostitutes do drugs. That's life. If I was watching a film about a hooker I would wonder, "Does she do drugs?" "Did she do drugs?" "Will she do drugs again?" To answer those questions, Barbara Benedek created a scene in which Edward suspects that Vivian is taking drugs. He confronts her and finds out that she is just using dental floss to take some strawberry seeds out of her teeth. A hygiene addict, not a drug addict. She confesses that she used to do drugs but stopped when she was fourteen. It was an interesting short scene that answered everybody's questions about drugs.

I ran into a similar problem with condoms. Anybody watching a modern movie about two unmarried people sleeping together for the first time is going to wonder if they used a condom. In 1989, when we made *Pretty Woman*, a director was being socially irresponsible if he told his story while ignoring the risk of AIDS and pregnancy. So in *Pretty Woman* we had the level-headed Vivian pull a potpourri of condoms out of her boot and offer Edward his choice. In this case we weren't masking the issue with dental floss; we nailed it right on the head. Vivian, the hooker, brought her own condoms. They used one. Problem solved.

When I wasn't worrying about dental floss or condoms on *Pretty Woman*, I was trying to make sure that everyone understood the story was a fairy tale. I knew it. The actors knew it. The studio knew it. We just had to make sure that the audience was aware. To do this, I started and ended the movie with a street person rapping. His tune told a tale of Hollywood as a place where people come to make their dreams come true; *Pretty Woman* is the story about one who did. Even though many people working on the movie tried to get me to take out those scenes, I fought to keep the two rap scenes in because they said, "You're watching a fairy tale and we know it. We're not pretending to be anything else." Being honest is the best way I know how to handle skepticism. Don't pretend with them. Be truthful and let the audience make its own judgment.

The film audience is quick, thanks to training from television and cable, and your actors should be, too. I like to use a few actors who can say a lot of words fast. I've often found that if a scene calls for two people to be in a room, one of them better have energy. Casting fast-talking actors also can help you cover more ground with the plot. If you've got a star who speaks slowly, you better pair him with another one who can pick up the pace. Matt Dillon talked slowly but Richard Crenna could be quick. Barbara Hershey spoke deliberately but Bette Midler could rattle off a dozen lines without taking a breath. Jackie Gleason strung out only one line in the time it took Tom Hanks to recite a page of dialogue. After the ability to act well, it's a trait that I look for on an actor's résumé: "Can say a lot of words fast with diction and honesty."

Using energetic actors is one way to fix a flat scene, but there are more. I carry around a list of scene savers that I call my "Ups":

I punch it up by adding more jokes.

I dress it up by bringing in extras.

I speed it up by cutting some of the dialogue or action.

I break it up by moving half of the dialogue to another setting.

I get the actors up and move them to find a more interesting way to stage the scene.

I mess it up by pulling a prank to make an actor more comfortable and release the crew's tension.

I score it up by adding music to enhance the dialogue or cover the dialogue completely and let the music carry it.

With so many ways to fix a scene, is there a reason for a director to knowingly shoot a bad one? Maybe not but we do. We let a less than perfect scene slide into one of my television shows at least once a month because we were pressed for time: If we didn't get the show ready, they'd put another show in our time slot, or worse, a rerun. With studio movies, when you have millions of dollars and up to a year to get it right, you should be able to find a solution. This doesn't always add up to a great movie, but at least you should know that you gave it your best in every scene.

A great asset in making a movie is getting the actors to help you. As a director, I tend to lead the actors instead of mapping out all the answers. I point. I suggest. I hint and gently nudge them in the direction I want them to go. This is the way I worked with Gleason in *Nothing in Common*. He had far more experience at everything than I did, and at first I was intimidated by his cachet. What could I possibly tell the Great One about acting that he hadn't already done or thought of or heard of before? (Particularly after he announced to the whole cast and crew that he *liked* to be called the "Great One.") Out of trepidation I decided to direct by suggestion.

In the movie, Gleason's character, Max Basner, a 1980s Willy Loman, gets fired from his job as a children's clothing salesman. This scene, shot on a ferry boat, shows how sad Max is about losing his job. We wanted to focus on Max's despair—the slim chance of his being able to get another job at his age. We were looking for something for Max to do that would be symbolic of despair, yet subtle—a gesture or a line but keep it simple. I sat down with Gleason to talk over the scene.

"So, Max is sad, right?" I said.

Gleason nodded.

"And he's probably still carrying his souvenir pens with his name on them. The ones he used to hand out to his customers, right?"

Gleason nodded.

"So, what would you want to do with the pens after you were fired?"

He was silent for a moment.

"Why don't I throw them overboard?" Gleason said.

At this point, I stood up and turned toward the crew.

"Hey, everybody, Jackie has a wonderful idea. Let's shoot it."

After we shot him throwing the pens overboard, he called to me.

Smiling, he said, "Garry, what kind of wonderful idea am I going to have tomorrow?"

He knew I was leading him and letting him be the star, but that was the way we worked. You can discover the answer together. There are no awards for who gets it first. Just get it.

There are also no gold stars for directing a movie perfectly because it can't be done. Each movie is different and you're always learning. Here is a brief list of some of the odd but useful things I have learned:

- Use whipped cream instead of soap in nude shower scenes because it doesn't make body makeup run.
- Always shoot a restaurant scene in a booth instead of at a table, which takes four times longer to light.
- Don't have a serious conversation with an actor when his agent is around.
- When shooting a scene where the actor is eating, try to frame the closeup above the plate so you won't have to match the food between shots. Trying to match a plateful of turkey, stuffing, mashed potatoes, and cranberry sauce after each take would cause even Mother Teresa to curse.
- When an actor has to clean up a floor, use a broom instead of a mop; it takes less time to clean and dry for take two.
- Unless shooting a horror film, don't use a fish-eye lens (a lens that distorts grotesquely) on a building. (I tried it on the Regent Beverly Wilshire Hotel in *Pretty Woman* and it made the hotel look like it belonged in a movie about a prostitute who gets her throat slashed.)

- Don't black out a room (seal it from light) without air-conditioning. The crew gets hot. Hot crews are lazy. Lazy crews are slow. Slow crews cost time and money.
- Remember to be careful shooting a scene where smoke is involved after August because by then it will be windy and might ruin your scene.
- Use makeup sparingly in love scenes because it rubs off and smears like a child's finger paint.
- Try not to shoot dialogue inside an airport because it's difficult to get them to turn off the public address system.
- Don't let actors walk around the set in bare feet during love scenes because their soles will get dirty and it looks cheap on film.
- Actors should only mount a movie horse from the left side because that's the way the horses have been trained. I learned this the hard way by setting up a shot from the right side and the horse trainer looked at me like I had never directed a movie before.
- Girls climbing up walls or ladders should wear pants, not skirts to avoid accidents and allow for low-angle shots.
- Always shoot at least one take of a stunt in slow motion.
- Horses can't hit camera marks like actors and cars can. Try not to let actors drive cars at all. They're usually so busy trying to hit their mark that they can't act. Tom Hanks was a great driver. Al Pacino wasn't. Don't risk it.
- At least once, shoot a phone sequence with the receiver over the actor's mouth so you can add any voice-over lines later.
- Try not to use boats in the background of scenes because it takes forever for them to turn around for the second take.
- Don't use tan costumes on pale-skinned actors because they look like beige eggs on film.

These are the little nagging aspects of filmmaking that a director can learn mostly through experience. There's one problem, however, that I personally find on every film: I hate towing car shots or inside a car scenes. They can only be described as the root canal of filmmaking. There are three kinds of towing shots: 1) You are on one truck with the equipment and the actors are on another truck with the car. 2) You let the car drive and follow it with your truck. 3) You and the car are on the same flatbed truck. In all three ways, you must have a team of policemen, usually on motorcycles, accompany you and another truck for the hair and makeup crew. With all of the logistics and time it takes to get everything in sync, a towing shot can take longer than a cross-country drive.

We shot one of our *Pretty Woman* limo scenes at four in the morning in Hollywood. During the shoot, a drunk driver who was trying to pass our caravan, side-swiped one of our police motorcycle escorts and then drove off. Of course, all the other police escorts chased the drunk driver. The cop who had been hit on the bike was all right, but suddenly there we were at four in the morning with big stars, expensive equipment, and no police escorts. By law, we had to stop shooting. Finally, after they caught the driver, they came back and we were able to resume our shoot. A director should always be ready for the unexpected to slow him up and then find a way to make up the time.

Later the same evening I had a fight with a member of the costume crew in another scene. She had outfitted Richard Gere in a suit with a vest, but when he was sitting in the limousine the vest bunched up and made him look like he had a very fat stomach. I told her it was dark in the limo and to get rid of the vest, but she refused because she said it wouldn't match the scenes we had already shot. I was exhausted and about to lose it and I said, "I don't care. Just get rid of the vest." She refused again, so I got crazy and took the vest and threw it into a lane of oncoming traffic. I considered the case closed. Early the next morning after we had finished shooting, I went to my car and found the vest tied around my side-view mirror. At least my crew had a sense of humor, but it still didn't change my opinion of towing car shots. The only good thing about inside the car shots is the actors don't necessarily have to wear pants.

One of the tools that can help a director is product placement. (I can hear you purists hissing already, but give me a chance to explain.) Product placement is the practice where companies give you money for putting their product in your film. The money goes into the movie's budget and gives the director a chance to shoot new scenes or enhance existing ones. (This is different from a McDonald's merchandising tie-in where you might buy a milk shake served in a cup carrying the logo of a film.)

I've found that if you do it right, and sparingly, product placement can be effective without being intrusive or looking like a commercial. Remember the French movie *A Man and a Woman?* Although this is one of my favorite movies, it is really a commercial for a new car. More money doesn't always make a movie better. Every production has budget constraints and product placement is one option to help you stay afloat when all else fails. When you see a Coca-Cola can in a movie, it didn't get there just by luck.

I try to tie the products I use to my story. In *Nothing in Common*, Max Basner eats Life cereal, which symbolized the movie's theme. In *Pretty Woman*, I used several cars and also made a deal with a clothing designer to supply us with some expensive suits for the extras. They sent over plenty of suits, but they were all size 42. To remedy the problem, we could either renegotiate the deal or put out a casting call for men size 42. When was the last time you were at a polo match and everyone wore the same size suit? Although the clothing company agreed to send us a new batch of suits in different sizes, a good director should always remember to ask specific questions (e.g., "What sizes will we get?") before he signs a deal.

Product placement doesn't work on every movie. But on *Frankie and Johnny*, the "above line costs" (salaries for the director, producers, writers, and stars) were so expensive that the "below line costs" (crew salaries and all production costs) accounted for a much smaller part of the budget. So I thought we could find some extra money with product placement.

There weren't many scenes in *Frankie and Johnny* that could have accommodated brand-name products. The movie was about poor blue-collar workers who lived in cheap apartments. I asked my producers, "Who's going to give me money for product placement? A company that makes meat loaf? A brand of rice pudding? A toothpaste manufacturer? Kleenex?" I did get about ten dollars from a company that made cleanser but that was about it. The bottom line on product placement is that if you can use it without being too obvious or hurting your story, then take the money.

A film is not a democracy. I repeat: A film is not a democracy. Democracy is good for a country but not a film. Never let anyone tell you differently. Someone has to be the boss and I think that to make the best movies, the director should be that boss. I've been a writer, an actor, and a producer and I still think that the director should be the boss on a movie.

In *Pretty Woman*, after Edward encourages Vivian to go on a shopping spree, she comes across a snippety and condescending saleswoman. The script called for Vivian to give the saleswoman the finger. The producers urged me to shoot the scene as written. Julia, however, thought that giving the finger was too callous and she wanted to say a line that one of the writers had given her, "It's amazing how you could have a ten-foot pole up your ass and it doesn't even show." A bit too literal perhaps, but still a sincere suggestion.

I listened, smiled, and nodded to everyone, but I had an overview of the movie. I knew that later in the movie Vivian would come back, all dressed up in her new clothes, and take her revenge on the saleswoman. If Vivian was rude the first time, then the second time wouldn't be as effective. To make my way work, in the first confrontation she had to walk out with her tail between her legs, totally devastated. This would give the audience the incentive to root for her to come back.

You're never sure, however, that you're right. What if her scene coming back later had to be cut from the movie? I ended up quickly shooting the scene three different ways: once with the finger, once with the hostile line, and once where she left with a whimper. The producers were content. Julia was happy. And I got my shot. I chose to use my version and had Vivian return later to triumph over the saleswoman.

INTERIOR SNOTTY BOUTIQUE—DAY
(Vivian enters. The SNOBBY SALESWOMEN are waiting on CUSTOMERS. Vivian approaches one of them.)

VIVIAN

Hi.
(One saleswoman looks up at her. Smiles pleasantly.
Recognizes a serious shopper.)

VIVIAN

Remember me?

SNOBBY SALESWOMAN

No, I'm sorry.

VIVIAN

I came in here the other day. You wouldn't wait on me.
(The saleswoman remembers.)

VIVIAN

You work on commission, right?
(The saleswoman nods. Vivian holds up several shopping
bags.)

VIVIAN

Big mistake. *Big. Huge.*
(She breezes out of the store.)

Audiences cheered when she got her revenge. Eleven years of
Happy Days had taught me how to make the audience root for a
character. When an audience laughs, it means that a character did
something funny. But when the audience laughs and cheers, that
means they love the character. There's a big difference.

Shooting a movie can be so intense that sometimes a director
doubts his ability. You think, "The studio is paying me all of this
money. I'm in charge of all these people and I'm really not sure
what I'm doing." The day we shot the ending to *Pretty Woman*
was my worst day on the picture. I had already decided to have my
lovers meet on a fire escape, complete with opera music playing in

the background to set the tone. However, the day we shot the scene, Julia was having trouble getting down the fire escape because of her slippery shoes and Richard was having trouble getting up without getting his suit filthy. It was not a perfect day.

I proceeded to shoot the scene eight times and each time I saw different members of the crew rolling their eyes because they thought the scene was too corny. The truth was that the crew, the producers, and even the actors weren't thrilled with the ending. I even felt a sense of doom about the scene myself. I knew that if it didn't work, I would have to stay up all night, rewrite a new ending, and beg Disney for more money to reshoot. Even product placement can't help you when you don't have an ending. No movie ever *ended* on the closeup of a can of Coca-Cola.

Before I gave up, I wanted to shoot the scene one last time. By now I had added pigeons, which the prop department attracted by throwing bread crumbs into the street. With pigeons in place and working for scale, everybody was ready. The opera music piped through speakers was playing loudly in the street, the cameraman was on his Titan crane, and the policemen, whom we'd hired for the day to stop cars from driving into our shot, were standing by. I yelled "Action!" and the scene began. Richard drove up in the limousine, then climbed the fire escape toward Julia. Everything went according to plan. I yelled "Cut!" and looked at my crew to see what they thought. I had hoped for some sign of approval, but all I saw was a group of bored people.

Then as I turned around, I saw that one of the policemen had tears in his eyes. I walked over to find out why.

"What's the matter?" I asked him.

"Mr. Marshall, the opera music. The pigeons. The two lovers up there. It just gave me goose bumps," he said.

I knew then that I had my ending to *Pretty Woman*. The cast and crew weren't my audience. My audience was that policeman and his friends who would go to their local theater on a Saturday night. I knew my picture had a chance if it could give an ordinary guy goose bumps.

Chapter Twelve

Editing a Movie and Remembering Matching Is for Sissies

Can You Cut from the Two Gay Guys to the Cuddly Doggie a Little Faster?

Three little words, "It's a wrap," can often make film people cry. This is because the end of a movie shoot is like the last day of camp: There are tearful good-byes; the usual exchange of addresses, phone numbers, and gifts; and one last hurrah at the cast party where everyone shares a laugh at the gag reel's montage of insider jokes. The cast and most of the crew are done with their work and wax nostalgic. "It's a wrap," says the assistant director and they pack up their gear and head to other film projects or home to pick out a new font for their résumés. But for the director the work has just begun. This is the time for many directors when the movie truly gets made.

First, I usually take a few weeks off to look into my wife's eyes after having spent the last twelve weeks talking to her earlobes, and then I head for the editing room. Editing can be disappointing if you discover that you didn't get the footage you wanted, but more often it's my favorite part of moviemaking: It's when you get to see if your story makes sense. Some directors consider postproduction the finishing-up stage, but I'm still creating. The way I look at it the success or failure of my films can be broken down to 25 percent preproduction, 25 percent shoot, and 50 percent postproduction.

Sometimes no matter how much you prepare or shoot, either the pieces don't fit or you're missing a piece. But never panic because until you finish the editing or until the studio takes it away from you, there are ways to improve it. Always! You can reshoot a closeup, loop in dialogue, add music to a scene, or reedit your footage and cut out a scene. You can even revoice the entire performance of an actor if you have to. Since my movies are usually made or broken in the editing room, I've learned to maintain as much control as possible during this process.

Unfortunately, *Overboard* suffered in postproduction. The movie was supposed to be about a mother and her children. But because of our high-profile casting choices (Goldie Hawn and Kurt Russell), we chose to balance the love story and the comedy together with the children. When we finished editing, producers Anthea Sylbert, Alexandra Rose, and I were pleased with our story, a lighthearted romantic family comedy for young people.

MGM, however, was not as charmed with my finished product. It turns out they wanted an adult movie they could market to a sophisticated audience. At this point in my movie career I didn't have much clout. They sent me back to the editing room with instructions to cut the film down and to push Goldie and Kurt. They were stars and studios know how to easily sell stars. Selling stories is harder. Also, whenever executives don't know what to do with a comedy, they say, "Make it shorter." Then you go in and trim all of the characters' back stories to make the film tighter, and you're left with characters who look like "sticks," as film critic Gene Siskel likes to call them.

Reluctantly, I cut *Overboard* down to an hour fifty minutes, but I probably should have fought harder to keep my length. In the shorter version we had no choice but to jam in the love story with the kids story and it was a tight squeeze. As it turned out,

Mutual mumbling:
mapping shots on the set of
Beaches with cinematographer
Dante Spinotti.

My son, Scott, risking
his allowance if he
doesn't keep Bette
Midler dry during a
scene from *Beaches*.

Cheerfully building my
career as a women's
director with two of the
best you can get, Barbara
Hershey and Bette Midler.

On *Pretty Woman*, I encouraged Julia Roberts to work with lots of props that her character wouldn't be familiar with. In the beginning she resisted and would say to the propman, "Oh, hide those opera glasses or Garry will make me do something crazy with them." By the end she was grabbing objects from the propman's cart and saying, "What can I do with this, Garry?"

Julia Roberts on the set of *Pretty Woman* for Touchstone Pictures, the division of Disney Studios where you can make movies with a few curse words.

Two men daydreaming and getting paid for it. With Richard Gere on the set of *Pretty Woman*.

Day 14 of *Pretty Woman*. Discussing the big shopping spree on Rodeo Drive in Beverly Hills with Julia Roberts.

Huddling before an emotional scene with Al Pacino and Michelle Pfeiffer on the set of *Frankie and Johnny.*

Al Pacino and I discuss the safety of using a real meat slicer in a sequence from *Frankie and Johnny.*

Laughing in a bowling alley with Michelle Pfeiffer during *Frankie and Johnny* after she threw a strike on the first take.

Whoopi Goldberg listening to me say "Peppy and cheap" in a scene from *Soapdish*. Whoopi and I also acted together in *Jumpin' Jack Flash*.

My sister Penny directing Tom Hanks and me in a scene from *A League of Their Own*.

Combining both nepotism and erotica, my wife, Barbara, appeared as an island guest with Dana Delany and Stephanie Niznik in *Exit to Eden*, a Savoy film. My wife chose the most conservative costume available.

Trying on dominatrix outfits with Rosie O'Donnell and Iman on the set of *Exit to Eden*. You don't give much direction to a woman in leather carrying a whip.

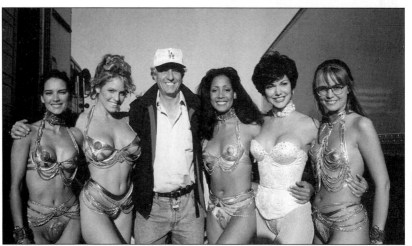

Some of the citizens of *Eden:* Not since *Blansky's Beauties* have I worked with so many attractive actresses.

Sometimes people get me to come to an event by saying that Penny is going to be there when she isn't, or by telling her that I'm coming when I'm not. On this night, we both showed up.

Albert Brooks trying to make me believe in Santi Claus on the set of his much revered movie *Lost in America*.

Here I am acting as the head of the network, Stan Lansing, on *Murphy Brown* with Candice Bergen and Joe Regalbuto. Joe also appeared in several episodes of *Mork & Mindy* as Neptune, an evil alien .

The hypochondriac and the nurse sharing a quiet moment of calm
in between movies.

Overboard was a big hit when it played on television and in video stores where it was rented by guess who? Young kids who loved the family part of the story.

A common problem is that long films don't test well with preview audiences, but I think that longer movies, both comedies and dramas, are usually stronger. Movies that run eighty-eight minutes are not usually movies that take home an Oscar (unless it's a movie directed by Woody Allen). So fight hard to keep your length. Today's film audience is trained to watch a movie for two hours, which is the average length of a mainstream studio picture. After two hours they want to go to the bathroom. The last part of your movie had better be interesting because you're fighting bladders.

On all my movies I've teamed up with producer Nick Abdo for my postproduction work; however, the time varies from movie to movie. But the dynamics are always the same: The director wants more time and the studio wants to give him less. I had about five months' editing time each on *Young Doctors in Love*, *Overboard*, *Beaches*, and *Pretty Woman*; eight months on *Nothing in Common*; ten months on *Exit to Eden*; twelve luxurious months on *The Flamingo Kid*; and on *Frankie and Johnny* a mere three and a half months, which nearly killed me *and* the movie. Usually five months is enough time to edit a picture, but only when I had all those months on *The Flamingo Kid* did I feel like I had ample time to get each scene the way I wanted it, each frame on target. With comedy, timing is sensitive because a single frame can mean the difference between a joke that works and one that doesn't. On *Frankie and Johnny*, because of the terrible editing schedule, there are still a few scenes where the timing is off but I still won most of the battles.

Part of a director's job is to hire an editor. At the interviews, they all look wonderful, but once you start work there are, with exceptions, two basic kinds of editors: The first kind says or insinuates, "Hello, I'm the editor. Give me the film. Okay, these shots are terrible. I don't know what I can do with this. How am I going to edit this crap?" The second kind of editor comes in and says, "Hello, I'm the editor. You are the director. My job is to save your ass and cover up your mistakes. We'll try this. We'll try that and it will be fine." The first editor can make your life miserable and the second editor can make your film better. A director doesn't need to hear an editor tell him that he made a mistake because the director already knows it; he was *there*. A director needs an editor who can tell him how to fix his mistakes.

Find an editor with whom you can work quickly and who eats similar food since you spend six months together in a dark room. But more important, find an editor who understands your vision and who's not afraid to tell you to reshoot a scene. Sometimes a movie requires a reshoot to make a moment work.

During postproduction on *Frankie and Johnny* two terrific editors named Battle Davis and Jacqueline Cambas came to me and said, "We have a problem. When Johnny tells Frankie that he was too frightened to get out of the car when he went to see his children, we can't get the emotion. You only filmed two sizes of that shot and it wasn't enough. We need a tighter closeup." That's good editing. They told me what was wrong and what to do about it. I had to either change my mind and forget the emotion or reshoot. I felt the emotion was central to the scene, so we reshot the tighter closeup.

Together, the director and editor also have to stress pace and clarity. If a movie is clear but too slow, the audience will get restless. That's why so many movies have car chases in the second half—to change the pace and wake up the audience. Have you ever seen a quiet car chase?

All directors, from the graduate student with no experience to the veteran with a dozen credits, make mistakes. Michael Ritchie, who directed *The Bad News Bears*, once said, "Matching is for sissies," which means that if your goal is to get your story across, you can't be preoccupied with matching every shot cinematically. Like directing, editing is not an exact science.

When you edit, you have to use all of the tools—sound effects, music, dialogue, and images—to tell your story. The director's job is to make the choices. Brian De Palma once said, "I regard film as a medium more akin to music and dance than literature. The character and story to me are not the primary focus." However, when I edit I *focus* on things like: performance, story, and character. Rather than protect scenes with expensive fireworks displays, wild stunts, or ocean panoramas, I'll sacrifice those scenes to enhance an actor's performance, even if it is just a line, expression, or gesture. I hire editors who can instinctively pick out the best performances from the dailies but when you pick this way, you wind up with some editorial mismatches or flubs.

My movies often appear in those blooper books, but so what! From a business standpoint, it's not such a bad thing to be in those flub books. People read them and then rent your movie to see if they can pick out all the mistakes. A flub can be a slight cinematic slip-up or a major gaffe. In *Pretty Woman*, there's a scene when Vivian tries to leave Edward and the camera's change of focus is late and quite noticeable. I had another take in which the focus was perfect, smooth as silk. However, I felt obliged to use the late one because the acting was better. It's important to me that the actors get to put their best performance forward. If that means a little late focus once in a while, then so be it. I'd rather the audience say, "What a brilliant performance, but there were some mismatches" than for them to knock the performance. Performances are remembered by audiences; mismatches are remembered by other editors.

Pretty Woman boasts a plethora of mismatches. There's a scene in the penthouse when Vivian is eating breakfast. At first, she picks up a croissant but in the next shot she takes a bite from a pancake. I shot it the right way, but I purposely chose to edit it mismatched because the takes I picked made the scene more powerful. Later, when Edward and Vivian are in the park, she takes his shoes and socks off, but in the next shot his shoes and socks are miraculously back on. I had a shot of her putting the shoes and socks back on, but it took too long and ruined the pace so I cut it out.

There also are a few flubs in *Frankie and Johnny*, such as Al Pacino's bandanna flipping on and off in one of the diner scenes and later the intrusion of a microphone boom in Frankie's apartment. But I feel a director should first do anything he can to protect an actor's performance, and then try to do the best he can with the rest. That's what editing comes down to for me. I've never stood outside a movie theater and heard someone say, "Let's send our friends to this movie because all the focuses are perfect." But that doesn't mean you don't try to get everything perfect.

The editors who impress me are the ones who can make the changes I ask for, and then give me more. I like it when an editor says, "Garry, here's the way you wanted the scene and here's my way. My version I put together on my own time." What an editor does on his own is sometimes better than my original idea. An editor who takes a risk, shares his opinion, and gives it a shot can set himself apart. I encourage the assistant editors to take a gamble too. The more versions of a scene I have to choose from, the better my odds are of putting together a winning scene. (The editor who says "I didn't try it your way, but here's my way" is the editor I fire.)

One way to help turn a scene around is by editing with sound. Some directors use sound only occasionally as a tool, but I use it often and look for editors who have experience cutting sound. You can make endless changes with sound editing, whether it is inserting a voice-over wild line (a favorite practice of mine that has earned me the nickname "Willy Wild Line") or just filling dead air on screen.

In television, often because of censorship, we had to fit a new line into an actor's mouth at the last minute. With the growing number of television alumni who are becoming film directors today, however, sound editing is being used more and more to enhance movies, particularly comedies. Just check out a comedy and see how many jokes are said while you're looking at the back of someone's head. That means the lines were put in during post-production. In the opening ten minutes of *A League of Their Own*, five great laughs are spoken over the back of people's heads or over scenery. Check it out.

Sound editing can give a director the up to the last second freedom to change his mind. In *Pretty Woman* (working with my favorite editor, Priscilla Nedd-Friendly), we were able to shift an entire scene with just the sound of a phone click. In the film's opening sequence, Edward is talking to his girlfriend on the telephone. In the version we shot he says, "Good-bye, Jessica," and then slams down the phone, hanging up on her because he was annoyed that she blew off his party. Once in the editing room we realized that the scene depicted Edward as too mean and heartless; not exactly the impression we wanted the audience to get at the beginning of the movie.

It would have been the wrong choice because later when he went to pick up Vivian, the audience wouldn't have rooted for their romance to unfold. Basically, he was a little too harsh to be a romantic lead so early in the picture. So instead of asking the studio for more money to reshoot the scene, we fixed it with sound editing. We moved up the phone click so Edward's girlfriend hangs up on *him* first. In the new version she says in a voice-over, "That's fine, Edward. Good-bye" and hangs up. Then he says on camera, "Good-bye, Jessica" to a sad dial tone. By switching the click, we changed the mood of the scene, made our hero more vulnerable, and got the picture off to a stronger start.

One of the best things about movies and one of the worst things about movies . . . is music. I've directed some films, such as *Beaches* and *Pretty Woman*, in which the sound tracks made me proud and went on to win gold and platinum records and praise from the audience and disc jockeys. However, other sound tracks have made me feel ashamed of what I chose. The one lesson I've learned the hard way is that a director has to maintain control of the music.

Every time I've put someone else in charge by saying things like "You know more about music. You handle it," I've gotten into trouble. There are people out there who call themselves musical experts, but beware: I feel only the director knows what music will go best with the scene that he has shot. A director must treat music as if it was one of his gold scenes; compromise on other things, but spend extra money and time if you have to to get the music right.

In *The Flamingo Kid* we used music to set the tone for the whole movie. It was a period film and we took extra care in picking out songs from the 1960s that complemented our story. We also were counting on the music to frame the time in history for our two target audiences, middle-aged people feeling nostalgic and young people possibly hearing the tunes for the first time. We ended up with an array of more than twenty-five songs by groups such as Hank Ballard and the Midnighters, The Impressions, and The Chiffons that not only put the audience in the right mood but also pushed the story along at an entertaining pace.

When music is working well, as it does in *The Flamingo Kid*, the audience won't be able to tell you what made a particular scene work for them. They'll just describe how the scene made them feel. Music played a key role in *The Flamingo Kid* when Jeffrey discovers Phil Brody is cheating. Again working with Priscilla Nedd-Friendly, who has a skill for finding the right performance and selecting music to match, we made more than fifty cuts in the scene and used music to help smooth out the transitions. With the wrong music a scene very often feels choppy.

My background is mostly with jazz and Dixieland, and I don't follow all contemporary music. I knew a little about music from the 1950s and 1960s, so I was able to muddle through *The Flamingo Kid*. But when it came to *Nothing in Common*, a picture current to the times, I deferred all musical judgment to the producers and music department made up of "experts." Delegating responsibility is one thing, but giving away the final decision is another. On *Nothing in Common*, I stopped paying attention to the music and it got completely out of control. The music itself wasn't bad; it just had nothing in common with the movie.

Instead of choosing songs that blended thematically with the picture, the "experts" selected music that they thought would become popular hits. Over a scene when Tom Hanks bumps into his former girlfriend, Bess Armstrong, I wanted to go with an old Air Supply song to conjure up the memories of a lost romance. We had used the song in previews and it moved the audience to tears so we knew it worked. But I was persuaded that by using a new song we could get more air time on radio stations and video channels like MTV, and that kids would dance to it.

The sound track didn't catch on anywhere. The kids didn't dance and the filmmakers didn't dance. The problem in film is that in postproduction the music divides the creative powers (studio executives, producers, and the director) into two different camps. Half the people are making a movie and the other half are making a record album. It's the director's job to scream, "We're making a movie here, not a record album."

A song only has to be in a movie for four seconds to make it into the sound track album. They need ten to twelve songs to make a record, so they try to jam them in wherever they can. In *Nothing in Common*, Tom Hanks pulls up in his Jeep with the radio on and turns off the ignition. The song that was playing on his car stereo, only about four seconds long, made it onto the album. That's why people buy film sound tracks and then say, "Where the hell was that song in the movie?" When music fits a movie perfectly, you know it right away: *The Pink Panther* music set a funny tone for the whole picture. In *Chariots of Fire*, the music made a track meet art. The music in *Doctor Zhivago* made a bitter cold winter look romantic.

My mother taught me that music works when it gives you the chills. At the end of her dance recitals in the Bronx, there was always a big finale: twelve chubby eight-year-olds doing the splits and singing "God Bless America," which brought down the house. My mother didn't study music. She didn't learn the history of music. In fact, she couldn't even read music, but she understood its emotion and power and eventually I learned that too. I taught myself to choose music and ask myself, "Does this music fit the scene?" instead of "Will this song make a nice video or sound good coming out of a car stereo in a traffic jam?"

Yet sometimes you need music that doesn't give you the chills but rather makes the audience be more attentive to the dialogue or the visual. In that case, I often use Antonio Vivaldi's classic *The Four Seasons*. It's very long, not too busy, can lay a mat underneath a scene without busting any punch lines, and the rights are modestly priced. In 1984, *The Four Seasons* was voted the "Most Boring Composition" by New York radio listeners, and that's why I like it. It doesn't get in the way of anything else going on. I've used it in *Pretty Woman*, *Frankie and Johnny*, and *Exit to Eden* to add dignity and lightness to various scenes. Viva Vivaldi!

• • •

The music on *Beaches* was far superior to music on any film I ever directed thanks to the help of Bette Midler, her musical arranger Marc Shaiman, and music producer Arif Mardin. Bette is very impulsive; one night she called me around 8 P.M. to ask me to come to Marc's house to talk about some music for the movie. I was tired and grouchy and the last thing I wanted to do was get back in my car and drive to a discussion. But Bette then said she'd sing the songs to me, so I went.

Bette and Marc performed a selection of songs for an audience of one—me. We wanted songs that would highlight the movie's theme of female friendship as well as showcase Bette's extraordinary musical range. She sang songs from the 1940s, such as Cole Porter's "I've Still Got My Health," and "Under the Boardwalk" from the 1960s and I listened and smiled, pleased with the selections. But when Bette sang her version of "Wind Beneath My Wings," I began to cry and I told her, "This one is very nice." I knew immediately it would be the most powerful song in the film. However, along with producer Bonnie Bruckheimer, we decided that Bette couldn't possibly sing the song on camera. The power and emotion she gave to it made the song too strong for the screen. If we had allowed her to sing the song on camera, her performance would have taken the audience right out of the story. It would have been Bette Midler singing, not C. C. Bloom. Instead, we decided to lace "Wind Beneath My Wings" over images of C.C. after her friend dies. Later C.C. would sing "Glory of Love," which the executive producer, Teri Schwartz, suggested, on camera as the film's finale. "Wind Beneath My Wings" made people reach for their handkerchiefs, but they also kept one eye on the screen.

When Priscilla Nedd-Friendly edited *Pretty Woman*, we were able to achieve the same musical balance we had found working on *The Flamingo Kid*. While some editors view music as a chore, Priscilla is challenged by it. Katzenberg called the editing suite one day and said he had the rights to three songs: "She's a Lady," "Lady Is a Tramp," and "Pretty Woman." He wanted us to listen to them and then select one as the title for our film. The shooting script was called

Three Thousand, but Katzenberg said, "I'm not calling this movie *Three Thousand*. You can't hum it." Test audiences had agreed.

The easy part was choosing the song: "Pretty Woman" was clearly the best fit. The hard part was finding a place to put the song in the movie. Often a title song is placed either at the beginning or end of a movie, but "Pretty Woman" didn't fit in either place so we tried the middle. I left Priscilla alone to try it in a few different places and when I came back she showed me a clip of the song played over the shopping-spree sequence. When I heard that drumbeat and saw Julia walking down the street lugging those shopping bags and looking gorgeous, I knew immediately that it was the perfect place for "Pretty Woman."

Selecting music for a movie is not a general skill that a director can master because you have to start from scratch on each film. It's an everyday battle and on *Frankie and Johnny* my side lost, again. When we started postproduction we signed Marvin Hamlisch to write the musical score. I was optimistic because *The Way We Were* has to rank as one of the best scores ever written. However, thanks to a less than expected music budget and at the time Paramount's less than capable music department (known for making even the most level-headed director curse), the music in *Frankie and Johnny* turned out to be a gigantic disappointment (and that's being kind).

Paramount told Marvin, "Don't write too pretty. *Frankie and Johnny* is about a waitress and a cook. Don't do all of the violins and all of that lush music that you usually write." Marvin was insulted and said, "What do you think? Only rich people hear violins when they kiss and poor people hear an accordion? Everybody hears violins when they're in love!" Marvin is a professional and despite the initial tension, he wrote a beautiful score for us. That was the good news.

The bad news was that the studio was too cheap to hire Carly Simon, the artist he wanted. Paramount signed Terence Trent D'Arby. Although an excellent performer, D'Arby agreed to sing in the film, but not on the CD or cassette, possibly because it conflicted with his own record deal. How the studio could make this kind of deal with him still stuns me. A director must stay on top of the music and always remember the good guys: If you find an editor with a talent for selecting music or come across a studio with a competent and well-funded music department, try to use them again. Disney's Chris Montan, whom I worked with on *Beaches* and *Pretty Woman*, has proven to me to be the best music coordinator. James Newton Howard, who also worked on *Pretty Woman*, and newcomer Jim Dunne were tops for me when it came to music composing.

The most painful part of editing a movie is learning that you have to cut your favorite scene. While editing *Beaches*, we had to cut one of the funniest moments in the movie because it was so honest that it took the audience right out of the picture. In the scene, C. C. Bloom, filled to the brim with envy, says to Hillary, "You're smart. You're beautiful," and then Bette ad-libbed, "and you have hair that moves."

In previews, the hair line got big laughs because the audience could sense the honesty of Bette's delivery. In real life, she is obsessed with her hair and wishes she had been born with hair that moved around instead of just lying there. But this was a serious and emotional scene following a long separation between the two friends and it just didn't need a treacle cutter; a laugh would not have been appropriate. Even though the scene made preview audiences laugh, it threw them out of the scene. So we ended up taking the line out. Disney used the line in the movie's trailer anyway, operating under the rationale that it's okay to throw the audience out of a trailer but not out of a movie.

This moment in *Beaches* was not the first, and certainly not the last, funny or poignant line I ever had to cut. I've shot entire subplots that started out strong but never made it into the movie. This happens, and it's better to find out if something doesn't work before a movie's release than after. In *Nothing in Common*, we had a subplot about Tom Hanks's mother, played by Eva Marie Saint, who started dating again after thirty years of marriage. Eva played the part beautifully but her story line didn't fit in our film. We cut many of her scenes because they competed with the movie's primary father-son plot. I didn't realize this during the shoot, but once we hit the editing room and put the pieces together, I said sadly, "Trim the mother."

In *Pretty Woman*, I insisted that we add a sequence showing Edward on Vivian's turf. I thought it was important for the movie's balance to show Edward inside Vivian's rough-and-tough neighborhood, just as we had seen her inside his refined world that only money could buy. We shot for three days on a sleazy nightclub set, but it wasn't until I got to the editing room that I discovered we didn't need those scenes to tell our story. The audience didn't care where Vivian came from. They just wanted to see where she was headed.

Many how-to-write-a-screenplay books stress the importance of showing as *much* as you can about a character, but the best way to make a movie is to see how *little* you can reveal and still convey a great character. The trick is to try to make a character clear using a minimum amount of writing and time. Anybody can reveal a character in one hundred scenes, but the great screenwriters and directors do it in two or three scenes.

In the editing room you sometimes have to cut out characters altogether. The biggest, most difficult edit I ever had to make was in *Frankie and Johnny*. In the screenplay, Terrence McNally had given Johnny two friends: Les, a drug dealer who had done time in jail with Johnny, and Penny, his codependent girlfriend. Les and Penny, played by Tim Hopper and Laurie Metcalf, represented Johnny's dark past. Their purpose in the movie was to try to lure Johnny away from his future with Frankie.

I shot the scenes, but once I began editing I realized we didn't need the subplot. They took away from the strength of Frankie and Johnny's love story. No director enjoys cutting out an actor's performance from a movie, especially when it's good (or the actor is a relative), but in this case it was necessary to protect the main story. For example, in *Pretty Woman* it wasn't necessary to film a scene showing how Vivian became a prostitute because it was a concept the audience could understand. But in *Exit to Eden*, we had to explain how Lisa (Dana Delany) became a dominatrix because many people didn't know what it meant or how or why someone would become such a thing. The more unfamiliar the character, the more back story a director needs to reveal.

On the other hand, in certain instances a director *will* include a scene in a movie even when it moves away from the main story.

A digression might be included because of its beauty or because it's simply an exceptional or amusing scene that overshadows the boundaries of the story. Once we started filming *Exit to Eden*, Rosie O'Donnell's character proved to be so popular in dailies that we gave her a love interest. It wasn't something we had originally planned, and it didn't really affect the plot, but it gave another dimension to her character that we simply couldn't pass up.

A special movie can become an ordinary movie when studio executives, armed with stacks of research, demand the director cut out anything that's not integral to the plot. The irony here is that if you ask moviegoers what makes a film special, they usually recall the quirky, spontaneous moments that have nothing whatsoever to do with the story, like when Julia gets her hand stuck in the jewelry box in *Pretty Woman*, Lauren Bacall whistles in *To Have and Have Not*, or Albert Brooks sits on his coattail so his collar won't rise up in *Broadcast News*. These are the moments that turn movies into hits. But there also are moments that can throw you out of the story. How do you determine what to keep in or out? Talent? Luck? Maybe a little of both.

When a director completes a rough cut, in most cases he then shows it at a series of previews for studio executives (who give a barrage of copious, often irrelevant notes) and test audiences (who inevitably love the scenes you hate and hate the scenes you love). It's not easy to preview your film and ask the opinions of strangers; that's why some directors don't preview at all, but I do. Editing and postproduction can get very lonely day after day and the vacuum can make a director question his cinematic choices. You think, "Am I really far off?" "Am I wrong about this scene?" "Am I making a terrible decision?" You get to the point where you need some feedback from real people.

I've found that when your film is still very rough, the first and best test audience is a small group of old friends or colleagues whom you respect. It's invaluable for a director to surround himself with a group of tried and trusted confidants, in the business and out, who will watch your movie and give you their straightforward opinion, good or bad. My group includes my wife, Barbara, my kids, my sis-

ters Penny and Ronny, James Brooks, Lowell Ganz, Harvey Miller, Bob
Brunner, Polly Platt, Blair Richwood, John Collins, Henry and Stacey
Winkler, Marilyn Katzenberg, and others, depending on their schedules.

This little group and I sit through their films and they sit
through mine like students swapping term papers before handing
them in to a professor. I like to show them my work during rough
cuts, when I'm still putting together the pieces of my story and
there's still time to make changes. Save more polished previews for
others but show the first draft, no matter how uneven, to your support group.

Marilyn Katzenberg, an elegant and refreshingly rare non-
show-biz woman, is one of the few people in Hollywood who has
a supreme sense of balance. When we first tested *Pretty Woman*,
all the Disney executives got very excited when they read the audience numbers. They ran around cheering. "We have a hit! We have
a hit!" But in the middle of their celebration, Marilyn issued a
warning of caution: "Remember *Lifeguard*." When her husband,
Jeffrey, had been an executive at Paramount several years earlier,
Lifeguard, a movie about an aging California lifeguard played by
Sam Elliott, had tested higher than any other movie in
Paramount's history; but it turned out to be a flop. So when others start to pop Champagne corks prematurely, I look to Marilyn
for patience.

Sitting through a rough cut of another director's picture is
never easy, especially when she's your sister. I sat through a four-
and-a-half-hour assemblage of Penny's film *Big* and it was far
from the smooth, well-crafted comedy that made it to theaters and
set records at the box office. Penny sat through a two-and-a-half-
hour screening of *Exit to Eden* and when she saw the scene in
which Dana Delany spanks Paul Mercurio's naked behind, Penny
uttered the immortal line "Our family's first naked people picture." When my daughter Kathleen asked her boyfriend, Kevin, in
the theater as the lights came up what he thought of the same
scene he said, "Give me a minute. I'm from the Midwest."

While I'm sharing my movie with friends and test groups, the
studio is usually trying to give me notes, such as "Women like this
scene but men hate it" or "This will play well in the Midwest." I
was particularly leery of the research man on *Exit to Eden* who

was the same man who predicted that *Starman* would be a bigger hit than *E.T.*

My ending for *Frankie and Johnny* almost didn't survive because of notes from Paramount. I ended the picture with a montage of shots showing the main characters in bed, some with lovers, some alone. The studio made noise about a shot of Frankie's two gay neighbors, Tim and Bobby (played by Nathan Lane and Sean O'Bryan). In the scene I showed the two men simply holding each other, and then panned down to their dog at the end of the bed.

"Can you cut the scene with the two homosexuals?" a Paramount executive asked. "It might offend some people."

"No," I said. The men were an important part of the film.

"Well . . . hmmmm . . . can you cut from the two gay guys to the cuddly doggie a little faster?"

"No," I said.

Trying to hide homosexuality behind the face of a cute puppy was a battle I had to win. I did.

Studios love research, but I don't usually share in their enthusiasm for numbers and focus groups. Sometimes, however, preview audiences can help point out a problem and possibly initiate plans for a reshoot. I originally had a rather frilly ice-skating ending to *Exit to Eden* that landed on the cutting-room floor after preview audiences thought it was a satire of Olympic skater Tonya Harding. They kept waiting for dominatrix Lisa to get whacked on the knee. Lesson: 1994 was the wrong year for ice-skating images. The ending also didn't work because Lisa quit her job and left the island with Elliot. Some test audiences responded to the ending with, "Why would she leave such a good job?" In the unstable job market, the audience perceived dominatrix as a very good profession. We reshot the ending to show that Lisa and Elliot stayed on the island together and she kept her job.

You can't test your movie in Los Angeles or you'll end up with a bunch of notes from amateur filmmakers. You have to travel to a city like Paramus, New Jersey, where it is easier to round up an audience full of real people who will give you their honest opinions. When Penny first previewed *A League of Their Own*, she ended the movie with a scene of the women being admitted to the Baseball Hall of Fame. The audiences didn't really care about the Baseball Hall of Fame; they wanted to know what happened to the two sisters. So Penny shot an additional scene between the two sisters in the locker room, and then ended the movie with their reunion at the Hall of Fame. I think it was Woody Allen who said, "Always plan a movie and then add two weeks of reshoot." Preview audiences seem to support this idea.

When we first showed *Pretty Woman* to preview audiences, we were afraid that in the last scene, when Edward climbs up the fire escape to rescue Vivian, the audience might become confused and wonder where the opera music was coming from. To clarify the scene, I had already shot an insert of the chauffeur's hand placing an opera cassette into a tape deck in the limousine. For today's filmmakers, inserts are a cross between a safety net and a guardian angel. (Think what *High Noon* would be without the insert of the clock, or what *Speed* would be without the shot of the speedometer.) But in this case I didn't use the insert in the preview because it was cinematically clumsy.

Following one of the previews, a moderator asked a small focus group what they thought of the ending.

"In the last scene, where do you think the opera music is coming from?" the moderator asked.

"The stereo speakers in Edward's limousine," a man wearing a striped shirt answered.

"No way," interrupted another guy in a leather jacket. "A limousine like that wouldn't have speakers that powerful."

"Maybe it's a specially designed limousine with high-tech speakers," a woman with too much makeup offered.

"No way. I know you'd never find speakers that powerful in a limo," the leather jacket insisted.

"Well, let's consider the other possibilities," said the moderator.

"Who gives a shit!" interrupted a teenage girl from the back of the group. "Vivian and Edward got together and that's what matters. I don't care about the speakers. I care about the lovers. I care about the fact that they got together!"

The girl's response was all I needed to hear. I left the shot of the limo tape deck on the cutting-room floor. Research can remind a director that he's making a movie for an audience, and for *them* passion is usually more convincing than logic.

As we approach the year 2000, it's becoming clearer and clearer that because so many movies are being made now, the timing for the release of a movie can mean the big difference between a hit and a flop. More people than I ever imagined saw *Pretty Woman* and not enough saw *Frankie and Johnny.* I give part of the credit and the blame to timing. *Pretty Woman* opened in the spring at a time in history when people were yearning for a fairy tale. *Frankie and Johnny* opened the weekend of October 12, 1991, during the Clarence Thomas–Anita Hill Senate hearings when people were glued to their television sets and had all the entertainment they needed right there. *Frankie and Johnny* was released in video stores the week of April 29, 1992, the same time as the first Rodney King verdict, which set off the Los Angeles riots. *Frankie and Johnny* won the prize for most looted cassette. Despite Paramount's full-out and expensive marketing campaign, people didn't go to *Frankie and Johnny,* the movie I consider my best filmmaking. The fact that they went to *Pretty Woman* was much to the credit of Disney's marketing team.

I'll never forget the moment when the poster for *Pretty Woman* was unveiled for me and a roomful of Disney brass and how startled I was as a marketing executive leaped from his seat and rushed over to the poster with a Magic Marker. He then colored in Richard Gere's gray hair black. Everyone else in the room nodded in agreement, except me: I was the only one in the room with gray hair.

Release dates are usually out of a director's control. *The Flamingo Kid,* a comedy about a cabana boy that was clearly a summer film, was released by Twentieth Century Fox at Christmastime, and it was by design rather than mistake. The studio's rationale was that the film would make a splash during the holidays. They felt that when it's thirty degrees below zero outside, people would go to see kids running around in their swim suits. Wrong again. While the picture didn't open big, it was later spurred on by good reviews and positive word of mouth.

Another aspect of postproduction over which the director has little control is the trailer. A director usually puts together some scenes he thinks will sell his movie, and then the studio has a nasty habit of whitewashing the trailer before it's released in theaters. In *Exit to Eden*, they made me change the phrase "an erotic island" to the more generic "an exotic island." In *Terms of Endearment*, they made James Brooks take out all of the hospital scenes so the trailer would appear to be promoting a comedy instead of the comedy-drama it really was.

I also think that trailers are a detriment to humor because they show just the punch lines from a film without the setups. I usually have to fight with a studio because they try to shove as many jokes as they can into a trailer, and I struggle to take them all out. Jokes that are funny in a trailer aren't funny in a movie because they're too cheap or easy. The movie *The Ref* was a very funny film, but the jokes in its trailer weren't.

Only a handful of directors get trailer approval, and I'm not quite there yet. (On *Exit to Eden* at least they consulted me.) In the end all you can hope for is that the studio doesn't screw up your trailer. In all fairness there are times when the trailer is much better than the movie. Someday PBS will do a salute to the best trailers.

The way studios test trailers is ridiculous. They set up televisions in shopping malls. As customers walk by, they try to grab them.

"Sir, would you like to come watch the trailer for a new major motion picture?"

"No. I'm going to buy socks."

"Come on. Please."

"But I'm really in a hurry."

"It will only take a minute."

It's not a scientific method. The process requires abducting people in malls who would rather be buying socks.

These days if your picture doesn't make its money back in the first three weeks, theaters usually dump it. When I started directing, it seemed like they gave movies more time to find an audience. But today, a film that opens in 1,700 theaters better make money fast or after three weeks it will drop down to 1,000 theaters, and then 200, and then it will disappear altogether.

One of the ways a director promotes his movie is through press junkets. When I first directed, each studio would send out each movie on its own press junket; but now to save money films piggyback on junkets. Penny took her movie *Renaissance Man* on a Disney junket along with *Angels in the Outfield*, a baseball movie, and *The Lion King*. On these junkets reporters get very tired interviewing so many different people. One afternoon Penny sat down for an interview and was asked, "Ms. Marshall, it's interesting that you would choose to direct another baseball movie so soon after directing *A League of Their Own.*" Penny was incensed. "Hello! My movie is *Renaissance Man.* It's about guys in the army." These big press junkets leave a lot to be desired.

A director has to work with what the studio gives him, and he has to help wage a stronger publicity campaign when the box office returns are less than expected. The minute I see one of my films in trouble I say, "How fast can publicity get me on *Today?*" It's an unwritten and hushed-up rule that you should use at least one actor in your movie who feels comfortable doing promotion on talk shows. Also sometimes actors don't like the picture, so they refuse to publicize it, which has prompted many studios to write publicity requirements into a star's contract.

Some stars, such as Al Pacino and Michelle Pfeiffer, simply hate doing publicity and it is pointless to force them because they will come across as uncomfortable, even if they love the movie. Superstars like Al and Michelle just wanted to be actors and weren't cut out to go on *The Tonight Show* and do cute patter. Other stars, Rosie O'Donnell and Dan Aykroyd, for example, enjoy doing publicity and can sometimes drive people into theaters just by a single appearance.

A director, obviously, has little control over the reviews. In general, my films don't earn the best reviews but they usually make money at the box office. Many years ago, Francis Ford Coppola declared that after a financially successful movie, the industry allows a director three or four subsequent flops before the work stops coming. Recently, a reporter asked Francis if he still felt that was true. Francis replied, "No. They give you ten now."

I received terrific reviews for *Frankie and Johnny* and *Nothing in Common* while *Pretty Woman* and *Beaches* made the most money. Ironically, *Pretty Woman* and *Beaches* received mixed reviews, some knocking my "manipulative blend" of drama and comedy, others applauding the blend.

Whenever you go into the arena you get all kinds of criticism. But I hoped they would never say that I did a quicky job or that I sloughed it. No matter what, I always try to give the audience and my employer their money's worth.

Young Doctors in Love, *Overboard*, and *Exit to Eden* didn't make strong showings at the box office or with the critics. At a time when I was known for making audiences laugh and cry with my movies, I took a new approach with *Exit to Eden*. I tried to make them laugh and become aroused. Unfortunately, the film was received as a kind of Benny Hill-style bathroom comedy instead of the more sensual blend of humor and erotica that I had intended. With *Exit to Eden*, the box office numbers were bad and the reviews were even worse. I was the first director to bring S & M to a mainstream audience and the critics spanked me for it.

My movie that came the closest to making money and getting good reviews was *The Flamingo Kid*. These days every film is bound to get at least one good review and then, even if it's from a grass-roots paper in Kalamazoo, the studio blows it up and puts it in the ad for the movie. But a director can't become obsessed with reviews, because with critics you simply can't win with any consistency. I've gotten good reviews (*"Pretty Woman* is the most satisfying romantic comedy in years"—Vincent Canby and about *Nothing in Common*, "Uncommonly splendid. Director Garry Marshall mixes comedy and drama with admirable ease"—Guy Flatley, *Cosmopolitan*) and bad (about a *Chrysler Theatre* TV special called "Think Pretty," "Even Fred Astaire's dazzling feet could not lift Marshall and Belson's script up above mediocre"—The *Hollywood Reporter*" and about *Frankie and Johnny*, "Prime time cuteness permeates the movie like an air freshener. People don't speak, they quip. This is 'Happy Days' with an apron on"—The *Washington Post*). My favorite review of all wasn't from a critic but from a woman in Florida who wrote me a letter. "I love 'Pretty Woman.' Finally a romantic movie that doesn't have huffing, puffing, and sweating in the love scenes." I've learned to accept all kinds of reviews, but five years ago, I decided not to read them until six months after a project. The studio (or sometimes a mean friend) tells me if they were generally good or bad, but I don't actually read them until six months later. (Except for *Exit to Eden*, which was nine months later.)

The truth is that the review that hurt me the most wasn't even a review about me. Early in her acting career, my daughter Kathleen appeared in a production of *Pastorale* in a fifty-seat theater in Chicago. Local critic Stephanie Shaw hated the whole play and the whole cast. She wrote that the play "pushes past migraine: You might stay at home and chew ground glass for two hours and achieve the same effect. And you wouldn't have to park." I felt like Harry Truman after the critics panned daughter Margaret.

What makes me proud, and what keeps me making movies, is not two thumbs up, four stars out of four, or a glowing review in The *New York Times*, but rather listening to the audience laugh or cry. One of the best places to hear people's reaction to a movie, other than in the audience, is in the bathroom. That's where they share their opinion with friends. Following each preview screening, I send my assistant Diane Frazen into the ladies room and I go to the men's and we hang out by the sinks listening to people.

Restroom conversation can be very illuminating and entertaining for a director. After *Pretty Woman*, I heard, "You think there really are hookers that pretty?" Following *Beaches* one man said, "I'm so fucking embarrassed that I cried in front of my girlfriend." At *Overboard*, I heard, "I wonder if Goldie Hawn would send me an autographed picture of her butt." And *Exit to Eden* prompted one irate man to say, "That movie was so bad that Garry Marshall doesn't even deserve to be Penny Marshall's father."

After *Frankie and Johnny*, I heard two men discussing the actors' performances.

"I really liked Al De Niro, but I didn't like Joanie."

"Joanie? Which one was she?"

"You know, Frankie was the short-order cook and Joanie was the waitress, Sally Field."

"That was Michelle Pfeiffer."

"Whatever. But I really liked that Al De Niro only I wish he would have killed somebody in this picture. I like it when he does that."

The parking lot is also a good place to listen to an audience. When a movie of mine is released, my wife and I go to a theater in our neighborhood and stand in the shadows outside the exit door, eavesdropping as the audience heads to their cars. After a showing of *Nothing in Common* one night, I overheard a woman tell a friend, "Such guilt that film gave me! Now I have to call my father. I haven't spoken to him in ten years."

There is no greater thrill for a director than to see six hundred people laughing out loud at images that he put together. When they laugh at the same movie in Denver, Phoenix, Los Angeles, and New York, time after time, you know that you're getting through. I'm also interested in hearing an audience's silence. There were a couple of dead silences in *Beaches*, when you could hear the tissues coming out of pockets and purses. And there were several silences in *Pretty Woman* and *Exit to Eden*. It's exciting to be in a theater when nobody moves and you realize you helped create that emotion.

I can direct. I can produce. I can act. I can play the drums. But I *have* to write. I became a director in the first place because I wanted to write with a camera. To be a director is to find your own voice. Marketing you can learn as you go along.

I can't give you the ingredients for a surefire hit, tell you who will be the next big box office sensation, or anticipate what kind of love story will attract men ages eighteen to thirty-five. I still haven't figured out a way for a family comedy to win an Academy Award. My job is to tell a story. Jeffrey Katzenberg once said to me, "Garry, we're in the same business but different functions. Your job is to make a good movie, and my job is to get the asses into the seats. If we both do our jobs well, then we'll have a hit."

When *Pretty Woman* passed the $100 million mark, it was rumored that Katzenberg, thrilled with the film's good fortune, got up on the boardroom table at Disney and did a tap dance to cele-

brate the benchmark. When I heard the news, I couldn't help won-
dering what Walt Disney might have thought of *Pretty Woman*. He
probably would have said, "A duck? No. A mouse? No. The highest grossing movie in Disney's history has to be about a hooker!"
Pretty Woman's success was later surpassed at the box office by
The Lion King, which probably would have been a great comfort
to Mr. Disney.

Chapter Thirteen

How to Work Steadily for Thirty-five Years in Hollywood by Using the Myth of Sisyphus

Life Is More Important Than Show Business

Some people look at a glass and see it half empty while others see it half full. I always figured that no matter what was in the glass, I was probably allergic to it. My attitude was to enjoy life as long as I could before I broke out in hives. So far I've spent more than thirty-five years in show business and along the way I've had some highs such as the success of *Happy Days* and *Pretty Woman,* and some lows like the beating up of my play *The Roast* and film *Exit to Eden,* but I've continued to be employed. To me the thought of being out of work always outweighed the fear of ending up with another *Me and the Chimp.* I was never afraid of failure, but I was horrified at idleness.

My personal motto has always been that "life is more important than show business." This industry will make constant demands on every minute of your time, but one of the reasons I've stayed around so long is because I wouldn't let it. I believe that your personal life has to take precedence over your professional life for you to achieve success in both. If I had the choice of attending a star-studded Hollywood premiere where I could meet plenty of career-advancing A-list contacts or an elementary school play where my kid wears a Greek toga and says one inaudible line, I'd pick the play every time. There are always more laughs at school plays.

This "family is all" philosophy is said with some irony because there were so many late nights during the 1970s when I was producing and show business became far more important than my wife and children. The night we shot the pilot presentation for *Laverne & Shirley*, the strength of my marriage was sorely tested. It was a Friday night and we wrapped up shooting a *Happy Days* episode around 11 P.M., and then we went on to shoot a very rough ten-minute pilot to give the network an idea of *Laverne & Shirley*. Barbara didn't know about the pilot and thought I would be ready to leave as usual around 11 P.M. when *Happy Days* was finished. She was waiting on the Paramount lot with a packed station wagon and three groggy kids ready to go on a vacation to Palm Springs when I went outside to shoot the titles.

Around midnight, I could tell that she was losing patience.

"Honey, I just need some opening titles and then I'll be ready to go," I said.

"Can you do it fast? I've got cranky kids in the car and you're about to have a cranky wife, too," Barbara said sweetly.

"I've got an idea," I said. "You print neat. Can you draw the words 'Laverne & Shirley' on this piece of cardboard and I'll shoot it as the title?"

As my wife wrote out the girls' names with a felt-tipped pen, I tried to figure out something for Penny and Cindy to do behind the title shot. Penny came up with the idea of the girls doing the funny little schlemiel-schlimazel walk that she and Ronny used to do in the Bronx when they were kids.

"Great. Penny, you teach the routine to Cindy. Somebody hold the sign, and then I'll shoot it and we'll all be out of here."

So I did a long panning shot (we had no time to make dolly

tracks) of the girls doing the walk, and ended on the closeup of a cardboard sign that said "Laverne & Shirley." If you listen very closely to Penny and Cindy saying "schlemiel-schlimazel," underneath you can hear one of my kids whining, "Hurry up, Dad!"

We sent this rough pilot off to ABC, and I was able to enjoy my vacation in Palm Springs with my family. Shortly after we sold *Laverne & Shirley* to the network, we dumped my wife's cardboard sign in favor of more professional graphics, but that schlemiel-schlimazel walk lasted the entire eight-year run of the series.

When I worked in television, I found myself constantly balancing the responsibilities of being a producer as well as a dad. I would come home late at night, exhausted from a day wrestling with four television shows, to find a book report on *To Kill a Mockingbird* or *Wuthering Heights* lying on the stairs leading to my bedroom. No matter how tired I was, I always tried to find the time and energy to read it so it would be ready before school the next morning. If I didn't, I'd usually find a nasty note in my bowl of oatmeal. A child doesn't understand the excuse "The network is breathing down my neck." Kids only know, "I have a book report due tomorrow and Daddy promised to help me with it." So I helped because I'm happiest when they do something well.

My own dad rarely encouraged me or helped me with my homework because he was usually out entertaining clients from his advertising firm. But sometimes he would make me happy by bringing home a present, like some stamps for my collection. Unfortunately, he brought home the same pack of Swiss stamps that he had given me a few weeks before, so I knew he really wasn't paying total attention. I tried my best to vary my kids' stamps.

One area where my kids never wanted my help was in the carpool. The day their mother was confined to her bed with a 102-degree fever, the kids still tried to drag her out to the station wagon, saying, "Please don't let Daddy drive carpool. He drives too slow around the curves. Even school buses pass him." I ended up driving anyway and watched through the rearview mirror as a carload full of impatient kids tapped their little fingers on school books and said, "Could you go a little faster, Mr. Marshall? We'd like to get there before lunch." I also was deficient in the math department, so I had to get help from the outside. Lowell Ganz once said that when the *Happy Days* writers weren't pitching ideas for new episodes, they were doing the Marshall kids' algebra homework.

For a creative person working in Hollywood, children can be great levelers. You are driving home from work feeling like you own the whole freeway because your show finally made it to the top of the Nielsen ratings, but when you find that your kid has a fever, the good feeling takes a nose dive. This happens to me at least once every flu season. And then there was the time my family and I flew to Chicago to see the production of *Shelves*, the first play I had written, and my son, Scott, became sick with pneumonia and had to be taken to a nearby hospital. There I was in a tuxedo experiencing the dream of a lifetime, hearing my words onstage for the first time, but I couldn't enjoy it because my son was a mile away in an oxygen tent wheezing like Darth Vader.

Many milestones in my life are marked not by accomplishments but by the number of times our kids got stitches. One night Barbara and I were all dressed up and ready to go to a play starring Will Hutchins. (Will had played the lead in *Hey Landlord!*) We would have met Jerry Belson at the theater if it hadn't been for the accident: When five-year-old Lori came running toward us to say good-bye, she tripped on the carpeting, fell on the floor, and cut her eye open on the bottom edge of the front door. As we tried to stop the bleeding, we called the pediatrician and he agreed to meet us at his office. Later that night I called Jerry at home to apologize for missing the play.

"Jerry, I'm sorry. Lori cut her eye and she bled all over the place. We had to rush her to the doctor to get stitches," I said.

"You had a better time than I did," said Jerry quietly.

Sometimes kids can remind you who you are. When our children were small, we used to spend a lot of time in Palm Springs, which helped me relax and get away from work. People who grow up in the concrete scenery of the Bronx really love deserts. One afternoon I was sitting by the hotel pool with the kids and noticed that my four-year-old daughter, Kathi, was chatting with an older woman. Kathi was always the most extroverted of our three kids and would strike up a conversation with anyone from the gas station attendant to the head of ABC. At the age of three when a studio guard told her that Tony Randall had made a rule that no children were allowed backstage on *The Odd Couple*, Kathi pointed her little finger at the guard's kneecap and said, "My daddy is Garry Marshall. He's the boss."

So that day in Palm Springs when I saw her talking with the woman, I didn't think much of it. However, a few minutes later when the woman and Kathi headed toward my chaise longue, I began to worry. I thought, "Oh no. This lady has figured out who I am and she's probably going to give me a script."

I was surprised when she reached out her hand simply to shake mine.

"Mr. Wathi," said the woman, "I just had the most wonderful conversation with your daughter. She's adorable."

"Thank you," I said, smiled, shook her hand, and tried to mask my confusion over the fact that she had just called me "Mr. Wathi." She had me confused with someone else.

As soon as the woman headed back to her room, I pulled my daughter aside.

"Kathi, what did you say to that lady?"

"She asked me what my name was and I said Kathi Wathi."

"Why?"

"Daddy, you always call me Kathi Wathi," she said, innocently.

I've been married to the same woman for more than thirty years and what's saved our marriage, aside from the fact that her medical training as a nurse has saved my life on more than one occasion, is that she's not in show business and she's a better driver than I am. Barbara has created a life for our family outside of the Hollywood mainstream.

One night in 1977, Barbara was in the studio watching as we filmed an episode of my short-lived series *Blansky's Beauties*, about a group of gorgeous Las Vegas show girls. There were about a dozen actresses wearing skimpy costumes running around on the set below while Barbara sat in her usual seat in the front row of the audience reading a book between takes. As I was setting up another shot, a woman in the audience turned to my wife and said, "Your husband works with so many beautiful women. Doesn't it make you nervous?" Barbara barely looked up from her book and said, "Wait until they see him eat."

I've been told that my eating habits are legendary. I'm not an intentional slob; sometimes I'm just concentrating so hard that I forget to chew or swallow and food often lands on my clothes or yours. Cindy Williams wanted written into her *Laverne & Shirley* contract that she didn't have to have lunch with me if I was eating something "white." Following *Frankie and Johnny*, Michelle Pfeiffer said in a magazine interview that "Garry is quite a good director, but you have to brush him off after lunch." And after working on *Wrong Turn at Lungfish* with Lowell Ganz, he said, "It's best when eating with Garry to wear a poncho." I think that lobster bibs are among the greatest things ever invented, and I wish I could wear one at every meal.

When my wife's not helping brush me off herself, she reminds me that at home I'm just another warm body: My chair at the breakfast table doesn't say DIRECTOR on it. Because she's a nurse, Barbara thinks that the only bad thing in life is if you get very sick. Poor Nielsen ratings and bad movie reviews are irrelevant. Good health is all that matters. When I met Barbara in the early 1960s, she was working at Los Angeles's first intensive care unit at Cedars of Lebanon Hospital. I would come home from work on *The Joey Bishop Show* feeling depressed and say, "Honey, Joey didn't like two of my jokes today." Barbara replied, "Two people died in my unit today." One night about four in the morning she was part of the intensive care team that saved the great comedy actor Peter Sellers's life after he went into cardiac arrest; he lived eighteen more years and made people laugh. That night Barbara became a friend of comedy.

In the end credits of every one of my movies I give a special thanks to "Barbara Sue Wells," that's my wife's maiden name. Although most studios try to discourage on-screen thanks, I always get around this by having it written into my contract because I know I wouldn't have a movie at all without her help. Aside from the strenuous pre- and postproduction schedules, the twelve or more weeks that it takes to shoot a movie can be the most difficult on your family.

I used to stay at home and drive my family crazy by waking at dawn to make early morning calls or stumbling in yelling at the dogs just before sunrise following an all-night shoot. Barbara has solved that problem: She throws me out of the house. She books me a room at a nearby hotel. I usually become so self-involved when I'm directing that staying at home is more of a nuisance than a comfort. But whether I'm sleeping at home or bunking at a Sheraton or Hilton, Barbara makes everything else in my life calm. She absorbs and deflects the day-to-day hassles and minutia so I can direct a movie. That's why I always thank her in the end credits: It's a credit for twelve weeks of keeping my world calm.

You have to be constantly on the lookout for ways to add balance to your life and one way is through sports. Recently, I was talking with a young film director at a party and we got into a discussion about sports and movies. He told me that his experience at tennis had helped him direct his first movie because as an athlete he knew what it was like to be losing love-forty and come back to win the game. In movies, a director is down love-forty almost every single day; sometimes he wins the game and other times he doesn't. But a director, and any player in show business, has to know that when his back is to the wall he's capable of coming back to win the set or he doesn't have a prayer to succeed.

For me there is no greater release from work pressure than to go out and hit a ball hard. Sports are the quickest way to take my mind off problematic plot lines and budget squabbles. Shortly after Barbara and I got married I became involved with sports in Los Angeles because I wasn't any good at sitting around a cocktail party with a drink in my hand.

The problem with a show business cocktail party was that I never knew when it was over. I was spending 90 percent of my time at work waiting on the words "maybe" and "if." But in sports both answers are more exact: You either win or lose, and most of the time after three sets, nine innings, or four quarters it's over. There's no "maybe" you won or "We'll wait until the grosses or ratings come in to see *if* you won or lost." I like the security that comes from sports closure.

During the 1973 Writers Guild strike, half the membership wrote books and the other half learned to play tennis. Along with some of the other writers and producers from *The Odd Couple*, I played tennis at Bruce Johnson's house. When the strike was over and we went back to the set, I continued to play tennis on the weekends, and sports basically became my social life. Instead of holding a conversation over a martini, I met people across the net.

My social life was threatened at the age of forty because I ripped a ligament in my knee playing basketball and a doctor told me that I would never play sports again. Determined that I wouldn't let one doctor's opinion sideline me for the rest of my life, I went to different doctors until I finally found one who gave me a different answer. I'm now sixty and I still play tennis, basketball, and softball. I've run into that first doctor a few times, usually when I'm wearing my tennis shorts or basketball jersey, and he's gone out of his way to avoid eye contact with me.

Just because you're playing ball doesn't mean that you can't get some business done, too. Basketball was the reason I got the script for *The Flamingo Kid*. For the last twenty years I've hosted a basketball game every Saturday morning on the half-court at my house. *Esquire* magazine labeled the get-together "a legendary schmooze game," and it has attracted an eclectic mix from Norm Nixon and Meadowlark Lemon to Ron Howard and Tony Danza.

I've made a lot of good friends playing basketball, including manager Mark Harris, entrepreneur Adam Linter, and Hector Elizondo. Hector has become such a regular in my movies that his credit for *Exit to Eden* reads "As Usual, Hector Elizondo." Shooting hoops was how I met Earvin "Magic" Johnson, and I attended his executive basketball camp. I also had the honor of being the oldest man on the court in Maui at the Jerry West/Magic Johnson camp; teammates included Pat Boone and a man who I think ran guns in South America.

As much as I loved the game, my dreams of shooting hoops for the rest of my life were cut short: Just before my sixtieth birthday I took a wrong turn on my basketball court and aggravated my twenty-year-old knee injury. I now have to wear a brace when I play, so it takes me a little longer to suit up for a game.

You're never too old to play ball in Hollywood. I belong to two softball leagues. The one on Saturday is called the Over the Hill League for players who have celebrated at least their fortieth birthday. I play first base for the Pacemakers in this league, which includes the Transplants, Kardiac Kids, Flatliners, and Angels.

On Sunday, I play second base for an even older team, the Outlaws, in the Fifty to Death League, which schedules all of its games early before it gets too hot. A rule of the league is that if a team scores five runs in one inning, the inning is automatically over (because of the risk of heat stroke), except for the last inning when we play until somebody wins. Although I've never seen it happen, we also have a rule that says if a player dies when the ball is in play, it's a ground rule double. In the Fifty to Death League when a player asks his teammate "How are you doing?" the standard answer is "I'm here."

In show business you need stamina and when I started out I had very little. When I arrived in Hollywood I was smoking two packs of cigarettes a day and could only list potato chips as the vegetable in my diet. As time went by and I produced my own television shows, to say that I was unhealthy would have been an understatement: I reached a pinnacle of four packs of cigarettes a day, which I smoked continually from the time I woke until I hit REM at night. Everything I did was predicated on lighting a cigarette first. Things got so bad that a doctor prescribed a 1,500-calorie nutritional shake that I drank three times between my regular meals to try to put on a few pounds, but I still lost weight.

I tried many times to quit smoking and have the distinction of being one of the only people to have failed the Schick stop-smoking method three times; it rivals my record at the DMV for failed driving tests. The Schick staff found me such a challenge that the fourth time they asked me back for free, but I said no. I tried several other stop-smoking programs, but being competitive I would only stay in them long enough to beat the other participants, and then I'd go back to smoking. Secretly I think I kept on smoking because I worried that if I stopped I might not be able to be creative.

In 1981, while directing *Young Doctors in Love*, my wife showed up on the set, after I had passed out from exhaustion, and said quietly, "We're going home now. No more shooting today." I realized I had to stop smoking or I simply wouldn't have the stamina to direct again. On *Young Doctors*, I had worked with an actress named Carol Williard, who said she could help me. Her philosophy was that instead of making smoking a pleasure you were depriving yourself of, it should be a habit you chose not to do. For one year I worked with Carol and she made me walk around with a pack of True Blue cigarettes in my shirt pocket. I could smoke them whenever I wanted, but I chose not to. On April 7, 1983, I threw away the pack forever.

Stopping was probably the most difficult thing I ever had to do, but it paid off. I was not only able to write, but also went on to direct *The Flamingo Kid* smoke-free and haven't smoked in more than ten years. Working with my microbiotic producer Alexandra Rose, my diet also improved, and today I snack on rice cakes and tuna fish instead of Mallomars and candy bars. At my favorite Italian restaurant, Vitello's in North Hollywood, there's even a rather healthy dish named after me: pollo alla Garry Marshall—chicken, peas, pasta, and fresh tomato sauce. I like it because it's green and red and reminds me of Christmas.

Although I've conquered some problems, I'm still troubled by allergies. When I have total control over what I eat, there's no problem, but when I visit other people's homes it can become dicey. Often hostesses try to fool me, thinking I'm just a hypochondriac. A well-intentioned hostess threw a dinner party and promised me that there was no mustard in the food. She later tried to hide her guilty face in a dish towel as the ambulance drivers carried me out on a stretcher after eating one of her secret-recipe, mustard-laced Swedish meatballs. We don't eat at her house anymore.

I once went to a fancy dinner party where ten guests sat around a table with a lazy Susan covered with pots of food in the center and a large glass of red wine at every place. The theme food was Indian and the pots were filled with spicy curries, most of which I couldn't eat and made me nervous just to smell. However, across the table I spotted a pot containing some plain white rice; it looked safe, so I quickly spun the lazy Susan to bring the pot my way.

Unfortunately, I was a little overzealous: When I gave a spin one of the pot handles was sticking out and it decapitated every wine glass on the table. Suddenly, ten people had red wine in their laps and they were all looking at me. I've never been invited back to that house.

In the privacy of my own home I've been known to put ketchup on my spaghetti instead of tomato sauce. It's a habit I inherited from my mother, who convinced us when we were kids that ketchup actually was tomato sauce when she was too busy to go to the market. When I'm not eating at home I steer clear of the life-threatening effects of mustard and mayonnaise by opting for my condiments of choice—ketchup or peanut butter, a difficult order to fill in French restaurants and sushi bars.

My eating habits often draw curious stares in public. There was pointing and whispering the night I listened to Barbra Streisand sing at a $1,000-a-plate fund-raiser and during the performance my wife unwrapped a cream cheese and olive sandwich for me because I was allergic to the $1,000 plate of food.

Along with my physical health, I have to watch out for my mental health. Sometimes the stress can become overwhelming, and there have been several times when I was concentrating so hard on a project that I simply lost all rational judgment. When I worked in television Nickodell's, a restaurant near Paramount, kept a supply of paper bags on hand for me to breathe into when I had an occasional anxiety attack. My wife said that I've probably had three nervous breakdowns in my career, but I was too busy to take the time to notice them.

During *The Odd Couple* days, I drove into my driveway late one night feeling exhausted from a day of fighting with the studio. I stepped out of the car, headed for the house, and saw something funny: a tricycle. I found this strange because at the time, my kids rode ten-speeds. I looked up and realized that I wasn't at *my* house but at the house we had moved from the previous month. I quickly tiptoed back to my car and left without being discovered. When I later told my wife what had happened she said, "Are you crazy? They could have mistaken you for a prowler and shot you. Stop daydreaming!" I nodded but quietly mumbled, "Daydreaming is what I do for a living."

If you're prone to losing it like I am, you have to surround yourself with people who can protect you. In 1969, on the Paramount lot, I met a secretary named Diane who worked for a casting director who was known for having a penchant for liquid lunches. Whenever the casting director made a mistake, Diane was there to pick up the pieces. Even though I'm not a heavy drinker, I figured if Diane could take care of that lady she could certainly watch over a bumbling, mumbling guy like me. Diane Frazen has been my executive assistant for more than twenty-five years and protected me from evil network executives, self-serving producers, and mayonnaise. Sometimes, however, even the people you hire to protect you can forget.

We shot part of *Overboard* on location in the woods of Mendocino, California. One day at lunch while we were watching dailies in a dark room, I asked Diane to hand me a bottle of Evian water from her tote bag. As I watched the images of Goldie and Kurt on the screen, I took a big swig of Evian. Suddenly, I tasted something terrible. "Diane, what the hell am I drinking?" When one of the editors turned on the lights, Diane realized what she had done: Earlier she had bought some supplies for our two apartments and had split up the dish washing liquid into empty Evian bottles so we could share it. This caused me, preoccupied in the dark, to drink liquid soap. Instinct told me that you can't command any authority in front of a large group of people if you have bubbles coming out of your mouth. So I ran to the restroom to spit. The editors found the sight of a director spouting bubbles the funniest frame of the entire picture.

While I was directing *Wrong Turn at Lungfish*, I stayed at a hotel in New York. One morning I picked up the hotel's hair dryer, which was mounted on the bathroom wall, and started to dry my hair. I was brushing my hair and pointing the dryer toward it, but after a few seconds I realized that no air was coming out of the dryer. I was trying to dry my hair with the telephone receiver. Scary, huh? And during the *Frankie and Johnny* shoot I toweled off in the shower but forgot one thing: to turn off the water.

I was watching some footage of *Exit to Eden* in a dark editing room one day and noticed some white dots on my black jeans. Thinking that I had spilled some lunch on my pants, I absentmindedly brushed them off and turned my attention back to the film. A few seconds later I looked down and the white dots were still there.

I brushed them again, but they still wouldn't go away. Then I put some soda water on a handkerchief and rubbed them harder. After lots of rubbing and patting I finally realized that the white dots were actually shadows from the sun coming through the venetian blinds in the editing studio. I looked at the young editing apprentice, who suspected the problem from the very beginning but who was too afraid to tell the director he was losing his mind. Creative concentration is good but you have to look up once in a while and take a break.

For years I believed that to make television shows and movies, a person always had to be in a pure creative state as free from responsibility as a child. I thought a creative person's mind needed to be free to think of stories rather than numbers and decimal points. From the moment I could afford it, I hired a business management firm to handle my finances. To me, balancing books seemed too tedious for a free-wheeling television writer and producer, so while I was charting plans for Fonzie and Richie, I had a couple of guys adding up how much money Fonzie and Richie were making for me.

While the financial high point in my life was *Pretty Woman*, the lowest was the day in December 1985 when I was editing *Nothing in Common* and found out I was broke. My business advisers had lost almost all of the money I had made in television on real estate. They also put me in debt. In 1986, I ended up owing big time and was sued twenty-eight times by various real estate people. I then went through about four years of a financial roller-coaster ride trying to pay back the bank. For the first time in my career, I had to choose jobs not based on the quality of the script or the stars involved, but because I needed to pay off debts.

Although I had always dreamed of working with Goldie Hawn, one of my reasons for directing *Overboard* was because MGM promised to pay me very well. Also during this shaky time I started going to psychics for advice, made regular visits to a little church in my neighborhood for support, hugged my wife a lot, and took a series of odd jobs for money. I even directed a music video starring the Latin rock group Menudo for the movie *Cannonball Run II*. As I stood on the set trying to explain to several non-English-speaking teenage boys how a papier-mâché cannonball was going to roll over their stomachs, I felt I had reached the abyss of my creativity. But I survived.

Jeffrey Katzenberg, Michael Eisner, and Frank Wells at Disney helped get me financially on my feet again by giving me scripts like *Beaches* and *Pretty Woman* and by often paying part of my salary in advance. During this time when I trusted almost no one, I turned to one of my childhood friends from the Bronx Falcons, a brilliant lawyer named Martin Garbus. He helped me swim the waters of lawsuits, subpoenas, depositions, and near bankruptcy. Throughout my financial plummeting the strongest safety net of all was one person . . . my sister Penny. She was always there for me through thick and very, very thin.

I thought I could concentrate solely on my creativity and hire someone else to totally handle my business interests, but I was wrong. You can't do that or you will get screwed.

In my thinking, passion for your work rather than for money will do you much better and may *also* lead to your financial goals. I never wanted a yacht because it would make me seasick. I never wanted a very nice car because I hate driving. I never wanted expensive clothes because I figured why pay three hundred dollars for a silk shirt when I was going to stain it. But I loved to work. And that work is done in an earthquake-safe office on the first floor with Fudgcicles in the freezer. I always wanted to work close to where I lived so I could either walk to the office or drive on surface streets with a minimum of left turns. My office is stuffed with memorabilia from my television series, movies, and plays because my wife decided long ago that anything with a likeness of Mork or Oscar Madison belonged at the office. Show business is not big in our home life, although Jack Klugman and Alan Thicke are two stars I often socialize with.

I have a nice collection of sports pictures on the walls, including an autograph of one of my all-time heroes, Joe DiMaggio. When I was fourteen my friend Harvey Keenan and I were the first ones in line at Yankee Stadium when tickets went on sale for Joe DiMaggio Day. We were able to get great seats, right down in front. A few minutes into the first inning an older guy from our neighborhood came down to talk to us with his date, a leggy brunet girl who had never been to a ball game before. The guy offered Harvey and me twenty dollars each for our seats. We figured we needed the money, so we gathered up our stuff and moved to the back of the stadium where we stood on two cardboard milk cartons and watched the rest of the game. DiMaggio hit a towering home run and I always regretted giving up those great seats. I learned two things that day: You shouldn't sacrifice your dream to money and a good way to impress a leggy brunette.

There is space on my desk at my office reserved for four small busts. They are of people who have inspired me: John F. Kennedy, Napoleon Bonaparte, William Shakespeare, and Buddha. What I liked about Kennedy was that he knew how to tap into youth. He understood that you can't be afraid of young people because they're weird or different, and that's really what my career in television was all about, attracting and working with bright, talented, and sometimes weird young people.

I always liked General Bonaparte and read books about his great war campaigns. He was able to lead a lot of people to do things they really didn't want to do, and that's a television producer in a sentence. However, where Napoleon went wrong was that he convinced himself that he was smarter than everyone else and believed his own parchment clippings.

Shakespeare was the greatest storyteller. He didn't just write one or two plays and hang up his quill. Shakespeare wrote play after play, and that has always been my dream: to keep producing new work year after year. In show business the players with longevity are the people who can consistently deliver the goods. There are plenty of people who write one good script or direct one decent movie and then are never heard from again.

It's the prolific storytellers who I've always looked up to.

Although I'm not a very religious person, I've always had a statue of Buddha on my desk. Buddha represents to me the sharing of peace and kindness without asking for anything in return. He also reminds me that there's something bigger than us out there, bigger than a network or a studio or even Hollywood super-agent Mike Ovitz.

And finally, I have a small statue of Sisyphus on my desk. The statue depicts a man in Hades who was forced to repeatedly push a large boulder up a hill. Each time he reaches the top of the hill, the rock falls back down to the bottom, and he has to go back down the hill and push it up again. This myth is probably the source of my positive attitude toward show business. When the guy is walking back down the hill to get the boulder again, he has a choice. He can say, "I'm sweaty and hot and I have to push that damn boulder up again" or he can say, "Here's a nice break. I don't have to push the rock again until I get to the bottom. I can walk down the hill, whistling and pushing nothing." I've always tried to make great use of my "walking down the hill time" because often that's the happiest it gets.

In the mid-1970s when I was a television producer and had the three top-rated shows on television, I had a visit from a woman from the Bronx named Lillian Dreyfuss, the mother of one of my childhood friends, David Dreyfuss. Mrs. Dreyfuss was a short, attractive, dark-haired woman who always wore high heels to make herself appear taller and she pulled her hair back in a bun.

In those days I always became very excited when people I had known in the Bronx visited me at my Paramount office. I would take them on a tour of the studio and introduce them to all the actors. The last time Mrs. Dreyfuss had seen me I was probably about fourteen years old and playing stickball in the gutter or being carried off by an ambulance. When she came to visit that day, I really wanted her to see how a sick little boy had grown up to achieve some success. After our tour of the studio lot where Henry Winkler kissed her hand and Robin Williams made her blush by putting on her sunglasses, Mrs. Dreyfuss and I walked over to my office where I offered to make her a malted, the flavor of her choice.

As she stared around my office taking in all of the framed pictures and memorabilia from my shows, it seemed like she wanted to say something about my success. I thought maybe she would say how much she had liked the warmth of *Happy Days*, the antics of *Laverne & Shirley*, the irreverence of *Mork & Mindy*, or the romance of *Angie*. But the Bronx has never been a very sentimental place, so I wasn't that surprised when she summed up my whole career by saying, "You're a big shot now. Garry, you really stepped in it."

May you all step in it, too.

WORK HISTORY

FILM

Director:
Young Doctors in Love (executive producer) . . . . (1982)
Flamingo Kid (coscreenwriter) . . . . (1984)
Nothing in Common . . . . (1986)
Overboard. . . . . (1987)
Beaches. . . . . (1988)
Pretty Woman . . . . (1990)
Frankie and Johnny (producer) . . . . (1991)
Exit to Eden (producer). . . . . (1994)

Writer and Producer *(with Jerry Belson):*
How Sweet It Is. . . . . (1968)
The Grasshopper. . . . . (1970)

TELEVISION

Writer:
The Jack Paar Show (Tonight Show) . . . . (1960-1961)
The Joey Bishop Show . . . . (1962-1964)
The Bill Dana Show. . . . . (1963-1964)
The Danny Thomas Show . . . . (1963-1964)
The Dick Van Dyke Show . . . . (1963-1965)
The Lucy Show. . . . . (1964-1966)
Chrysler Theatre: Think Pretty . . . . (1964)
Gomer Pyle, U.S.M.C. . . . . (1964)
I Spy . . . . (1965)
Sheriff Who?? . . . . (1971)
Evil Roy Slade: TV Movie . . . . (1971)
Love, American Style. . . . . (1971-1972)
(some segments written as Samuro Mitsubi)

Creator and Executive Producer *(television series):*

Hey Landlord! . . . .(1966-1967)
The Odd Couple (developed for TV) . . . .(1970-1975)
Barefoot in the Park (developed) . . . .(1970-1971)
Mc and the Chimp . . . .(1972)
The Little People/The Brian Keith Show . . . .(1972-1974)
Happy Days . . . .(1974-1984)
Laverne & Shirley . . . .(1976-1983)
Blansky's Beauties . . . .(1977)
Who's Watching the Kids . . . .(1978-1979)
Mork & Mindy . . . .(1978-1982)
Angie . . . .(1979-1980)
The New Odd Couple . . . .(1982-1983)
Joanie Loves Chachi . . . .(1982-1983)
Nothing in Common . . . .(1987)

THEATER

Shelves (playwright)
. . . . (1978: Pheasant Run Playhouse, St. Charles, IL)
The Roast (cowriter with Jerry Belson)
. . . . (1980: Broadway's Winter Garden Theatre, NYC)
Wrong Turn at Lungfish (director/cowriter with Lowell Ganz)
. . . . (1990: Steppenwolf Theatre, Chicago)
. . . . (1992: Coronet Theatre, Los Angeles)
. . . . (1993: Promenade Theatre, New York)

ACTING

Psych-Out . . . .(1968)
Maryjane . . . .(1968)
The Escape Artist . . . .(1982)
Lost in America . . . .(1985)
Jumpin' Jack Flash . . . .(1986)
Soapdish . . . .(1991)
A League of Their Own . . . .(1992)
Hocus Pocus . . . .(1993)
Murphy Brown (recurring role) . . . .(1994-1995)

INDEX